PLATFORM

P R E S S
DOYLESTOWN
PENNSYLVANIA

The
SELFISH PATH TO
ROMANCE

HOW TO LOVE
with PASSION *and* REASON

EDWIN A. LOCKE *and* ELLEN KENNER

www.SelfishRomance.com

Published in the United States by
Platform Press
The nonfiction imprint of
Winans Kuenstler Publishing, LLC
Doylestown, Pennsylvania 18901 USA
(215) 500-1989
www.wkpublishing.com

Platform Press and colophon are registered trademarks

ISBN: 978-0-9824117-5-9

First Edition

This publication is intended to provide authoritative
information on the subject of personal behavior and
relationship issues. However, it is sold with the understanding
that neither the Author nor the Publisher is engaged in
rendering psychological, counseling, or any other professional
services by publishing this book. The Author and Publisher
specifically disclaim any liability, loss, or risk incurred as a
consequence, directly or indirectly, of the use and application
of contents and concepts contained in this work.

The portrait of Ayn Rand appearing on page ix is reproduced
with the gracious permission of the artist, Robert Tracy, who
created the original oils-on-board work in 1999.

The biography on page ix was adapted with permission from
the Ayn Rand Institute website: www.AynRand.org.

The image on the cover is of a bronze sculpture called "The
Offering" by Malvina Hoffman (1885-1966), from the
collection of Harris and Ellen Kenner.

Dedicated to our soul mates,
Cathy Durham and Harris Kenner,
who have brought us the greatest joy and
happiness we have ever experienced.

"It is one's own personal, selfish happiness that one seeks, earns, and derives from love."

—Ayn Rand

Table of Contents

Table of Contents

Preface

*T*housands of books have been written on the topic of
romantic love, and many of them offer valuable insights
into what makes successful romantic relationships
possible. However, virtually all such books are quite selective in their
coverage—they deal with certain elements of the love relationship
but not others. In reality, romantic love is an integrated whole,
consisting of many interrelated aspects. If any aspect is missing in the
relationship, the lack of it may undermine the romance. Our goal was
to include what we consider to be all the essential elements.

There are several features of this book that are wholly or
relatively unique. We bring an original perspective—based on Ayn
Rand's philosophy of Objectivism—to the topic of romantic love. Ayn
Rand was a world-famous novelist whose most well-known novels
were *The Fountainhead* (1943) and *Atlas Shrugged* (1957). Both books
are still best sellers today. She was also an original and revolutionary
philosopher. Although she did not have a fully developed theory of
romantic love, she had many important insights about love. Her most
revolutionary idea is that love is based on egoism and not, as is taken
as an axiom by most people, on altruism. We show why altruism
destroys love. Another revolutionary idea of Ayn Rand's is that there
is no inherent contradiction or conflict between our emotions and
reason; thus love and reason can be fully integrated.

We give explicit credit for any ideas that come from Ayn Rand's writings. Otherwise, the points we make are based on our own clinical experience, Dr. Kenner's radio show, and other sources (which are referenced).

For those interested in history, we give a brief overview of the history of romantic love. Romantic love, defined (in the modern sense) as the mutual enjoyment of emotional and sexual intimacy between self-chosen and equal partners, is actually a very recent and truly marvelous discovery in human history—although the concept is not fully understood even today. Our goal in this book is to deepen that understanding.

We explain the need for romantic love based on the visibility principle. Many people view love as involving the need for approval or validation, but we show that visibility—which was first identified by the philosopher Aristotle—is something quite different.

We address the moral basis of love. It is conventionally held that love has little to do with moral character, but we argue that moral character is essential to a successful romantic relationship. (Ayn Rand also stresses this point).

We discuss whether love has actual causes that can be consciously identified or whether, as is commonly held, it is just a matter of mindless and inexplicable "chemistry." We show that love's causes can be identified by introspection.

We make a claim that may be surprising to some: Love is not an unconditional gift but actually has to be earned. We explain in detail what one has to do to earn it, including creating one's own moral character. This point is tied to Ayn Rand's "trader" principle, which is based on the idea of trading value for value.

We define what a romantic soul mate is and discuss how to recognize your soul mate.

We demonstrate that a romantic relationship can endure only if it is accompanied by conscious thinking, on a regular basis, about how to promote and strengthen it, and why love cannot endure if partners count only on the emotion of love to support the relationship. We show how to actively promote romantic love.

We explain what makes a happy sexual relationship

possible—and it is not just a matter of using the right sexual positions. Knowing about sexual anatomy is indeed important, but the issue goes much deeper than that: to the actual relationship between mind and body.

Finally, although most love books recognize that conflict can arise between romantic partners, we show why some conflict between partners is inevitable and how conflicts can, in many cases, be rationally resolved.

We use many case examples in the book. The examples are sharply focused on the differences between couples, in order to clearly isolate and stress the points we want to make. These case examples were drawn principally from four sources: our own clinical experience, Dr. Kenner's radio show, our own personal experiences and those of friends and acquaintances, and letters to advice columnists. Many examples are composites of individuals, and we dramatized a small number of cases in order to illustrate a point in the clearest possible terms. In all cases we disguised details to protect privacy.

One more point: although our examples pertain to heterosexual couples, we believe that the principles described in this book apply equally to same-sex couples. We did not use any same-sex examples simply because our experience is limited in this area.

We offer this book as a guide for strengthening your romantic happiness. Putting the ideas and skills you learn here consistently into practice in your own personal life may be helped along, if needed by a skilled therapist. We cite a great many self-help resources in the endnotes. All offer varying degrees of good advice; however, there are occasional passages in some of these books with which we strongly disagree—for example, passages advocating humility or selflessness. Our mentioning these resources should not be taken to imply that in all cases we agree with everything an author says.

We hope that you will discover new insights about romantic love and that these insights will make your own romantic life happier and more fulfilling.

Edwin A. Locke   Ellen Kenner
Westlake Village, California   North Scituate, Rhode Island

About the Authors

Edwin A. Locke, PhD, is a noted and widely published scholar in the field of psychology, with fifteen years of clinical experience and more than three decades as a professor of psychology and of management at the University of Maryland. He is also a scholar and advocate of the works of Ayn Rand, has written and spoken extensively about her philosophy, and has been a senior writer for the Ayn Rand Institute.

He is a Fellow of the American Psychological Association and of the American Psychological Society, has been recognized by his peers with many scholarly awards, and frequently speaks at conferences on the topic of setting goals for life and happiness.

He earned his PhD from Cornell University and his BA from Harvard University. Dr. Locke lives in California.

Ellen Kenner, PhD is a licensed clinical psychologist with a private practice in Rhode Island and host of the nationally-syndicated radio talk show, "The Rational Basis of Happiness®." Her specialty is exploring how to apply the rational, pro-happiness philosophy of Ayn Rand's Objectivism to mental health issues.

Dr. Kenner has been a speaker at Objectivist conferences for many years and has presented several workshops on romance and family issues. She makes frequent media appearances.

Dr. Kenner earned her PhD from the University of Rhode Island and her BA from Brown University.

Acknowledgments

We owe a debt of gratitude to many individuals who contributed to this book—a work that has been eight years in the making. We owe a very special debt to Mary Ann Sures who read every chapter of an early draft in extraordinarily meticulous detail and made many hundreds of valuable suggestions for clarifications and improvements. The book benefited enormously from her help. We are also tremendously indebted to Thomas A. Bowden who read an early draft of the entire book and made many important and insightful suggestions for improvement.

Dr. Robert Mayhew was very helpful in providing information about love in ancient Greece. Dr. Allan Gotthelf was very helpful in referring us to and clarifying Aristotle's ideas on friendship, as well as providing additional information about ancient Greece. Our spouses, Dr. Cathy Durham and Harris Kenner, read every chapter and gave us many valuable insights. Dr. Dina Schein Federman and Dr. Ann Porto gave us helpful feedback on early versions of our book and openly shared their enthusiasm about the ideas. Kathy St. Jean and Randy Deats, and Laura Mottola Kenner offered many beneficial suggestions. Dr. Jonathan Rosman and Naomi Kenner provided helpful insights on several chapters. Dr. Tara Smith provided us with a richer philosophical understanding of kindness, generosity, and charity in relation to virtue. Marcia Yudkin, with her extensive knowledge of the publishing world, offered us valuable guidance. We are grateful to Fran Fisher who did significant work to reduce the length of our manuscript. We have tremendous respect for the outstanding work Donna Montrezza has done in the copyediting and enriching of our manuscript and for the pure joy of working with her.

We owe a special debt of gratitude to our publishers, Foster Winans and Walt Kuenstler, who shepherded us through earlier versions of the book to the final version by providing us with many important suggestions for refinement, and guided us through the transition from raw manuscript to published book. They helped us with countless valuable suggestions, great enthusiasm, and additional help as needed. Also, special thanks go to Foster Winans and Whitney Cookman for the design of the cover, and to Raquel Pidal who helped with the manuscript and with book distribution.

Of course, we are entirely responsible for the final version of the book, including any errors or unclarity that might remain.

About Ayn Rand

*A*yn Rand, whose writings and philosophy inspired the authors to create this book and have inspired millions of people the world over, was born in St. Petersburg, Russia, on February 2, 1905. She was eyewitness to both the Kerensky Revolution, she supported, and—in 1917—the Bolshevik Revolution, which she denounced.

She graduated from the University of Petrograd in 1924 after experiencing the disintegration of free inquiry and a communist takeover of the university. Soon after, she traveled to the United States to visit relatives in New York City, spent six months with relatives in Chicago, and then left for Hollywood to pursue a career as a screenwriter.

She sold her first screenplay, "Red Pawn," to Universal Pictures in 1932 and saw her first stage play, *Night of January 16th*, produced in Hollywood and then on Broadway. Her first novel, *We the Living*, based on her years living under Soviet tyranny, was published in 1936 in the U.S. and England.

Her next work was an anti-collectivist novelette, *Anthem*, followed by the phenomenally successful *The Fountainhead* which earned her lasting recognition as a champion of individualism.

Her last work of fiction, *Atlas Shrugged,* was published in 1957 and is considered her greatest achievement, dramatizing her philosophy in an intellectual mystery story that integrated ethics, metaphysics, epistemology, politics, economics, and sex.

Thereafter, Ayn Rand wrote and lectured on her philosophy—Objectivism—which she characterized as "a philosophy for living on earth." She published and edited her own periodicals from 1962 to 1976, including essays which provided much of the material for her six books on Objectivism, including *The Virtue of Selfishness*. Ayn Rand died on March 6, 1982, in her New York City apartment.

Every book by Ayn Rand published in her lifetime is still in print, and hundreds of thousands of copies are sold each year, so far totaling more than 25 million. Her vision and philosophy changed many lives and launched a philosophic movement that has had a continuing and growing impact on American culture.

Introduction

MANY PEOPLE'S EXPERIENCE WITH love is shrouded in mystery, but we believe love can be rationally understood, fostered, and cherished.

An ideal romantic relationship can be one of life's greatest and most enduring pleasures. The experience and intimacy of love is expressed beautifully in this adapted version of the sixteenth-century poem "My True-Love Hath My Heart" by Sir Philip Sidney:

> *My true-love hath my heart, and I have his.*
> *By just exchanging one to the other given.*
> *I hold his dear, and mine he cannot miss,*
> *There never was a better bargain driven.*
> *His heart in me keeps him and me in one;*
> *My heart in him his thoughts and senses guides;*
> *He loves my heart, for once it was his own;*
> *I cherish his because in me it bides;*
> *My true-love hath my heart, and I have his.*[1]

Many people have never felt this way about another person but most of us long to experience such passion and intimacy.

Sadly, failed romances often bring enormous pain and suffering, because the needs involved are so fundamental and the expectations so high.

Even in the contemporary Western world where people have the freedom to choose their own partners, many romantic relationships, including marriages, fail. In the United States about half of all marriages end in divorce. But this does not mean that the fifty percent who stay married are happy. Many unhappily married people stay together because of inertia, duty, children, fear, self-doubt, or financial or emotional insecurity. We believe that the number of fully happy, totally fulfilled couples is far lower than fifty percent, with the rest experiencing varying degrees of satisfaction, ranging from mild happiness to mutual toleration of one another to mutual contempt.

No one enters a romantic relationship or marriage with the expectation that the initial feelings of passion and joy will fade away to indifference or even turn to contempt. We look forward to a romance in which every day is a joy. We dream that this happy state will last until "death do us part." Yet few such dreams come true. Why don't they? Because romantic relationships are very complex: they involve two people:

- with free will
- with different backgrounds and at least somewhat different beliefs, values, personalities, habits, and interests
- with the capacity for independent thought
- with the ability to change ("for better or worse")
- who deal with each other every single day as total entities, usually over an extended period of years

With so many factors involved, many things can go wrong—and they do. Many people have no idea why, and they either struggle along in pain and disappointment, dreaming of an unfulfilled longing, or they give up and conclude, "I guess it wasn't meant to be."

This isn't surprising. After all, it was thousands of years before today's concept of romantic love was discovered. Let's take a brief stroll through history and see how contradictory ideas, false turns and dead ends have undermined the concept of romantic love.

A Brief History of Romantic Love

Romantic love (including the sexual aspect), especially between mutually chosen partners who view one another as equals, is a very recent development—as well as a glorious achievement—in human history.[2]

In ancient Greece, although there could be close friendships of character between husband and wife, women were considered inferior to men, and marriages were usually economic arrangements. Wives were usually viewed as housekeepers and bearers of children.[3]

For men, friendships with other men were considered to be more important than relationships with women. Heterosexual passion, where it existed, was reserved for "companions" (high-class prostitutes or courtesans), who were often witty, well educated and expert at giving men pleasure. Even then, however, if a man's love (Eros) for a woman became too passionate, it was considered a sign of madness.

In early Roman times, wives were considered mere chattel, and husbands could do anything they wanted, including beat them, enslave them, and even, in some cases, kill them. Later, Roman women acquired more freedom, including economic rights and the right to divorce, but romantic love in marriage was not highly regarded. Like the Greeks, the Romans believed that passionate love was madness. The most "pleasurable" form of what passed for "romance" was considered to be adultery—a game played with anyone and everyone a man or woman could seduce.

Both the Greeks and the Romans practiced so-called love between men and young boys. It is believed that the boys were typically in their early teens. (There were lesbian relationships also, but we know less about these.) We know that in Greece there could be "passion" in such relationships, but it was based mainly on the physical attractiveness of the boy. Often, however, it was simply a relationship of usefulness. The man was the boy's tutor or would give him money or presents and the boy would give him physical pleasure.[4]

Today, of course, this constitutes sexual abuse; young boys do not qualify as consenting adults.⁵ Also, as in every civilization, there were romantic attachments between same-sex adults.

As the Roman Empire crumbled around 500 A.D. and Western civilization descended into the Dark Ages, the influence of Christianity, particularly the philosophy of Augustine, rapidly increased. Augustine's widely accepted view was that the body, and therefore sexual pleasure, was evil and corrupt. Paul (Corinthians 1:7) had expressed earlier the view that virginity was preferable to marriage. Jerome (Letter 22) agreed, but believed marriage with sex could be useful as a means of creating more virgins! Later Christians favored marriage, but the purest type of marriage was considered to be "spiritual" or "continent," that is, sexless. Virginity was regarded as the highest feminine virtue. Sex was "permitted" reluctantly, providing its sole goal was to create children. Loving one's wife too much was asserted to be the equivalent of adultery.

Toward the end of the eleventh century, as the Dark Ages drew to a close, the concept of "courtly love" arose in France and spread to other countries. It involved a profound respect for and worship of women. But it was a strange kind of worship; it was asexual and was clearly influenced by the Christian viewpoint. A knight might spend years seeking the love of his ideal lady, but even if he succeeded, he would never marry the object of his worship. It is reported that in some cases, he might even lie naked in bed with her but without consummation. Denial was considered more virtuous than gratification. No such worship of women was extended to the marital relationship, which was thought to be sullied by sex, and marital sex itself was simply a woman's duty.

In the thirteenth century, Christian philosopher Thomas Aquinas (and others) helped pave the way for the Renaissance by bringing Aristotle's philosophy, especially respect for reason, into Christian thought. To him, marriage and celibacy were morally equal—a definite step up from the view dominant in the Dark Ages.

In the Renaissance, which began in the fourteenth century, a respect for reason began to challenge religious dogma. The arts flourished and freedom gradually increased, culminating in the triumph of reason in the eighteenth century, the Age of Enlightenment. The Renaissance, however, did not immediately free women from medieval influence. A great dichotomy arose: the woman as pure virgin versus the woman as evil witch. During the Inquisition many thousands of so-called witches were burned at the stake. The alleged source of woman's evil? Her "carnal lust"— her capacity for sexual pleasure and her alleged capacity to cause sexual problems, such as impotence, in men. Gradually, this lose-lose dichotomy began to erode. People talked and wrote about romantic love in relation to marriage, as in Shakespeare's *Romeo and Juliet*. There was extensive discussion of whether marriages should be arranged by the parents—divorced from romantic attraction and usually for economic reasons—or based on the personal, romantic desires of the couple.

The Catholic view of the philosophy of love and sex was also challenged by the sixteenth-century Protestant Reformation, which gave rise to Puritanism. The Puritans generally regarded pleasure with grave suspicion; for example, they had rules and even laws forbidding or severely limiting stage plays, card games, singing, dancing, fancy dress and hairstyles, and jewelry. But in one particular respect, Puritanism represented an advance over the Catholic view. Contrary to popular belief, Puritans were not against and actually endorsed romantic love, including sex, so long as sex was confined to married couples. They condemned lifetime virginity as a Catholic conceit. However, in Puritan communities, sex outside of marriage—fornication between unmarried couples, or adultery—was condemned and could result in ostracism (portrayed in Hawthorne's *The Scarlet Letter*), severe punishment, or even death. Furthermore, although the Puritans believed that husband and wife should enjoy sex as well as each other's companionship, wives were still expected to be subordinate to their husbands.

The eighteenth century, the Age of Enlightenment, was a critical turning point in Western civilization. The power of Puritanism and religion gradually faded, and pleasure became more respectable under the influence of Enlightenment thought. It was the triumph of reason and freedom of the mind over tradition and religious dogma.

However, the Enlightenment did not resolve all of the problems faced by women in relation to romance. Women, unlike men, were not regarded as fully capable of reason. The ideal woman was supposed to be modest, meek, sweet, and in need of protection and domination by a strong but kindly gentleman. Romantic love was an accepted part of marriage, but it was not considered a love between equals.

This inequality carried over into the nineteenth century and the Victorian era. Marriage itself was valued, but attitudes towards sex regressed to pre-Puritan levels. Sex—even in the marital context—was considered low, indecent, and even disgusting, at least for women. Husbands could enjoy sexual pleasure, but wives were not supposed to. The female "enjoyment" of sex was only for prostitutes, many of whom were kept busy by sexually frustrated husbands.

Eventually the Victorian influence waned. Women began to acquire the same legal rights as men, and women's sexual pleasure became respectable, especially in America, where the pursuit of happiness was considered a natural right. The divorce rate in the latter part of the nineteenth century greatly increased, most likely because more people came to value happiness and felt less constrained to stay married solely out of duty. Marriage, love, and sex gradually became more unified as the twentieth century began. Romantic love among relatively equal partners (by historical standards), with enjoyable sex as an ideal had triumphed at last—or had it? Not quite.

A strong feminist movement arose in the 1960s, factions of which replaced the medieval view that women were evil with the assertion that men were evil. Sex, it was claimed, reflected men's attempts to dominate women and was akin to rape. One radical feminist wrote, "Maybe life is tragic and the God who does not exist made women inferior so that men could . . . [penetrate] us."[6] The problem, according to this feminist, stems from the fact that men and women have different sexual anatomies.

In reality, different does not mean unequal, and different anatomies do not prevent—and in fact make possible—sexual pleasure between equal partners. Many feminists were even opposed to marriage and the bearing of children, fearing that these also reflected subservience to men. This hostile view towards men has not entirely disappeared, but its popular appeal has faded. The most rational elements of the movement—that it is good for women to have careers and to be treated fairly in the job market and elsewhere—endured.

In the 1960s the counterculture movement arose. Hippies regarded sex as a strictly sensual, animal pleasure divorced from love, values, or intimacy. They viewed themselves as path-breaking rebels, but in reality their view of sex was not much different from that of the early Christians. They fully agreed with the medieval view that sex was an animal act divorced from the "spirit" or mind, but rather than condemning mindless sex, they glorified it, especially when it was combined with the use of hallucinatory drugs.

Religious spokesmen have retaliated against what came to be called "casual sex," which has clearly infiltrated our culture. They do so by preaching abstinence: no sex until marriage, based on Biblical teachings. In this respect, they have gone back to the Middle Ages and tied sex to supernatural permission. This is no solution. Marriage does not guarantee a close spiritual relationship any more than free love does. (By "spiritual" we mean tied to conscious convictions, values, and intimacy.) To understand romance, with or without marriage, and to make it flourish, we need reason—we need to know what to do on an everyday basis. That is what this book is about.

In the twentieth century, psychologists and psychoanalysts began to write about sex and romance, but many of them have only managed to confuse matters further. For some, love was akin to some form of neurosis. The two most influential figures have been Sigmund Freud and Eric Fromm. For Freud, sex was a brute instinct (implying we are all like the lower animals) and love involved investing sexual energy in a relationship without letting the brute instinct get out of hand. Fromm claimed that love stems from the terror of being separate from others (implying that we all long to become part of some super-human organism). In his view all human beings are fundamentally the same; therefore, it makes no difference whom we love (implying that one person will make us as happy as another).[7]

All this is nonsense. There is no sexual "instinct," only a potential for pleasure. Genuine love is not based on terror but on self-esteem and esteem for one's partner. And it certainly does make a difference who one's partner is. There are some contemporary psychologists who have very insightful things to say about love and sex, and we will refer to them throughout this book.

Questions

1. Have you ever been in at least one serious relationship that failed? More than one?

_____

_____

2. Do you fully understand the causes of these failures?

_____

_____

3. Have you ever had casual sex that, despite being pleasurable, left you feeling like something was missing?

_____

_____

Notes

1. This is our abridgement of an adaptation of the sixteenth-century sonnet "My True-Love Hath My Heart," from the collection *Arcadia*, by Sir Philip Sidney, 1554–1586. Available on many websites including: http//eir. library.utoronto.ca/rpo/display/poem1941.html and http://www.sonnets.org/ sidney.htm#125.

2. We are not denying that before modern Western civilization there existed some happy romantic relationships. But in the past and in non-Western countries even today (though some are gradually changing) marriages were often, if not typically, arranged. They were based on such factors as economic considerations, social status, tradition, family ties (marrying a cousin), and politics (especially among royalty). And the concept of women being fully equal to men in marriage was virtually unthinkable until well into the twentieth century. (In the few cases in which women have been rulers or "matriarchs" of a clan or family, the dominance hierarchy naturally was reversed.) If a true

romance did blossom in the absence of choice, it was a matter of good luck. Of course, there were undoubtedly instances where people did get to choose their partners despite cultural norms prohibiting or limiting choice, but these had to be the exception rather than the rule.

3. Much of our historical material on the history of love (up to the Victorian Age), unless otherwise indicated (as in the case of some of the material on the Greeks and Romans) comes from Morton Hunt's *The Natural History of Romantic Love* (New York: Doubleday [Norton], 1994).

4. K. J. Dover, *Greek Homosexuality* (Cambridge, MA: Harvard University Press, 1989).

5. Beverly James, *Treating Traumatized Children* (Lexington, MA: Lexington Books, 1989).

6. Andrea Dworkin, *Intercourse* (New York: Free Press, 1987), p. 143.

7. Fromm wrote a popular book called *The Art of Loving* (New York: Harper and Row, 1956), which we believe did a great disservice to the art of loving. Our views are antithetical to his in virtually every basic premise and detail.

Part I: The Basics

To say 'I love you' one must first know how to say the 'I.'
                    —Ayn Rand, *The Fountainhead*

CHAPTER 1

What Is Romantic Love?

R omantic love is not based on the need for approval, but on the need for visibility.

Ross, a bachelor, met Olivia, the divorced mother of two young boys, at a science museum. She was taking her boys through an exhibit about the Wright brothers, the first men to achieve powered, manned flight. He loved the way she explained what a great achievement it was and how many difficulties and failures the Wrights had to overcome before they succeeded. Ross saw the boys' eyes glowing with excitement as Olivia talked about the origin of manned flight.

Ross was so impressed that he went up to Olivia and said, "Excuse me, but I overheard you explaining the exhibit to the boys and they seem really excited about it. You're a wonderful mom to do this for them." Olivia was completely shocked, and for reasons she could not fathom, almost burst into tears, but managed a "Thank you." Her husband had deserted the family some years before, and she had felt totally invisible to him. When her husband abandoned her, he left the responsibility of child rearing in her hands. She obtained a full-time job but struggled financially as well as emotionally. Nevertheless, she had sworn to make up for the loss of the boys' dad by being a conscientious, benevolent mother. Out of the blue, Ross had made her feel visible in a way that was very important to her and in a manner she had never experienced before.

Ross himself felt visible because he saw how his remark had moved her. He wanted to find out more about her, so he asked Olivia if he could show the boys a space exhibit in the museum he knew well. Olivia agreed and they all had a great time. Then Ross asked if he could buy them all some ice cream in the cafeteria. They sat and talked, and he learned that Olivia was a single mom. He complimented her further on how happy and secure the boys seemed to be.

Olivia learned that Ross worked for NASA tracking space probes and that he had worked to get a PhD in aeronautical engineering. He paid his way through college because his parents refused to help; his father thought construction work, which he had done all his life, was good enough for his son. Ross passionately loved his work. Olivia told Ross how much she admired him for his ambition and his struggle to do what he wanted. Now it was Ross's turn to feel teary-eyed. His father had never appreciated his achievement and thus never made him feel visible for all that he had accomplished and for what he valued in himself.

"We seem to have a lot in common," Ross observed.

"What do you mean?" asked Olivia.

"We've both had to struggle against tough odds but we were determined to do what we thought was the right thing and to do it without bitterness—to keep joy in our lives."

"Yes," said Olivia, "you're right."

They both smiled and were aware that a bond was growing between them.

Ross said, "You're a lovely lady, and I'd love to do more with you and the boys—maybe a tour of NASA, and I would love to take you out alone too."

Olivia blushed. It had been many years since a man told her she was attractive and she suddenly felt visible as a woman. This was the beginning of a promising romance. In the short time they were together in the museum, both Olivia and Ross felt seen, or visible, in important ways.

Ross took Olivia and the boys on a tour of NASA, which they all loved, and Ross began to date Olivia. They were strongly attracted to one another and each date over many months strengthened their bond. When they made love they felt a joyous ecstasy unlike anything they had ever experienced.

Olivia and Ross fell in love. What exactly does that mean? What is romantic love?

> *Romantic love is a strong, emotionally intimate relationship between consenting adults that combines an intense valuing of a partner on the deepest level and the enjoyment of sexual pleasure with that partner.*

Both the strong degree of intimacy and the element of sexual pleasure set romance apart from other types of human relationships. A close relationship with another person that does not combine profound intimacy with sexual desire is not a romantic relationship. Many successful romantic relationships end in marriage, though not all (some couples choose to live together).

At some point in life almost everyone longs for romantic love. Romantic love is a never-ending subject of interest in novels, movies, paintings and sculpture, popular magazine articles and history books, as well as thousands of books and professional articles written by psychologists and other mental health professionals.

A subject that receives so much attention must involve an important human need. What is the nature of the need for romantic love? Why do you need and want it for yourself?

One flawed answer is that it is based on the need for approval stemming from children's dependence on their parents. If this were true, however, then mature, self-confident, independent people would be indifferent to romantic love—which is obviously not the case. In fact, confident people are the most likely to have successful romantic partnerships. People who are seriously psychologically dependent or needy have troubled relationships because others cannot fill their profound feelings of emptiness.

Another inadequate answer is that romantic love is based on the desire for the sensation of bodily pleasure. If sexual pleasure were just a physical need, people would not need the romantic aspect and would be fully content with sex toys and self-pleasuring. Again, this is obviously not so. Full, enduring sexual pleasure presupposes a personally valued partner.

The Visibility Principle

Why, then, does one need a romantic partner? An important clue comes from the ancient Greek philosopher Aristotle's discussion of the nature of friendship.[1] Aristotle noted, "All love for others is an extension of the love one has for oneself. . . . [The good man] has the same attitude toward the one he loves as he does toward himself, for his friend really is another self."[2] Aristotle reportedly said:

> The self-sufficient man will need someone to love ... [For] it is both a most difficult thing ... to attain a knowledge of oneself and also a most pleasant thing.
>
> ... And so, as when we wish to see our own face, we do so by looking into the mirror, in the same way when we wish to know ourselves we can obtain that knowledge by looking at the one we love. For the one we love, as we say, is another self.[3]

Aristotle further explains: "We are better able to observe our neighbors than ourselves, and their actions better than our own."[4] What does Aristotle mean here? Probably this: When we are alone, we experience ourselves from the inside, as a flow of mental processes, mental contents, actions, and other characteristics. We experience a continual succession of mental and physical states and actions.

Every mental process has content: we experience specific types of emotions (frustration, anxiety, pride, joy), thoughts about something particular (what the new job project entails), mental images and memories of people or things (recalling our childhood bedroom), sensory perceptions (of a garden, a wave washing ashore), convictions ("I'm not the type of person who would lie"), and choices ("I am going to admit to my partner that I was wrong in that argument"). We also constantly take action: eat meals, go to work, talk with friends, react to the actions of others.

Notice how much we experience ourselves from the inside. Alone, however, it is impossible to fully integrate these elements into a directly perceivable view of who we are as a total person.

How, then, can you actually see yourself fully as a self? Looking in an actual mirror, as Aristotle noted, reveals your physical self. But your total self is your body plus your mind and your character (virtues), including all your beliefs, values, methods of thinking, and all the choices and actions you take to develop and express your character. What, then, is the alternative to a literal mirror? Aristotle's answer is: the mirror of another person who is directly perceivable. If a friend shares your basic values and virtues, openly responds to them, and exemplifies them in action, then that friend provides you with a psychological mirror.[5] You can see yourself in that person. You not only feel understood, you experience your total self more fully, more objectively, as a result of another person's possessing the attributes you value and that person's responding to similar attributes in you. You can experience yourself directly as an entity, rather than as an ongoing succession of emotions, thoughts, and memories.

> *When you get to know another person very well,*
> *a person whose values are very similar to your own,*
> *you experience a mirror of your own soul.*

Just being in that person's presence is enjoyable. Not only do you experience yourself more fully, but you also experience that other person as a soul mate (a topic we will discuss in Part III).

A unique feature of romantic love, as contrasted with mere friendship, is that the feeling of visibility is even more all-encompassing and profound: not only does your partner respond to you sexually, as a man or woman, but also to your most intimate, deeply held values.

> *The bond with an ideal romantic partner*
> *is the most intimate bond you can experience.*

A business friend might respond to your business expertise, a golf friend to your golfing ability, a socializing friend to your pleasant personality, but only a romantic partner is able to know your total self, including not just your body but also the most intimate aspects of your soul. With a romantic soul mate, you get a "mirror" of yourself that even a close friend cannot provide. When a partner tells you what he or she appreciates about your character, in words (for example, giving you a warm, tender look and saying, "I love your warmth and sensuality") or in actions (for example, responding to you emotionally, intellectually, and sexually), your partner provides you with a unique and priceless psychological mirror.

Assuming that you are a good, self-respecting person, gaining this external perspective on your own character is more than deeply rewarding and motivating; it is irreplaceable. It gives you a type of self-awareness that you cannot get in any other way. Observe that this is a two-way mirror; you both benefit. Together, as psychological mirrors of one another's souls, you heighten your awareness both of yourself and of your partner. This intensifies your intimacy and adds joy and excitement to your life. In sum, only a romantic partner can give you total visibility as an individual.

But another person cannot be a mirror to your self unless you have a self to mirror. Melinda was an extremely shy, passive young adult. She had no hobbies and few acquaintances. There was nothing she really valued and no goals that she aspired to. She had an office job in which she spent most of the day doing mundane tasks that meant nothing to her. After work she kept to herself and watched TV to pass the time. She worked with Dylan, who had a crush on her. He assumed that she had a strong sense of herself and that her reticence hid a quiet self-confidence.

One day, he told her he was very attracted to her; he admired what seemed to be her quiet self-assurance. Melinda at first felt flattered but was then hit by a sudden wave of anxiety. Her mind was swimming with thoughts such as *I'm such a boring, do-nothing person—he doesn't know me at all. I'm not full of confidence—I'm just empty.* Melinda felt invisible because there was nothing of her self to see.

Nor can you get visibility by being with someone whose character is fundamentally different from your own (a co-worker you despise, a person who totally bores you, a date with whom you have nothing in common). Such a person's way of coming at the world is alien to your own; you will not feel an affinity for them or experience a reflection of yourself, and you certainly won't feel any romantic attraction to this person. To act as your mirror, another person must share important values with you.

> *It is no accident that one of the most painful complaints you can make about your partner is that "He (or She) makes me feel invisible, unimportant, like I don't exist."*

Invisibility is the negation of romantic love and of an important human need. (We'll come back to this issue in Part IV.)

In the story of Olivia and Ross, contrast how they felt about themselves in each other's presence with how Olivia felt when she was with her worthless ex-husband or how Ross felt in the presence of his uncaring father. The feeling of visibility was so important to each of them (though they did not consciously know what the principle was) and they had missed it so much that it brought each of them to the verge of tears when they experienced it through one another at the science museum. They were experiencing the fulfillment of deeply held but frustrated longings.

Observe that unlike Melinda, Ross and Olivia were not selfless. One of the themes of this book is that selflessness destroys romantic love: becoming a doormat will destroy your happiness. Such self-sacrificing has no place in romantic love. You may be thinking, *But that's what I've heard my whole life! To be a good partner, you have to learn to sacrifice . . .* Think again.

We hope we've got your attention, because you will discover for yourself, in the forthcoming pages, that to love and be loved, you need to truly value your self. You need to choose and pursue your own personal values.

Exercises

1. List up to three specific incidents during or after which you felt invisible to a romantic partner. What happened to make you feel this way? (For example, Eric took me to a party with his co-workers and didn't introduce me to any of them. He went off in a corner with his buddies, including his attractive secretary, and left me to introduce myself to a few people. I felt abandoned.)

a. _____

b. _____

c. _____

2. Now imagine that you could relive those three incidents. Identify exactly what you wished your partner would have said or done to make you feel visible in each case. (For example, I wish Eric had stayed with me and introduced me to the co-workers he liked the most. I wish he had said a few nice things about me in the introduction. I wish he had made it clear that I was his partner, rather than flirting with his secretary.)

a. _____

b. _____

c. _____

3. Notice how different you would have felt had your partner said or done these things. Think about how you can tell your current partner what you want to hear at times when you are starting to feel invisible. (For example, Eric, I feel like a fish out of water here. I would love it if you would introduce me to your friends.)

We will have more to say about visibility, communication, and self-valuing later in the book. For now, let us turn to that often-touted "virtue" that goes by several names—self-sacrifice, selflessness, altruism—and see whether being a good "martyr" makes for good romance—or not. Of course, there's a twist to the plot—with an outcome that may surprise you.

Notes

1. Aristotle, apparently, did write about romantic love, but these writings, along with many of his other works, were lost according to Aristotelian scholar Allan Gotthelf (see footnote 2).

2. Allan Gotthelf, "Love and Philosophy: Aristotelian vs. Platonic": This lecture was first written in 1975 and revised since; it has been given on more than twenty-five occasions at colleges and universities and to private groups, nationally and internationally. Dr. Gotthelf is a professor in the Department of History and Philosophy of Science at the University of Pittsburgh. The first part of this quote, "All love for others is an extension of the love one has for oneself," is from Aristotle's *Nicomachean Ethics* IX.1166a10; cf.1168b5. The second part, "[The good man] has the same attitude toward the one he loves as he does toward himself, for his friend really is another self," is from Aristotle's *Nicomachean Ethics* IX.1166a30–32. Translations by Allan Gotthelf, sometimes adapted from those by Martin Ostwald and others. Aristotle, *Nicomachean Ethics,* tr. by Martin Ostwald (New York: Random House, 1962; New York: The Bobbs Merrill Company, 1962).

3. Ibid., Aristotle, *Magna Moralia* II.1213a13–26. (Translations by Allan Gotthelf, sometimes adapted from those by Martin Ostwald and others.)

4. Ibid., Aristotle, *Magna Moralia* II.1169b34–1170a2. (Translations by Allan Gotthelf, sometimes adapted from those by Martin Ostwald and others.)

5. Based on Ayn Rand's private papers, there is evidence that she and Nathaniel Branden did additional work on the concept of visibility; see James S. Valliant, *The Passion of Ayn Rand's Critics* (Dallas, TX: Durban House, 2005, p. 219). It is impossible to determine with certainty exactly what each of them added to Aristotle's original idea, especially because they spent hundreds, if not thousands, of hours in discussions with each other. Ayn Rand used the term "mirror" in *Atlas Shrugged,* a term that Aristotle also used (see his quote above). Aristotle and Rand did not use the term "psychological visibility," so Branden's contribution may have been making explicit what was implicit in Aristotle and Rand (ibid., *Valliant,* p. 354).

---------------------- • CHAPTER 2 • ----------------------

Altruism and Narcissism: Two Approaches to Love That Do Not Work

On some level, you may have accepted the idea that love, in its purest and most exalted form, consists of sacrificing yourself to your loved one—dutifully putting your partner's needs, welfare, wants, desires, and values ahead of your own and giving up values that are personally important to you. You may believe that self-sacrifice is morally good.

Altruism

The moral code telling you to put others above yourself is known as altruism. Altruism does not mean politeness, kindness, consideration, or generosity. Literally, altruism means other-ism. Others come first; you come last. Consider the comments we've all heard:

> "He's so loving. He wants nothing for himself. He lives only to make his wife happy."

> "She's a dream girlfriend. She does whatever he wants. He's so lucky."

It is often argued that sacrificing yourself for others will bring you happiness. Does it? Consider some quotes from people in an altruistic relationship:

"I feel trapped. I feel like I've lost my self."

"I don't know who I am anymore—I'm just Joey's wife."

"I miss my old self—I used to have a sense of myself as a person. Now I live in the shadow of my wife—I'm afraid to speak up when I want something."

> *What's going on here is that the altruists in these examples are giving up their values and in the process losing their sense of identity.*

The end result is not happiness but unhappiness. Consider the case of Shannon.

"Have a good day, honey." Shannon gave Joe a quick kiss as he grabbed his coat and walked out the door. Looking out the window at her husband of fifteen years as he started his car and drove off to work, she realized how unhappy she was.

Just an hour earlier, Joe had asked her to "cozy-up"—code for helping him achieve orgasm. She had complied, burying her head in the pillow so he wouldn't see her eyes or facial grimaces as she silently repeated, over and over, *I hate sex! But even worse, we have perfect marriage! Like heck! I hate my life! I want to run away. I want a new life. . .*

Venting made Shannon feel better for a split second; then she felt an upsurge of guilt. *How dare you!* she thought. *Where would you be without him! Joe is so nice. You have two lovely sons with him. He gave you this house. You're financially secure. He even told you that you never have to work. YOU chose that boring office job! What the heck are you complaining about! You live in a nice neighborhood with lots of friends. Your parents love you. Even his family loves you. What more do you want!*

Shannon is the perfect wife and mother, the perfect daughter, the perfect friend, and the perfect neighbor. Everyone likes her, but she hates her life.

She heard herself moan, "I'm just being selfish. I should be grateful!" She took some deep breaths and the waves of anxiety ebbed into the pseudo-calm of temporary resignation. Joe was on his way to work—the day was hers. . . or was it? Glancing at her to-do list, she saw a long list of things she had planned to do for others. At the very bottom of the list was something for herself:

Home: Shop for groceries. Wash and iron Joe's shirts.
　　　Do dishes. Plan dinner.
Work: Make 20 copies of Mary's report for tomorrow's
　　　meeting. Prepare the 1,000-customer mailing, pick-up
　　　donuts for the coffee room and more toilet paper.
Kids: Buy soccer gear. Plan the next youth group meeting
　　　at the house. Buy Jared's teacher a get-well gift.
　　　Set up dentist appointments.
Mom and Dad: Pick up mom's medications at the pharmacy.
　　　Plan dinners for their Sunday visits this month.
Joe's sister: Offer to baby-sit for her on Tuesdays.
Friends/neighbors: Make dinner for Suzanne and
　　　get sympathy card for her. Plan the annual
　　　neighborhood yard sale. Buy Emily's mom a gift for her
　　　50th anniversary. Bake cupcakes for the animal shelter
　　　bake sale.
Sign up for the oil painting class on Monday evenings.

Shannon thought, *What if I sign up now?* Another glance at her list washed that thought away: *What's the use!* Then she heard the familiar chiding in her mind: *This is just self-pity. Grow up. Go finish the dishes.*

But something different was happening today. Shannon's thoughts were going in a new direction. She ripped her to-do list off the pad, grabbed a pen, and started writing furiously on a blank page:

I am NOT the perfect person—I'm the PERFECT HYPOCRITE!! I have tried so hard to please everyone else—so damn hard—and I resent them all. I am depressed, anxious—and angry. I'm always thinking: What does everyone else in my life want? Who is left out—ME! I feel like a servant—worse! I feel imprisoned in my perfect life. Why can't I focus on me! Because it's selfish, people say.

Shannon began to question whether her guilt about being selfish was connected to her aversion to sex. "Joe used to ask me repeatedly," she recalled, "what turned me on—I was too embarrassed to admit that anything turned me on—it seemed so selfish. I was supposed to please him. So I faked orgasms for a while. Now I don't even bother. I just dutifully submit."

The phoniness and the submission in her actions sickened her and she recognized that her phoniness bled into every aspect of her life. She put her pen to the paper to capture her thoughts:

> *I don't just fake sex, I fake everything. I tell people what they want to hear, not what I genuinely think.*

I'm dishonest. And it's a burden. I have to figure out what makes everyone happy, then try to please them. I hate people! They rob me of my time, my energy—they rob me of me.

Shannon laid down her pad of paper and glanced over at a travel magazine on the coffee table. The cover featured a slender, tanned woman wearing a business suit and carrying a portfolio with a cityscape in the background.

Tears rolled down her cheeks as she remembered her dream of becoming a fashion designer. She picked up the magazine and flipped to a photo of an artist who was painting two smiling children at a playground. She wished she could paint like that artist—another suppressed dream. On another page, she saw a couple lovingly embracing. The woman didn't look like *she* was faking romantic happiness. Shannon sobbed even harder. All the images spoke of hidden, frustrated desires.

New thoughts began to emerge: *Maybe it's not entirely other people's fault. After all, I'm the one who chooses to sacrifice.*

Could this idea of sacrificing myself, altruism, be self-damaging?

Could it be that my moral code—the one I worked so hard to achieve—is actually the problem?

She was beginning to see that this was a much wider issue. Gradually, she reached a startling conclusion: Maybe altruism was the reason she was so unhappy! It had led her to give up her values. It ruined her sex life, her career aspirations, her joy in life—even her capacity to think for herself.

She now saw clearly that she believed she was being morally "good" when she gave up her values. Altruism actually made her feel worthless, except for a temporary high when she was sacrificing her values in selfless service to others. Later she felt resentful and empty—and even more worthless. When she imagined doing things for her selfish pleasure, she felt morally guilty. Shannon realized she had more thinking to do.

We will revisit Shannon and Joe later.

In subtle and some not so subtle ways, many of us have fallen into the "altruism is moral" trap: moments when we betray ourselves in the name of being "good." We then suffer as Shannon does.

> *Being "good" by sacrificing one's values*
> *destroys romance and happiness.*

What happens to romance when both partners sacrifice? Let's look at altruism from a two-person perspective. Joanie and Bob have been married for two years and both feel that true love requires self-sacrifice.

"Hey, love," Bob said warmly as Joanie felt him wrap his muscular arms around her slender waist. She noticed that he'd returned home from work with a playful glint in his eyes. "A good day?" Joanie asked. "A good month!" Bob announced. "I found out today that I got those major accounts I've worked so hard on. My boss is so thrilled that he gave me a nice bonus. Now we can take that trip to Venice!" Bob's energy was contagious and Joanie turned around and gave him a passionate kiss.

As another reward for his success, Bob had promised to treat himself to a day of golf with his friend Jeff. He told Joanie about his plans for golf and watched her rolling her eyes. "Why the sour face? We can wine and dine at the Club tomorrow night. . . and then snuggle afterwards."

"Golf, Bob? With the sink leaking, the grass going to seed, both cars needing a wash, I thought you would want to stay home."

Confused, Bob said, "The sink is barely leaking and I planned on fixing it Sunday morning. The mowing I can do after work on Tuesday."

She shot back, "You are so selfish!"

Here she goes again, Bob thought, *accusing me of being "selfish" because I'm doing something I love. What a killjoy!* His marriage was important to him, he dutifully admonished himself, so reluctantly and resentfully, he called Jeff back and canceled. Now it was Joanie's turn to feel Bob's iciness towards her the rest of the night. There was no talk of celebrating, of eating out and snuggling—or of Venice.

Joanie woke up the next morning to find Bob in a sullen mood. "Why are you so upset? So you missed your stupid golf game. There are a hundred things you could be doing around here instead!"

Joanie's stomach tightened into a knot of guilt, as she thought, *Why do I pick on him all the time? Why can't he play golf? But—why can't he do his chores happily and willingly?*

The rest of the afternoon they did not speak to one another. The silence was broken by the cheery sound of Joanie's cell phone. Joanie answered, and Bob saw her brighten up as she said, "I can't wait to go to the theater tomorrow! Tell Becca and Sarah that I want that front row seat!" She loved musicals and romantic dramas. Her joy overshadowed her tension with Bob. She hung up, spun around, and started singing.

Bob, who had absolutely no interest in theater, had been aware of her theater plans for weeks but they had slipped his mind. Like Joanie, he had been privately struggling between feelings of guilt and anger. He had been planning his own peace offering: "Honey, let's forget what happened and start fresh. Let's go to Ristorante Canova for a candlelight dinner tomorrow night—and we can talk about our trip to Venice."

Relieved that Bob was no longer giving her the silent treatment, Joanie chimed, "Oh, I'd love to Bob, but can we do it some other time? I've been looking forward to going out with the girls."

"Can't you give your ticket away? I'll bet your sister would love to go to the show. I hope I'm more important than your friends." Bob couldn't help but feel a twinge of "got you back."

Joanie responded with a hardened edge in her voice, "I've had this night booked for a while, Bob. You know this."

Bob retorted, "Now who's selfish!" He walked out of the room without another word.

Joanie felt guilty. She wanted to go to the theater. But how could she enjoy it now? She called Cynthia back and told her to invite someone else.

Sunday evening arrived. Joanie went through the motions of a romantic dinner at Ristorante Canova. Back at home, Joanie felt that at least she should have sex with Bob. She did so but showed no enthusiasm. Bob asked what was troubling her. "I've got a headache," she lied, "I'm just not in the mood." Joanie was too confused to tell Bob the truth—that she resented not going to the theater and felt guilty for pressuring him to give up golf. Both ended up feeling gloomy, and their evening degenerated into silence. They went to sleep without talking further.

Notice what happened when both Joanie and Bob succumbed to dutifully giving up what they loved. This is altruism for two. They accused one another of being selfish if either pursued their own values. Notice that the more Joanie and Bob gave up, the more they mangled any genuine tenderness and love they felt for each other. You may have even forgotten their loving embrace at the outset of their story. They likely had forgotten it too. Altruism causes a vicious cycle that keeps stacking hurt upon hurt.

These two examples illustrate the basic pattern of altruistic romantic relationships.

Person A has something he or she values—something that is important, a source of pleasure and happiness (career, golf, theater).

Person B wants *A* to sacrifice the value—out of love.

Person A does not want to give up the value, but by viewing self-sacrifice (altruism) as morally proper, makes the sacrifice out of guilt.

Person A resents the sacrifice and *B* resents the resentment, because if *A* "really loved her (or him)," he (or she) would give up the value (golf, theater) gladly.

Both A and B end up unhappy and emotionally distant from one another.

Given the premise of self-sacrifice, there is no solution to such dilemmas. Self-sacrifice is renunciation of the valuable, of the important, of what you want—of yourself.

Don't be confused by thinking altruism simply means consideration and good will toward others. Treating your partner and others with kindness, tenderness, consideration, and generosity does not require sacrificing your values unless you do not actually value those others. You will want to treasure your partner (and those you care for) because they are selfish values. Happiness, whether in romance or in any other realm such as work or friendship, is impossible to achieve under the code of altruism because happiness stems from the achievement of one's values, not from giving them up. (This assumes that the values and goals one pursues are rational—a topic we'll explore later.)

The code of sacrifice promises happiness by advocating a contradiction: the demand that one give up that which makes happiness possible.

To quote Ayn Rand:

[Selfless love] would have to mean that you derive no personal pleasure or happiness from the company and the existence of the person you love, and that you are motivated only by self-sacrificial pity for that person's need of you. I don't have to point out to you that no one would be flattered by, nor would accept, a concept of that kind. Love is not self-sacrifice, but the most profound assertion of your own needs and values. It is for your own happiness that you need the person you love, and that is the greatest compliment, the greatest tribute you can pay to that person.[1]

An experienced marriage counselor-sex therapist agrees. David Schnarch writes, "Expecting your partner to sacrifice for you in the name of love kills marriage, sex, intimacy, and love."[2]

It should be noted that it is impossible to practice altruism consistently. To be perfectly altruistic, you would have to give up your money, your job, your hobbies, your house, and even your loved ones; after all, others might need them more than you. Of course, no one goes this far, but this leaves a professed altruist in a state of permanent guilt. Moral perfection, by altruistic standards, is impossible; the only path to "perfection" is total self-immolation.

Narcissism

If self-sacrifice doesn't work, what is the alternative? Would it be doing whatever you feel like doing and treating your partner and others as your servants?

Let's revisit Shannon as she considers this alternative. Shannon was still thinking: *Since sacrificing myself to others is making me miserable, how about turning the tables? Maybe I should make them all sacrifice to me? I could refuse to iron Joe's shirts and demand that he iron my blouses. Instead of getting dinner ready for the kids, I could tell them to cook it for me and clean the house too. Rather than helping the neighbors with baby-sitting, I could pressure them to sit just for my kids. Rather than driving Mom to the grocery store, I could insist that she drive me. As for my career plans, I could just take money out of our joint account without discussion and announce that I am going to art school.*

We suspect that your gut response is: How selfish! But let's look a bit closer. Would these actions be in Shannon's actual self-interest? What effect would such actions have on the relationships she values? If she felt unimportant as an altruist, wouldn't her loved ones feel unimportant as well when the tables were turned?

Is a "me only" policy any better than a "them only" policy? Aren't these two sides of the same sacrificial coin? In both cases, someone plays the role of the victim.

Let's consider Bob and Joanie. What if Bob decided to play golf no matter what promises he had made to Joanie about joint activities? What if he went drinking with his buddies several nights a week and told Joanie to make the needed house repairs herself, after doing his laundry and cooking his meals? And what if Joanie rebelled by going out with the girls several nights a week and told Bob to fix her meals and do her laundry? And let's add that both would raid their joint bank account at will to buy things they each wanted. Give this marriage a few more months at the most. Again, what we conventionally called selfish is actually self-destructive. Such behavior would ruin a potentially good marriage and thus work against both their interests.

To illustrate the point further, let's visit a new couple, Carol and Tom. On Saturday morning Tom announces that he's going sailing all day. Carol is shocked because they had already agreed to shop for furniture. Tom dismisses her objection and says, "I don't want to do that—maybe some other time." After sailing, Tom sits in the yacht club lounge with his buddies, drinking beer and boasting, mainly with fictional stories, of his great prowess at sailing, fishing, and golfing, as well as his job achievements and his successes with women he has "on the side."

After drinking himself into a semi-stupor, he drives home erratically and demands to know when dinner will be served. Dinner conversation turns into a huge argument about Tom's "selfishness." After dinner Tom demands sex but Carol refuses, and he stalks off angrily to the basement to watch TV and drink more beer.

Consider a similar scenario from the other side. Carol insists that they spend far more money than they actually have—by running up huge credit card bills on jewelry and fine clothes for herself, buying an expensive car, and throwing lavish dinner parties to which she invites people Tom hates. During the dinners she tells jokes at Tom's expense. She pressures him to move to a more exclusive neighborhood even though they can't afford it. What Tom wants is totally irrelevant to her. She's infuriated by what she considers his neglect and by the slightest criticism from him. What is at the core of their lousy marriage? The problem is that both Tom and Carol are "me only" people, in other words, narcissists.

"Me-only" people are no better off than "them-only" people. Neither approach leads to happiness.

What specifically is narcissism? Narcissism is a psychological pattern characterized by the following:

- Feelings of grandiosity and superiority
- The need for constant attention
- Exhibitionism
- Fantasies of unlimited success and omnipotence
- Constant envy of other people
- Feelings of entitlement
- Exploitation of others
- Lack of empathy

Exhibiting some of these behaviors some of the time does not make you a full-fledged narcissist. Sometimes you can properly feel lack of empathy (for example, toward a person who hurt you). Sometimes when you are overly stressed you may be hypersensitive to criticism or need special attention for a short period of time, but you and your partner know it is "out of character" for you—it is not a pattern. Such moments do not make you a narcissist. Like other traits, narcissism exists on a continuum. The more of these characteristics a person has and the more frequently they are exhibited, the more of a narcissist that person is.

Observe that narcissists appear self-centered in the sense that they want everyone to gratify their wishes. But they lack genuine self-esteem, any real sense of themselves or their own worth, and they desperately need other people to relieve them of their doubts.[3] This relief is short-lived because others cannot create the self-esteem they lack, so their desire for reassurance from others is insatiable and unremitting. The most accurate description of such people is not that they are self-centered but rather that they are self-doubt-centered.[4]

The problem with full-fledged narcissists as romantic partners is that they are incapable of truly valuing another person because they do not value themselves; they are fundamentally lacking in self-esteem and are obsessed with relieving their own anxieties. They don't know what it means to pursue a positive value—one that is not tied to relieving self-doubt. They "need" others—in a desperate sort of way—and they "use" them, but they cannot love them. They are not truly selfish because narcissists have no real sense of self. Their "self" is only a cauldron of fears and doubts—and grandiose, self-deceptive fantasies whose goal is to alleviate those doubts.

Loving a narcissist is a frustrating, painful and ultimately heartbreaking experience, because they have unlimited wants but nothing positive to offer another person.

The more narcissistic a person, the worse it is for romance. We should add that there are people we call "clueless" when it comes to relating to other people and yet who are not actual narcissists; nor are they suffering from any inborn disorders such as autism. They are typically people who have been deprived emotionally in childhood and thus are not in touch with their emotions and are impoverished when it comes to having their own values. This makes it hard for them to be sensitive to the emotions and values of others, simply because they do not know any better. Such people can get better if they are strongly motivated to do so, though they usually need professional help.

The "Magical" Affinity of Altruists and Narcissists

It is no accident that narcissists and altruists often have a magnetic attraction to one another. Can you see how perfect the fit is? The altruist feels the need to selflessly serve others and this is just what the narcissist wants. Narcissists want to be worshipped and gratified in every way possible, and this is just what altruists offer, thinking it demonstrates their moral virtue.

But the fact that they represent a fit does not make such relationships successful. The narcissist cannot be satisfied and may soon tire of just one worshipper. And the more selfless the worship the altruist offers, the greater the feeling of emptiness that results. Such people might stay together out of fear or inertia, but it won't be a relationship between self-respecting equals and it certainly won't be romantic.

So if neither altruism nor narcissism leads to a happy romantic relationship, what does? See the next chapter.

Below we offer exercises on detecting altruism and narcissism.

Exercises

Detecting Altruism

1. Think of a current relationship (or one in your past). Note a few instances in which you've sacrificed something important to you that you wish you hadn't. Examples:

- I wish I hadn't given up going to college for my husband.
- I wasn't ready to have children, yet I was afraid to let down my wife.
- I wish I hadn't missed that movie because my boyfriend wouldn't go with me.

_____

_____

2. When you sacrificed something that was important to you, how did you end up feeling?

About yourself: _____

_____

Toward your partner: _____

_____

3. It's helpful to detect what you actually say to yourself when you sacrifice your values. That way you can hear yourself starting to go down an altruistic path. What types of things do you say to yourself to cause you to self-betray? Here are some examples:

> *Resignation:* Oh, what's the use! I don't want any arguments
> *Appeasement:* I don't want to rock the boat. I just want to keep the peace.
> *Moral uncertainty:* Who knows what's right or wrong— guess I'd better play it safe.
> *Altruistic attacks against yourself:* I don't want to be selfish. That would be wrong.
> *Should statements/Duty statements:* It's my duty to please others.
> *Need-based statements:* Bob needs me to give up the theater so I can spend the evening with him.
> *Denying your values:* I don't really need to go to the theater. I can give it up.

List some things you say to yourself that cause you to sacrifice what's important to you:

_____

_____

Detecting Narcissism

1. Below is a list of warning signs of a "me-only" person. Choose your current partner, someone you dated in the past, or someone you might possibly date. Then, using the list below, circle any descriptions that fit this person. (Not every "me-only" person will exhibit all these traits all the time or to the same degree.)

- Acts arrogantly, domineering and intimidating.
- Needs to be the center of attention—to have undivided (and unearned) admiration.

- Talks "big," i.e., shows off and has a much exaggerated view of himself or herself.
- Acts as if other people owe him or her (a sense of entitlement).
- Presents as a "one-way street." Doesn't feel it's necessary to consider others' values.
- Manipulates to get whatever he or she wants.
- Has a quick trigger and takes minor slights very personally; hypersensitive to criticism.
- Has no empathy and refuses to put himself or herself "in your shoes."

2. When with this person, how do, or did, you feel?
About yourself: _____

_____

_____

Toward this person: _____

_____

_____

3. What could you say or do to preserve your dignity when dealing with a narcissist?

_____

_____

Notes

1. Ayn Rand, *Playboy Magazine* (interview of Ayn Rand by Alvin Toffler), March 1964.

2. David Schnarch, *Passionate Marriage* (New York: An Owl Book, Henry Holt and Co., 1997) p. 298.

3. Paper Swagger, *Harvard Magazine*, "Self Esteem, Real and Phony," Sept.–Oct., 2005, pp. 18, 22.

4. For an expanded discussion of the idea of being "self-doubt-centered," see Ayn Rand's essay: "Causality versus Duty," published in *Philosophy: Who Needs It* (New York: Bobbs-Merrill, 1982) New York: Signet, 1984, chap. 10.

CHAPTER 3

True Romantic Love Is Egoistic

*E*goism is your foundation for romantic happiness. By egoism we don't mean a mindless hedonism but a mutual valuing of yourself and your partner. Making love work, as we will see later, requires rational thought.

Shannon kept thinking about her situation in light of her new knowledge: *Since sacrificing myself to others is making me miserable, and sacrificing others to myself would also make me miserable—what's left? Being an altruist leaves me feeling unimportant. I've ended up hating both Joe and my life. Being a narcissist is just plain controlling and mean. How would I feel deep down if Joe pandered to me or cowered before me? I'd feel guilty. Then Joe would be in the position of being selfless, and I don't want to be on the giving or the receiving end of any sacrifices.*

What, then, do I need? Maybe I need to be more self-valuing, have more self-respect, more self-worth. Funny, this runs counter to everything I've ever heard! But I think that's exactly what I need and what Joe needs.

I want to wake up in the morning and feel, "This is a day in my life, a day I can't wait to enjoy." I want my to-do list filled with my chosen values, not sacrifices. And with Joe? I want to truly love and feel loved by him. I do want to be selfish—rationally selfish. And I want Joe to be the same.

Uprooting altruism and becoming more self-valuing and egoistic is no easy task. It's difficult to change life-long moral premises. One sentence Shannon found herself repeating was a line by Howard Roark, the hero in Ayn Rand's novel *The Fountainhead:*

> *"To say 'I love you' one must first know how to say the 'I.'"*[1]

Fast forward one year: Shannon is smiling, because in the past year, she has learned to value herself. She now understood that it was proper to design her own life by naming what matters most to her:

- Choosing and pursuing her own values
- Thinking for herself
- Speaking up for herself—tactfully
- Being honest—with herself and with others
- Setting proper boundaries with family, friends, and associates
- Going to night school to become a clothes designer
- Giving her children a good education and moral guidance, yet encouraging them not to obey blindly but to think for themselves
- Learning how to communicate well with Joe and growing closer to him emotionally

Shannon was changing, but that didn't mean that others around her were changing also. Shannon would answer her phone and hear the typical, "We need you to. . ." and "Could you just do me a little favor. . . ?" from her mother, her sister-in-law, her neighbors, her boss, and her friends. She learned how to be honest with them. When her sister-in-law cornered her and said: "Hey, Shannon, you're a dear! I'm planning a weekend getaway to the lake without the kids and I figured they could stay with you. I need a break!" Shannon gently responded, "It sounds like you've planned something fun. You'll need to find someone else to sit. You might call the college and see if they can recommend any students who might be available for the weekend. I find that I enjoy your company and the kids more when I'm not their regular sitter." Her sister-in-law shot back, "Can't you do this—for me—as a favor? After all, we're family and I prefer to have you as a sitter than a stranger." Shannon paused; that old trapped feeling descended on her. She then remembered to relax and stay true to herself, calmly saying, "I need to do myself a favor—and you a favor. I need to be honest with you. I want to enjoy your darling kids as an aunt, not as a perennial sitter. I felt obligated to help you out over the years at the expense of taking care of myself. I grew to resent it, and then I felt guilty about the resentment. Now I see the error I was making. This weekend I want some time with just Joe and our kids. My guess is that you've felt this way in your life too."

Shannon's sister-in-law looked both shocked and disappointed but did not argue further. In the past, Shannon would have collapsed into a puddle of guilt at even the thought of refusing. This time, she felt a warm, glowing sense of pride. She had stayed calm without attacking her sister-in-law. Her sister-in-law's annoyance was caused by her expectation that others would serve her needs. Shannon no longer agreed to be the servant and knew that it was her sister-in-law's unfair demands that she was properly rejecting.

When you selflessly, altruistically, play the role of the martyr, there must be someone who is receiving your sacrifices. Shannon continued thinking: *Why is it morally okay for others to accept my sacrifices? Aren't others being selfish in accepting them? Shouldn't they refuse my offers? Or if they accept, shouldn't they sacrifice back? But then nobody would ever get what they want. Something's wrong here.*

> *Shannon was beginning to grasp that altruism demands a double standard: you give, others take. Is there another way to deal with others? Yes—voluntary trade to mutual advantage. That way, both parties get what they want.*

Shannon used her healthy self-assertiveness to improve her sexual enjoyment with Joe. When Joe occasionally approached her in the morning to "cuddle," instead of dutifully submitting and muttering,

"I hate sex," privately to herself, Shannon now respected herself to say, "Hey, love, now's not a good time for me. I've got a busy day ahead and my mind is wrapped around that. Let's unwind tomorrow night. I'd love to take the evening off—for us." Joe was delighted. He was now married to a person with a self. For Shannon, it felt like she was dating Joe again. Shannon discovered her creative side in coming up with erotic fantasies that they both enjoyed. He loved the new woman she was becoming. They worked to mesh their schedules so that they could enjoy each other's company as equals. Not only did their sex life improve, but their whole relationship became more loving and intimate as well.

Shannon made other dramatic changes: She quit her boring job and worked part time with a dressmaker. Before work, she would spend an hour at the gym. She lost twenty pounds and looked shapely. She rarely snapped at her kids—and she gently apologized when she slipped up. She hadn't taken any art classes yet, but she put that goal on her wish list for the future. She was embracing her life.

Joe learned, too, that telling Shannon that she never had to work again was not a gift. She needed to discover and live her dreams. The boys enjoyed their mother's honesty and her growing confidence in them. She was no longer the "hovercraft mom"—trying to make their every choice for them. While still being very caring, she was letting them grow and use their own minds.

There were some setbacks but none that brought her all the way back to her old life. She was discovering more and more reasons to love her life. And now whenever she feels as though she is reverting to her old altruistic premises, she simply recalls the line from *The Fountainhead*: "To say 'I love you' one must first know how to say the 'I'"—and recaptures her newfound world.

Shannon and Joe were not the only couple struggling with altruism and narcissism. Let's revisit Bob and Joanie. Recall that Bob was celebrating a productive month at work, culminating in a nice bonus check. He and Joanie could now plan their dream trip to Venice. He also wanted to celebrate by playing golf on Saturday;

Joanie accused him of being "selfish" for choosing golf over chores. Bob gave up golf resentfully. Later, when Joanie enthusiastically reminded Joe that she had theater tickets to see a musical with some friends, Bob accused her of being "selfish" by putting her friends above dinner with him. Joanie gave up her tickets resentfully. Both were sacrificing to one another. With altruism as their guide, their romance was dying.

Let's give them a better ending. Imagine that Joanie had lovingly told Bob, "Enjoy your golf game. I know there are chores, but those can wait! Go celebrate!" And imagine Bob had said, "Joanie, I completely forgot about your theater plans. How about going to Canova's next Friday night?" What a different relationship they could be enjoying!

These examples show the dramatically different pattern that emerges when couples don't demand sacrifices of one another and don't capitulate to altruistic standards but instead maintain self-valuing and partner-valuing standards:

> Person A has something he or she values—something that is important, a source of pleasure and happiness (career, golf, theater).
> Person B wants A to pursue this value—out of love.
> Person A happily pursues the value.
> Person A loves the support of B—and is equally supportive when B wants to pursue his or her values.
> Both A and B end up happy and emotionally intimate.

We hope that you now see that there's a third choice of standards on which to base romance which is neither altruistic nor narcissistic. Genuine love is neither self-sacrificial nor narcissistic, but rationally egoistic.[2] This is true in three respects:

1. Being egoistic means that you have an ego, a self—that you are secure in your own person, that you have a firm sense of your own identity and pursue your own values.

2. It means that your partner is enormously important to you

personally.

3. Being rational means that you don't demand, even in trade, what is unfair or unreasonable (for example, that your partner give up a passionately loved career for your sake).

Romantic love is the most selfish of all emotions. It means that you care deeply about your partner's welfare, health, pleasure, success, and happiness. Your loved one is an irreplaceable personal treasure, someone to be nurtured and protected, with whom you want to grow and thrive as an equal partner for life. It's someone whom you miss when you are away and whom you delight in seeing upon your return. It is someone you love to talk to, to touch, to be near, to make love to, to take delight in. Without that person there would be a huge, irreplaceable void in your life because he or she makes your life complete. And all this applies to your partner's view of you.

To quote Rand, "One gains a profoundly personal, selfish joy from the mere existence of the person one loves. It is one's own personal, selfish happiness that one seeks, earns and derives from love."[3]

True love is egoism à deux—egoism for two.

Love is neither sacrifice nor exploitation. It's a relationship in which both parties are happy because they both get what they want.

❉   ❉   ❉   ❉   ❉

You may be thinking, *Okay, fine, but it's impossible for both partners to be happy if each one does every single thing he or she wants all the time.* Well, that depends upon what you mean by every single thing. For example, one should properly eliminate bad habits, such as being chronically late, failing to shower regularly, leaving smelly clothing and mold-covered dishes scattered about, living for booze, etc. Why? Because these are not rational values. People cannot rationally want to be irresponsible or a slob. Just try imagining the romantic lives of those who don't value themselves or value being responsible.

What about small, optional things? Let's say your partner was brought up in a poor home and hates to see the water running in the shower for more than five minutes. Or you like the bed made every day and your partner thinks it's not a big deal. These are examples of differences that all couples encounter. It's rational to make compromises on such things without either partner being a martyr. For example, your partner might grasp that you're now financially better off and that it's okay to enjoy a longer shower. Maybe you can shower together. Your partner may choose to make the bed or you may agree to make the bed together—or you could buy a featherbed cover that makes the task effortless. Alternatively, you can decide that it's not a big deal whether it's made at all.

What about big things such as career conflicts? Let's look at the case of John and Sue.

John was a successful Broadway actor who worked regularly and happily. On vacation he met and fell in love with Sue, who lived in a small town in Oregon. She ran her own business and loved it very much. There followed an intense, long-distance romance that lasted almost a year. Wanting a permanent relationship, Sue ultimately demanded that John quit his New York job and move to the West Coast to live with her. John complained that he could not pursue his acting career in Oregon and refused to give it up.

Sue was furious at John's refusal. Her underlying presumption was, *If you really love me, you will sacrifice your career for me.* John knew he would resent Sue if he did, but she was counting on his sacrifice to make her happy. She was oblivious to what giving up a career he loved would do to him. This conflict ended the relationship. Conventionally, one would call Sue "selfish," but observe that her demand was not, in fact, in her actual self-interest, because it destroyed a relationship that she greatly valued.

Now let's consider the case of John and Sue from a rationally egoistic perspective. First, Sue would not ask John to sacrifice his career for her. Rather, together they would think of solutions that would make them both happy. For example, they might decide to continue their long-distance romance until a solution could be found, or (if they were older) until one partner was ready to retire. They might consider whether Sue could restart her business successfully in

New York. They might consider both moving to another city where conditions for both their careers would be favorable. One of them might consider starting a new, personally valued career. If Sue were agreeable, John might consider living in Oregon between acting jobs. Observe that the goal is to ensure that each partner gets what he or she wants. Creative thinking is paramount. (In Part VI, we discuss in depth how couples can resolve conflicts effectively, including a discussion on basic methods of compromise.) If both parties selfishly and deeply value one another, barring unusual circumstances, they will not let geography ruin their relationship. They will figure out a way to make it work.[4]

A note on egoism: Of course you can give non-sacrificial favors. Let's look at this issue from a genuinely loving perspective. If you adore your partner, you will selfishly enjoy doing things to please him or her. This doesn't just mean ceasing the annoying, negative things (such as calling your partner "fatty'" or refusing to help around the house), but giving your partner positive values, such as listening attentively, writing love notes, and bringing flowers. (This is such an important topic that we devote all of Part IV to how to nurture your love for one another.)

Now you might be thinking: *But annoying habits and irresponsible behavior aren't the only sources of conflict. Big issues always arise—problems with finances, in-laws, kids, a couple's sex life.* We will address how to resolve the big ones in the chapters ahead.

Now that you understand that love is a profoundly selfish (but not narcissistic) value, what's next? We'll explore what causes that wonderful feeling of love in our next chapter.

Exercises

1. Being egoistic means that you're secure in your own person, that you have a firm sense of identity. Most people are self-critical and focus on personal flaws, for example: "I'm so disorganized!" "I'm never on time." "I'm so bad at math." "I'm not the best lover." There is good reason to do this when you are trying to improve yourself.

However, most people rarely pause to take stock of what they value in their own character. Take a moment to name a few things that you love about yourself. (Shannon might say: "I love that I am not afraid to question and to search for answers that will make me happier" or "I love that I have learned to be honest with Joe" or "I love that I chose a career I will enjoy.")

_____

_____

2. Being egoistic also means that your partner is enormously important to you personally. List a few things you value and admire in your partner. (Shannon might say: "Joe has a delightful sense of humor" and "Joe is honest—he was totally forthright in therapy" and "Joe is a loving father—he's actively involved in the boys' lives.")

_____

_____

Notes

1. Ayn Rand, *The Fountainhead* (New York: Signet, 1993), p. 376. The fuller text is:

> "I love you, Dominique. As selfishly as the fact that I exist. As selfishly as my lungs breathe air. I breathe for my own necessity, for the fuel of my body, for my survival. I've given you, not my sacrifice or my pity, but my ego and my naked need. This is the only way you can wish to be loved. This is the only way I can want you to love me. . . . To say 'I love you' one must know first how to say the 'I.'"

2. We distinguish rational egoism, which means concern with one's own interests, from egotism, which refers to boastful self-absorption. Egotism is similar in meaning to narcissism. We also distinguish rational egoism from hedonism, which is the mindless pursuit of pleasure based on the feelings of the moment. Hedonism is a dead end, as the hippies of the 1960s revealed. To choose values and pursue them you have to think, and the thinking has to be long range as well as short range if you want to be in control of your life.

3. Ayn Rand, "The Ethics of Emergencies," *The Virtue of Selfishness* (New York: Signet, 1964), p. 48.

4. Moving to another country would be a different matter, especially if one partner would have to move to a country he or she strongly disliked.

CHAPTER 4

Understanding Love

*R*omantic love is neither mysterious nor ineffable. The causes of romantic love can be (and need to be) understood through introspection—that is, looking inward at one's own thoughts and feelings.

You're preparing for a lovely evening with your partner. You decide to go to the movies to see a typical Hollywood romance. At the end of the movie, you feel deflated and depressed. Another movie with good-looking characters who fall in love quickly and end up in bed without knowing if there is anything to value in one another, apart from looks.

Is this what romance is all about—the superficial? The psychologically causeless? Hollywood's typical treatment of romance is generally consistent with the conventional view that love is mysterious, a matter of the heart, beyond reason and causal understanding—in short, that it is just some kind of ineffable chemistry. This mistaken view leads to many disastrous romantic relationships.

To make matters worse, researchers in the fields of neuroscience claim that love is basically a matter of brain activity, a primary mating drive, with your free will and choices minimized, reduced to evolutionary pushes and pulls from neurochemicals and brain systems. Your personal values and your mind—the part of you that perceives, reasons, and feels—are left out of the picture.

Although neurochemicals and brain pathways are obviously essential to the proper working of the mind, is there nothing more? Are we no different than animals? When you're with someone you adore, are you simply pair-bonding like baboons, responding to inanimate chemicals?

Why would anyone believe that love is basically brain activity? Or that love is solely a matter of the heart, of unanalyzable emotions? The reason is that emotions often do feel mysterious. They happen so fast! They are actually very quick, automatic reactions involving your *subconscious* personal knowledge, values, and standards.

Imagine you're a woman on a first date with a dashing, handsome man. You're immediately sexually and emotionally attracted to him—the chemistry seems solid. But then your friend in the police department warns you that this man is a well-known con man who has left broken and domestically abused women in his wake. What do you feel now? Notice what happens to your so-called chemistry. Your new knowledge changes your appraisal of him, according to your value standards, and your emotions change as a result—from admiration and pleasure to disgust—instantaneously. Chemicals did not cause your new knowledge.

Suppose you're a man on a first date with an attractive woman but know very little about her. During the evening, you discover that she is a single mom and raised two children on her own. The kids were sent to good schools because she wanted them to develop basic skills and the ability to think. When the time was right, she started a small business on her own. Through reading and taking online courses, she was helping to ensure that her business would be a success. In the course of discussing a problem she had with the business, you discover that she was always honest with customers even though lying at times could have brought her a short-term advantage. She seems totally genuine and is not trying to impress you.

With each new discovery, you are aware of very positive emotions. You are experiencing the beginning of love. Certainly there are brain chemicals at work here but they and the love were the result of the information you gained and appraised.

In both cases, your feelings changed when you discovered some negative or positive information about the other person's character. Chemical determinism was not the cause when you answered the question "Could he or she be the one?" with a no or a maybe. Let's take a closer look at the *psychology* of love.

Love is an emotion, and all emotions have consciously identifiable causes. However, certain factors make the causes of emotions (such as love, joy, sadness) especially difficult to identify.

As noted, emotions occur automatically and instantly, based on how we appraise people or situations. Emotions don't develop in slow motion. You catch your boyfriend in bed with your best friend and you are instantly flooded with anger. You reunite with your husband after he's returned from his military tour of duty and you immediately feel overjoyed.

The appraisals causing our emotions are not only automatic but also subconscious—outside of our immediate awareness. You feel irritated with your wife but may not be able to easily put into words what's specifically causing your irritation.

Emotions can be understood consciously but only through introspection—by focusing inward on our own mental contents and processes. Subconscious thoughts can be brought into awareness. Pedro thinks: *Aaron is flirting with my wife and I feel fear. Why? I'm worried that she'll divorce me.* If Pedro had more self-confidence, his reaction might be quite different: *I like that my wife is attractive, and she's probably enjoying the attention from Aaron. But that's no threat to me because we deeply value one another and feel worthy of each other's love.*[1]

Introspection is a learned skill. Without it, you are doomed to feel at the mercy of mysterious, ever-changing, emotions. But with practice you can become very good at it.

We are all complex individuals, with many facets and layers. The outer layer is often what people want others to see but underneath they may be quite different. They may appear kind, honest, and self-confident but underneath they have a mean streak, poor morals, and profound self-doubts. They may also act inconsistently, some days acting warm and loving and other days cold and vindictive.

Alicia met Sam on a blind date. Sam was tall and slender, with an attractive smile and a pleasant, outgoing manner. Alicia was attracted to him as soon as she saw him but had no idea why. Everyone has an automatic, or "gut," emotional reaction—positive or negative—when they first meet another person. Alicia was responding to Sam's physical appearance and demeanor and was subconsciously inferring things about his personality. For example, she may have implicitly concluded that tall people are strong and masculine. Sam's smile may have conveyed to her that he was a kind and considerate person. His outgoing manner may have subconsciously conveyed to her that he would be enjoyable to talk to and that she would not have to draw him out of a shell. All of this was Alicia's first-level reaction, although she was clueless as to its causes.

After some preliminary chatting, Sam and Alicia discovered that they were from the same state and had gone to the same college. This drew Alicia a bit closer. She felt, but did not identify in words, that they may have shared something in common. Sam complimented her on her outfit and how beautiful she looked. This relieved her anxiety, because she had always been self-conscious about her looks. She now experienced a rather warm and comforting glow, helped along by her second glass of wine. Sam seemed like a really sweet guy. At this point they had gotten to a slightly deeper layer; she actually knew something—although not very much—about Sam other than that obviously he was good-looking.

They ordered dinner. Sam's order was not taken correctly and he spoke rudely to the waitress when the wrong entrée was delivered. Alicia was taken aback, but Sam put on another big smile and she pushed her doubts out of her mind and rationalized: *This just shows his masculine assertiveness.* Alicia did not identify why she felt upset or what it could mean about Sam.

Alicia asked Sam about his job. He was a government bureaucrat who seemed to enjoy the power he had over people. He also told her, "confidentially," the names of some famous people and organizations that his agency had had dealings with. At this point Alicia experienced conflicting emotions. She admired his success and his pride in his work; she liked the idea of an ambitious man who knew important people and who was friendly and complimentary. On the other hand, she felt anxious about his meanness to the waitress, his boastful attitude, and his revelation of private information.

At this point, she half-realized that she had gotten to a deeper layer of Sam but did not know what to make of her mixed feelings and chose not to analyze them further.

After dinner Sam took her to a nightclub for drinks and dancing. He was a marvelous dancer and she was immediately aroused. Alicia did not know how much of this was the dancing, the wine, or the feeling of being desired, but at this point she stopped thinking altogether and just let herself go.

Alicia felt as though she were falling in love. She fantasized about the two of them getting married and dancing in Hawaii on their honeymoon. Her reverie was broken when she noticed Sam ogling other women on the dance floor. This aroused some jealousy, but she suppressed her doubts and focused only on the feel of his body against hers. She felt safe and desirable.

Under the influence of alcohol, the dancing, and Sam's charming smile, they went back to his apartment and had sex. She experienced great sexual pleasure and apparently he did too. When she got back to her apartment later, it occurred to her that Sam had never asked her about her work and she felt a stab of resentment. But she didn't care. She felt she was madly in love with Sam. When she talked about him to her friends, they politely suggested that there were some red flags about Sam, but she paid no attention. When asked why she was in love, she shrugged and said, "I don't know. He just drives me wild. I can't explain it."

Sam and Alicia continued dating and had an exciting sexual

relationship, but there were ups and downs, especially when he insulted her about such things as her choice of shoes or snapped at her when she locked her keys in the car. Gradually, Sam began to distance himself from the relationship and the end came when Alicia's best friend confessed she had slept with Sam the night before. Alicia could not understand it. One day they were in love, and the next day they were not. It seemed inexplicable.

What went wrong?

Two things. First, there wasn't much basis for the relationship in the first place. Second, Alicia totally failed to identify her emotions or their causes, which could have given her the valuable clues that Sam was not the man for her.

Let's consider Sam first. Sam was a shallow person who liked to boast about his power over others, reveal confidential information about his work, and insult people who displeased him. It appeared that he was a womanizer as well. These facts make it clear that he had his own insecurities—elements of narcissism—and a lack of moral integrity. His whole appeal to Alicia was based on looks, charm, and the ability to dance well. These are, of course, desirable traits to have, but they didn't reveal the essence of his character.

Alicia did not ask herself why she was angry when he was rude to the waitress and later to her, which would have led her to question her initial assumptions—that he was a considerate person. She did not explore the anxious feelings she had about Sam's boastfulness, nor did she pay heed to forewarnings of his insecure personality and questionable moral character. She failed to introspect what it meant when she felt jealous about his ogling other women. If she had, she might have begun to suspect his womanizing tendencies. Had she analyzed her resentment at his failure to ask about her job, she might have begun to suspect that Sam was more interested in sex than in her as a whole person. She did not introspect well enough to realize that part of her attraction to Sam was that he temporarily relieved her feminine and intellectual self-doubts, which meant she was attracted by a negative—the removal of anxiety—as much as by his positive traits. She neglected to examine deeper layers of Sam's character and thus see that these negated his superficially desirable qualities.

If Alicia had taken the trouble to understand her emotional responses to Sam and their causes, she would not have been surprised by the outcome of the relationship and might have broken it off much earlier.

Let's consider another couple. Melissa met Pete at a dinner party. At first, Melissa did not have a strong gut feeling about Pete. He was average looking and quiet, although he had attractive blue eyes. She found herself seated next to him at dinner. He immediately began asking her questions and seemed genuinely interested in what she had to say. She was surprised to hear herself admit openly that she had recently been divorced and had been very hurt by it. She felt an immediate attraction to him; she knew that there was something about him that made her feel comfortable. Then she grasped the reason—he seemed to understand her. She felt visible. He confessed that he had been divorced himself and knew how hard it was to cope with the end of an important relationship.

Pete admitted that his divorce had been mainly his fault, but he did not offer any further details. This made her feel slightly anxious, and, unlike Alicia, she made a mental note to herself: *Better find out more about this at some point.*

She asked him about his work and learned he was a stockbroker. It was clear that he loved the process of discovering good, safe investments for his clients. She felt even more attracted to him and realized that she admired the pride he took in doing a good job without boasting.

Pete asked Melissa what she did for a living and she revealed that she was a lawyer who worked for a small business consortium. At his prodding, she told him about some ethical dilemmas she'd had to deal with. When she explained that she refused ever to deceive her clients, she was surprised that he said, "Good for you." She liked the fact that he appreciated her honesty: it implied that he took moral values seriously.

During dinner the caterer accidentally spilled wine on Pete's jacket. Melissa noticed the gracious manner in which he dealt with the incident. Afterwards he made a light joke about it and Melissa decided she liked his sense of humor.

After dinner they sat alone together on the host's patio. She decided to push for more details about Pete's divorce. He was reluctant to talk about it but finally admitted that he'd had an affair. This made Melissa feel afraid and angry. Her ex-husband had done the same thing to her. She definitely did not want to be hurt again, but she did not want to reach a final conclusion without more facts, so she asked about his motivation for the affair.

Pete explained that his wife had been cold and distant for many years for reasons he could not fully fathom. They had gone to counseling more than once, but it had not helped. It seemed as if they were simply not suited to one another in many small ways, and they had slowly grown apart. Pete longed for the affection that a marriage was supposed to have, and during a business trip he impulsively had a one-night stand with a co-worker. He confessed the affair to his wife upon his return, who then left him. He told Melissa, "If you think less of me for this, I don't blame you. I was wrong. It was a mistake that I will not repeat."

Pete's last words mitigated, but did not eliminate, Melissa's fear and anger. Although she appreciated the way he had owned up to his deception and had taken responsibility for what he had done, at the end of the evening her feelings were mixed. On the positive side, he took her seriously and he seemed to care about her as a person. He seemed to be self-sufficient; he did not need to show off or put on an act. He treated the caterer with respect, could laugh in the face of a small adversity, and make her laugh as well. On the negative side was the betrayal of his wife, something he had sworn never to repeat. Melissa understood the causes of both her positive and negative reactions to Pete and knew she would have to be cautious. She agreed to go out with him, but she knew that the relationship might not develop into a permanent one. She knew that she was not yet ready to have sex with him.

Of course, Pete was most likely a better type of person than Sam, and Melissa was a more secure person than Alicia. This made Melissa and Pete's relationship more promising. The important difference was that Melissa understood her emotional responses to Pete. She was attracted to him but not yet in love with him. She knew there were qualities that could lead her in that direction but there was possibly a quality that could make her completely lose interest.

Her feelings were not a matter of ineffable chemistry. She knew there were identifiable causes for her emotional responses.

As we said earlier, all emotions have causes, including love. Love, whether mistaken, as in Alicia's case, or potential, as in Melissa's case, is a response to subconscious estimates we make about the other person, estimates we can become aware of consciously—by introspection. This gives us a wealth of information that can be used to make good decisions. It is critically important to know what you are responding to when you feel love for someone or have doubts about someone.

Does analyzing our emotions take the mystery out of love and thereby ruin it? No—just the opposite.

> *Real love is based not on mystery*
> *or fantasy but on causality.*

When you know the reasons for your love (assuming they are rational reasons), the relationship is stronger and more secure. If you do not know why you respond to another, you will feel out of control and often confused. Emotional responses to your partner will come and go for no discernible reason and emotional conflicts will be irresolvable. Communication and intimacy will be undermined.

> *People want to be loved for specific reasons.*

It is up to each partner to identify why they love the other—and to say so. This last point raises a new question: Granted that love has causes, will just any cause do? No. Does it matter which traits you value and, on the other side of the coin, which traits you possess? Yes. There are very personal causal factors involved in love, but certain core traits are required to make any romantic relationship successful in the long run (see Chapters 5 through 7 for details). If you want to be loved, you have to do things to make yourself lovable. Egoistic love, the only real kind of love, is not a selfless gift. It is a trade, which means it has to be earned. In the next chapter, we discuss how to set the foundation for being lovable.

Exercises

1. Think of a time when a friend fell in love with somebody you knew was unsuited to him or her, ultimately leading to a failed relationship.

    a. What do you think your friend reacted to subconsciously that caused the initial attraction?

_____

    b. What did your friend miss by not introspecting better? What did you see that your friend did not?

_____

2. Think of a time when you fell in love but the relationship did not work out.

    a. What attracted you to this person at the outset?

_____

    b. Was there a point when you began to introspect and to see emotional reactions you had missed or suppressed at the outset? What were they?

_____

    c. What new knowledge did you gain about the person over time? How did this affect your emotional reactions?

_____

Notes

1. Introspection starts with asking yourself questions such as: What emotions am I feeling? Why do I feel sad or angry, guilty or happy? What triggered this feeling? How do I typically respond? What thoughts are going through my mind? Is there an alternative way to look at this situation based on all my facts? We will go into this issue in more detail in later chapters.

Part II: Making Yourself Lovable

*Love is the expression of one's values,
the greatest reward you can earn for
the moral qualities you have achieved
in your character and person.*

—Ayn Rand, *Atlas Shrugged*

CHAPTER 5

Building Moral Character

C ontrary to widespread belief, love is not a causeless gift but something that has to be earned.

You may have heard yourself say, "I want to be loved just the way I am." Unfortunately, "just the way you are" may include qualities that make you less lovable than you could be, or even unlovable. Love is not causeless; it is something you have to earn—but how? In this chapter, we'll discuss the starting point: moral character. Of course, there are many other factors involved in love, including common values and individual, personal preferences, which we will discuss in later chapters. Moral character, however, is the foundation and it is indispensable.

Suppose you've caught your wife in so many lies and she's broken so many promises that you can't believe anything she says. Or you discover your husband is cheating on you, spending money on things that you had agreed to decide on jointly, and only pretending to look for a job. What does dishonesty do to romantic love? It kills it. What do flaws like this in your partner do to your sense of feeling visible, valued, cherished? Can you trust or feel emotionally close to your dishonest partner? Could you desire intimacy with a person with a bad moral character?

Now you might be thinking: *But I have a friend whose husband is a cheat and she loves him anyway.* Is this love or dependency? Perhaps fear keeps her in the marriage: *I'm afraid to be alone or on my own.* Or self-contempt: *He's all I deserve.* Whatever it is, it is not a happy, intimate romantic relationship.

As we discuss moral qualities that will make you lovable, note that most of us have problems we want to fix, and many of us don't know where or how to begin. You don't need to be perfect in every respect to find a partner, but never settle for a deeply flawed self. Making yourself into a lovable person gives you the best chance for a happy, long-term romance. If you have some moral flaws that need fixing, make it a priority to correct them.

Dave needs to do that. As a young boy, he chose to steal money from his mother's purse while telling himself: *She's just my mother.* He perfected cheating in high school by copying his assigned papers from the Internet. *After all*, he rationalized, *other kids do this.* He two-timed his girlfriends, egging himself on with twisted thoughts: *I deserve to have fun—they won the jackpot with me!* When he got his first job, he stole credit for others' work, lied to customers, and stole company property: *I need to get ahead!* Eventually, he was caught and fired. Of course, he lied to his new girlfriend about why his job ended. She discovered the lie and dumped him. He was thoroughly untrustworthy. He was twenty-five years old with nothing to show for it. At this point, Dave still has a choice: re-make his own character or keep lying and cheating until he irretrievably ruins his life.

If Dave chooses to rebuild his character, where would he begin? What virtues should one practice—and why? What is a proper moral code? Why do you need one at all?

You need a moral code, because you're not born with any knowledge of right and wrong. You need moral values to guide your choices and actions. But where do you get a moral code?[1]

Most people automatically assume that moral codes come from religion. But there's a problem: How do you validate religious moral codes? You are told, for example, to take the Commandments in the Bible on faith, to just believe. But many feel enormous guilt questioning if what they've been taught is right or wrong. To go by faith means that you are not thinking or reasoning, but rather obeying. You ignore conflicting evidence; you push out of awareness any questions that may challenge your moral code. You ignore the need (or don't know how) to choose and validate the motor of your own life—your moral code.

What's the alternative to faith?

The alternative is valuing your ability to think, to question, to look at and logically integrate facts, to identify contradictions and resolve them—and to set proper goals and standards for your life (rationally prospering). A proper foundation for your life can be yours if you validate your moral values by reason.

The key question philosophers over the centuries faced was: What is the ultimate value, a value to which all others are the means? Should that value be self-sacrifice, martyrdom, suffering— as various religious doctrines assert? Not if genuine happiness is your goal. Novelist-philosopher Ayn Rand made the philosophical breakthrough by identifying that the ultimate standard of morality is life. She wrote: "It is only the concept of 'Life' that makes the concept of 'Value' possible."[2] It is because we face the alternative of life or death that things can be values or non-values to us. She showed that the purpose of having a proper moral code is to help us make choices that will promote our lives and our happiness. "Happiness," she said, "is the successful state of life."[3]

Note that the purpose of developing a proper moral code is not just to follow some do-gooder's list of the ways you should act for the sake of being virtuous. Virtue is not its own reward.

> *The purpose of rational virtues is the ability to make better choices that will achieve your own enduring happiness and survival. The selfish (or self-respecting) reward of virtue is to live successfully and happily on earth.*[4]

Core Virtues

Our list of moral virtues is drawn from Ayn Rand's philosophy of Objectivism. Her core virtues are rationality, honesty, integrity, independence, justice, productivity, and pride.[5]

Rationality is the all-encompassing, primary virtue, because reason (rational thinking) is one's main tool of survival. You need to think in order to gain the knowledge required to live. You can't survive on instinct because you don't have any. Being rational means you are willing to put forth the effort to think, to integrate your knowledge, to commit to looking at facts without evasion, neither expecting effects (money) without causes (working for a living), nor enacting causes (smoking) without considering their effects (serious health risks).

Attempting to have a romantic relationship with an irrational person is a living nightmare. You cannot reason with irrational people; facts and logical arguments have no effect on them. You cannot understand them because they are full of unresolved contradictions. They are unpredictable because they often act on whim. You cannot feel fully understood because they don't consistently use reason to understand you. All this is anathema to romance. Furthermore, irrationality will undermine all the other virtues because they are all aspects of rationality.

> *Irrationality, at the deepest level, amounts to the rejection of facts and logic, which means the rejection of reality.*

You may be thinking: *Well, okay, but we can't be rational all the time, can we? After all, we have emotions!* As we will see, emotions are not the enemy of rationality.

Honesty is the refusal to fake reality. It is essential in a romantic relationship. Without it you cannot have trust, which means you cannot rely on the character of your partner. How many times have you heard unhappy partners say, "I can't trust her" or "He broke my trust"? People typically lie for temporary gain in the hope that by denying reality, they can temporarily recreate it based on their wishes. But it can't be done, and you can't escape knowing that fact, even if you can deceive your partner *temporarily.* You are making yourself unlovable, and privately, you will not admire yourself.[6]

Integrity means being loyal to your rational convictions in action. A breach of integrity means acting against your own convictions. Having courage, that is, remaining true to your values in the face of threat, is an aspect of integrity. It also means not giving up your values for a momentary emotional high. A wife may profess to love her husband, but she brushes that off for a quick, mindless affair. A man may know he needs to exercise regularly, diet, and stop smoking, but he suppresses that knowledge for "just a moment"—every day, for years.

Breaches of integrity cost us our self-respect, not to mention our romantic happiness. When we let ourselves down again and again, we lose trust in ourselves and others lose trust in us.

Independence is your commitment to think for yourself and to earn your own keep. The proper basis for coming to conclusions in any area of your life (be it romance, career, moral beliefs, even practical decisions) is by not going *blindly* by what your parents, friends, neighbors, colleagues, or religious and political leaders tell you, but going by your own best, rational judgment. You may get very useful facts from others but you still need to judge others' claims for yourself. Independence is your refusal to accept any idea without evidence. Dependence is a mirror of what others want, and as a result, one loses control of one's life and destroys any sense of self.

Independence is not only thinking for yourself but also living by your own effort, which includes living within your means.

Justice means appraising and acting toward other people in accordance with facts; treating them as they deserve. Justice is reason applied to your relationships with others. It is based on what Ayn Rand calls "the trader principle." A "trader is a man who earns what he gets and does not give or take the undeserved."[7] The very foundation of love is a trade: you offer your virtue and other attributes in return for those of your partner. Ayn Rand writes, "Love is the expression of one's values, the greatest reward you can earn for the moral qualities you have achieved in your character and person, the emotional price paid by one man for the joy he receives from the virtues of another."[8]

Justice demands showing appropriate appreciation for your partner's character and actions and making them feel visible. It also means making sincere apologies when you have hurt or wronged them. In healthy romantic relationships, partners must practice the principle of justice or else resentments build and relationships deteriorate.

Productivity is the process of creating material values (goods or services). Living requires material values. If nobody worked, how would you get your home, food, clothes, car, or medical care? Material values are not just a matter of surviving at the subsistence level. The goods and services we buy are healthy sources of pleasure—books, appliances, jewelry, art, personal computers, massages, vacations, and much more. (We are *NOT* advocating using things, including money, as status symbols—this shows a lack of independence and makes you feel chronically insecure, because there is always someone who has more.)

Productivity requires having a long-range focus on a career, developing the skills you need to be employable and earn money. Your career gives you a sense of purpose and the financial ability to trade with others in order to sustain and enrich your life; it gives you a sense of pride in yourself.

Don't make the mistake of thinking that you're unlovable unless you have a job or career right now. You may be going through a tough personal time, be between jobs, or be unemployed by circumstances beyond your control. Or perhaps you're caring for children or elderly family members. If you are making a genuine effort to improve your situation, you may be perfectly lovable and moral.

> *Having a productive purpose gives meaning to your life. What's the meaning of your own life? It's the important, personal values and goals that you choose and pursue.*

Pride, according to Ayn Rand, *"is the sum of all virtues."*[9] Many people believe that pride is a vice. We all dislike pompous, boastful people, but these people feel false pride. Their pomposity and boastfulness serve to hide inner doubt. Martyrs can also feel false pride for having given up all self-value for the sake of others; but they end up feeling resentful, cynical, empty, and depressed.

We view real or earned pride as a virtue; it results from the desire to be moral, or more succinctly, a consequence of your "moral ambitiousness."[10] You earn a sense of pride by deliberately practicing the virtues we've discussed and building them into your character.

You can properly take pride in the practical accomplishments resulting from your virtues (a successful business venture, a successful romantic relationship). You can also take pride in having done your best even when things do not turn out as desired (a failed business venture, a failed romantic relationship); practical outcomes are not always fully in your control. Pride, like all the virtues, is available to everyone, whether rich or poor, highly educated or a high school dropout.

The main question to ask yourself is, given your situation and knowledge: Do you work to make yourself virtuous? If you do—you are building moral character and making yourself more fit to live and more lovable.

Does being virtuous mean one never acts out of character? No, but a moral person will recognize and admit their error, take steps to correct it, and make amends, if possible and appropriate. In sum, a rational (reality-oriented) moral code gives you the best chance to live happily and successfully.

> *"The purpose of morality is to teach you, not to suffer and die, but to enjoy yourself and live."* —Ayn Rand[11]

Note that the above list of virtues does not include traits that many people view as virtues. For example: What about helping others?[12] Obviously helping others is not a duty, since your life belongs to you, but it can be a selfish value. If you love somebody very much, it means that they are a top priority. Not to help your loved one, someone you selfishly value, would be a contradiction and a breach of integrity. In fact, you could be willing to risk your life for your loved one if your life would have no meaning without that person.

The same principle holds, though to a lesser degree, for friendship. If a friend, as Aristotle said, is another self, then you care deeply about that person and help your friend when he or she is in need. This does not mean your friend has a limitless right to your time, effort, and money; you help your friend in proportion to his or her value to you. And you are never obligated to drain your resources to help an irresponsible person.[13]

The Immorality of Threatening or Initiating Physical Force Against Others

Hitting, punching, kicking, raping, or any other means of physically coercing or threatening a partner (or any person) is the antithesis of reason and a violation of rights. The same goes for stealing and defrauding. Abusers may use threats or, in extreme cases, weapons to coerce or harm their victims; this makes them fundamentally immoral and unlovable.

Lydia had been an eminently successful property manager. She earned a good income by making wise investments and had built up a nice nest egg. Early in her marriage to Devon, she agreed to pool their finances and become a homemaker, hoping to start a family. To her surprise, Devon worked at nothing but a series of unchallenging jobs, punctuated by periods of unemployment during which he hung out with "the boys." His jobs did not pay enough to meet their expenses, so he simply spent her hard-earned money.

Furthermore, he became abusive. He would bark orders at her, criticize her relentlessly, and slap her around whenever she talked back. If she tried to call a friend or her parents, he would yank the phone away from her. He did not let her spend money without his permission. Sex was basically rape. She felt sick and trapped and often fantasized about escaping to a safe place. Before the marriage, Devon had seemed like a confident, take-charge guy, but she had not realized, until too late, what "take charge" meant to him. He was a control freak.

Abusers may initially act nice in order to con their partners into a relationship. Then they gradually escalate their abuse and insidiously undermine the confidence and trust of their partners until none is left. Lydia should not have just fantasized about running away, she should have walked out. (Using force in self-defense, when your life is in imminent danger and when you have no time to call the police, is legally warranted and morally justified.)

Abusers do not value their partners' happiness because they don't value themselves. Their goal is destruction. A physical abuser belongs in jail. A partner who is the victim of abuse or is threatened by abuse should call the police and flee to a safe place as soon as possible.[14]

Frequently, a partner will put up with abusive (or otherwise bad) behavior because the abusive partner sometimes acts in a respectful, considerate manner. The victim rationalizes that the abusive behavior is "not the real him (or her)." This is an unfortunate mistake. Abusive behavior is just as much a part of that person's character as the considerate behavior—and a very dangerous part because, unless corrected, it always undermines the rest. (This is discussed further in the Appendix).

Exercises

1. For each virtue, indicate on a scale of 1 (low) to 10 (high) how frequently you practice it, and then give one personal example for each virtue—or the lack thereof. For example:

Rationality: 7

• One night my husband and I discussed having a baby. I reminded myself that we'd only been married six months and had not saved any money yet. We loved our jobs and were not prepared to parent 24/7. I'm glad I gave it careful consideration and that we didn't act on impulse. It's something we can consider later.

• I acted on impulse when I bought my car. I liked the look of it and did not give it any careful thought. In hindsight I regret it. The car turned out to be a lemon.

a. Rationality:

_____

_____

b. Honesty:

_____

_____

c. Integrity:

_____

_____

d. Independence:

_____

_____

e. Productiveness (or sense of purpose):

_____

_____

f. Justice:

_____

_____

2. When you note examples of your own virtuous choices and actions, how do they sum up in terms of feeling earned pride?

_____

_____

3. What virtue do you most need to improve?

_____

_____

4. How would developing this virtue help your existing romantic relationship—or any future romantic relationship?

_____

_____

5. What would be the first step to take toward improving yourself?

_____

_____

Notes

1. For an excellent, clarifying discussion on why everyone needs a moral code, see Ayn Rand, *Philosophy: Who Needs It* (New York: Bobbs-Merrill, 1982). The title essay of this book is from an address given to cadets of the United States Military Academy at West Point on March 6, 1974. Ayn Rand stated the following:

> Nothing is given to man automatically, neither knowledge, nor self-confidence, nor inner serenity, nor the right way to use his mind. Every value he needs or wants has to be discovered, learned and acquired—even the proper posture of his body. In this context, I want to say that I have always admired the posture of West Point graduates, a posture that projects man in proud, disciplined control of his body. Well, philosophical training gives man the proper intellectual posture—a proud, disciplined control of his mind.

2. Ayn Rand, *Atlas Shrugged* (New York: Signet, 1957), p. 931.

3. Ayn Rand, *Atlas Shrugged* (New York: Signet, 1957), p. 940.

4. For information on a proper moral code, see Ayn Rand, "The Objectivist Ethics," *The Virtue of Selfishness* (New York: Signet, 1964). See also, Ayn Rand, *The Journals of Ayn Rand*, ed. David Harriman (New York: Dutton, 1997), p. 597, in which she states the following in a letter dated May 19, 1949:

> Man exists for his own happiness, and the definition of happiness proper to a human being is: a man's happiness must be based on his moral values. It must be the highest expression of his moral values possible to him.
>
> This is the difference between my morality and hedonism. The standard is not: "that is good which gives me pleasure, just because it gives me pleasure" (which is the standard of the dipsomaniac or the sex-chaser)—but "that is good which is the expression of my moral values, and that gives me pleasure." Since the proper moral code is based on man's nature and his survival, and since joy is the expression of his survival, this form of happiness can have no contradiction in it, it is both "short range" and "long range" (as all of man's life has to be), and it leads to the furtherance of his life, not to his destruction.

5. Leonard Peikoff, *Objectivism: The Philosophy of Ayn Rand* (New York: Dutton, 1991). Our discussion of virtue is based on chapters 6–9 of this book.

6. There are rare situations when it is moral to lie, such as when defending yourself against criminals. In such cases you are not pretending to yourself that the facts are other than they are, but you are lying to preserve or

protect values including your life from being destroyed by irrational people.

7. Ayn Rand, *Atlas Shrugged* (New York: Signet, 1957), p. 940. Also see Leonard Peikoff, *Objectivism: The Philosophy of Ayn Rand* (New York: Dutton, 1991). The trader principle is discussed in chapter 8, "Virtue," pp. 28–91.

8. Ayn Rand, *Atlas Shrugged* (New York: Signet, 1957), p. 950. Also see Leonard Peikoff, *Objectivism: The Philosophy of Ayn Rand* (New York: Dutton, 1991), p. 288.

9. Ayn Rand, *Atlas Shrugged* (New York: Signet, 1957), p. 974.

10. Leonard Peikoff, "Pride as Moral Ambitiousness," *Objectivism: The Philosophy of Ayn Rand* (New York: Dutton, 1991), p. 303. See also, Tara Smith, *Moral Ambition: Perfection and Pride* (audio tapes or CD sets available at www.aynrandbookstore.com).

11. Ayn Rand, *Atlas Shrugged* (New York: Signet, 1957), p. 932. The fuller text for this quote is:

> Happiness is the successful state of life, pain is an agent of death. Happiness is that state of consciousness which proceeds from the achievement of one's values. A morality that dares to tell you to find happiness in the renunciation of your happiness—to value the failure of your values—is an insolent negation of morality. A doctrine that gives you, as an ideal, the role of a sacrificial animal seeking slaughter on the altars of others, is giving you death as your standard. By the grace of reality and the nature of life, man—every man—is an end in himself, he exists for his own sake, and the achievement of his own happiness is his highest moral purpose.
>
> But neither life nor happiness can be achieved by the pursuit of irrational whims. Just as man is free to attempt to survive in any random manner, but will perish unless he lives as his nature requires, so he is free to seek his happiness in any mindless fraud, but the torture of frustration is all he will find, unless he seeks the happiness proper to man. The purpose of morality is to teach you, not to suffer and die, but to enjoy yourself and live.

12. Ayn Rand, "The Ethics of Emergencies," *The Virtue of Selfishness* (New York, Signet, 1964).

13. Tara Smith, "Implications for Certain Conventional Virtues: Charity, Generosity, Kindness, Temperence," *Ayn Rand's Normative Ethics: The Virtuous Egoist* (Cambridge: Cambridge University Press, 2006).

14. Leonard Peikoff, *Objectivism: The Philosophy of Ayn Rand* (New York: Dutton, 1991). For a more in-depth understanding of the evil of the initiation of physical force and its effect on the reasoning mind, see chapter 8, pp. 310–324.

CHAPTER 6

Developing Genuine Self-Esteem

S elf-esteem is a critical psychological need; it is your evaluation of yourself as a capable and worthy person. Some self-help books tell you to simply accept yourself as you are. That advice cannot work, because who you are (or are not) at this moment may be the problem!

Even if you consciously try not to judge yourself, your subconscious will do it for you. It is essential to know the right standards to judge yourself by to avoid suffering unnecessarily.

Self-esteem is vital to your happiness—including your romantic happiness. If you do not respect yourself, you will not feel worthy of being loved. To have self-esteem, start with the premise that you are, in principle, worthy of your own happiness. Reject as outrageous any doctrine that says you are born evil. In reality, you are born neutral— you create your own moral character. Further, if you have accepted the altruistic idea that you exist merely to please and serve others, you are doomed from the start, because you have decided that others are worthy of achieving their own values but you are not.

> *Selfless people cannot have self-esteem,*
> *because they have no self to esteem.*

How do you make yourself worthy? Genuine self-esteem comes from relying on your power to think.[1] This means, for example:

- Taking facts seriously—even when you don't like them. (Can you really afford that new car?)
- Exerting mental effort to gain knowledge rather than drifting through life in a daze. (Do you try to improve your job skills? Your knowledge of the world?)
- Thinking independently, rather than blindly following others out of passivity or fear of disapproval. (Do you ever pretend to agree with things that friends say even though you strongly disagree with them?)
- Thinking about the long-range consequences of your actions, not just about the short-range. (Are you thinking about plans for retirement? The health consequences of your lifestyle?)
- Making firm decisions about your life rather than drifting aimlessly. (Do you think about finding a job that you really enjoy?)
- Choosing your own values rather than thoughtlessly copying what others seek. (Do you copy your parents' or peers' values without thinking or do you choose your own?)
- Taking rational action to pursue your values—not being paralyzed by fear, doubt, or guilt. (Is there something that you really want in life, some rational value, but are afraid to go after?)
- Taking conscious pride in the achievements you have honestly earned. (Do you ever feel unwarranted guilt about a genuine achievement or about your moral virtues?)
- Developing your moral character, as we discussed in Chapter 5. (Do you lie when it's convenient? Do you routinely break promises?)
- Working to understand yourself. (Are you afraid of looking into your own mind?)

> *Genuine self-esteem does not depend simply on your practical successes and failures, but on your method of thinking and your choice to act on the basis of your best thinking. It means being in mental focus.*

You are in charge of whether and how you think. How you think affects the practical outcomes you achieve, but outcomes are not always fully in your control. What's important is that you do what is possible with what is in your control. If you earn your own self-esteem, you'll make yourself more lovable, and in the end, you'll attract more and better individuals as potential partners.

Faked Self-Esteem and Defensive Maneuvers

Self-esteem is an essential psychological need—no one can live with the conviction that they are fundamentally no good, so people who lack the real thing attempt to fake it. Let's take a quick look at three types of defenses: defense mechanisms, defense values, and defensive actions.

Defense Mechanisms: These are automatic or conscious mental orders or habits that prevent painful thoughts or emotions from entering awareness. A common one is repression: not allowing oneself to become consciously aware of one's emotions. Another is denial: refusing to acknowledge painful realities. Yet another is evasion: deliberately refusing to think or mentally focus when it is needed. A defensive person is always denying they made an error or did anything wrong—defending the illusion that they are perfect.

Defenses, though very tempting to most people, are irrational because they divorce the mind from reality. Defensiveness has disastrous effects on romantic relationships. For example, Josh forgets his wife Sarah's birthday. She is very upset, but instead of apologizing and trying to make amends, Josh piles on excuse after excuse and then gets mad at her for "overreacting."[2] This does not bode well for their relationship. If you are wrong or make an error, admit it. It may seem counterintuitive but this will *increase* your self-esteem because you are fully acknowledging reality.

Defense Values: People may use values that they possess or aspire to as substitutes for genuine self-esteem and to cover up self-doubt.[3] Examples are: money, looks, intelligence, popularity, fancy clothes, expensive cars, large houses in wealthy neighborhoods, social status, and sexual conquests. Not all these values are necessarily irrational. The problem is that they are held compulsively, even desperately. An expensive car can give you pleasure, but not if you just want to own it to show off. You are still the same person with or without the car. Whether others approve of you or not does not change who you are.

Maybe you are an astute role player, but if you engage in dishonest actions to please or fool others, your real self-esteem will decrease because you have betrayed your own soul (your mind, values, and judgment). What counts is what goes on inside.

> *Wanting appreciation for your good qualities and actions (wanting visibility) is the opposite of wanting approval to eliminate your self-doubts.*

The essence of love is not filling a self-esteem void but valuing genuine good traits in one another. Parents can greatly harm a child by acting irrationally and convincing the child that whatever goes wrong is the child's fault. Parents can also instill self-doubt and anxiety by not showing love and concern for their child. Some poorly treated children spend their lives trying to undo the damage by getting others to parent them, often their partners. This does not work. You need to learn to value yourself (perhaps with professional help).

On the other side of the approval coin, *you cannot get genuine self-esteem through disparaging others* (with put-downs, flaw-finding, or one-upmanship). Another person's flaws don't make you a better person. People who try to get self-esteem by putting others down are trying to hide their own moral vices and/or their own sense of inferiority. You earn self-esteem by your own thinking and actions, not through comparisons.

> *Self-esteem is not a matter of comparing yourself to anyone or gaining the illusion that you're okay by using defensive maneuvers.*

Some defense values can actually be rational values (intelligence, earning money, buying nice clothes) but held in a wrong way. For example, to hide a sense of inferiority, a person might try to constantly show off his intelligence, attempt to put down others of lesser ability, and never admit to mistakes. The tip-off as to whether something is a defense value is if it is pursued compulsively (*I must always be right, I must show off my wealth*) and defended desperately, if threatened, as if it were a matter of life and death (which in their psychological context, it is).

Defensive Actions: A prime example is the chronic use of alcohol and illicit drugs to reduce anxiety. Getting high temporarily blurs the pain and may even yield the illusion of pleasure, but such jolts lack the quality of pleasure based on actual achievements and do not lead to action that would remove the real cause of the pain. This is not to deny that you may genuinely need medicines for anxiety or depression but these should be used only under a doctor's care. Another example of defensive action is lashing out physically in order to exert power over those who threaten your fake self-esteem. Social withdrawal in order to escape the anxiety of dealing with other people is another defensive action. Withdrawing into a shell simply reinforces your feelings of inadequacy.

Temporary Blows to Self-Esteem—and Recovery

Is it possible for a person with self-esteem to suffer a temporary blow? Yes. This typically happens when we feel we've failed to gain or keep something we highly value (failed a test, lost a job, were jilted or abused). A generally confident man or woman may temporarily feel low and disoriented when rejected by a loved partner. Being rejected doesn't necessarily mean you're unlovable. Maybe you had the wrong partner. Keep this in full focus. You can grieve the loss while reminding yourself of your good traits. Many relationships that don't work are simply a matter of a wrong match. (We will give you ideas to help you pick the right partner in Part III.) Keep pursuing values in the face of setbacks. If a partner rejects you, you can put more time into a hobby, such as gardening or traveling, or take on a new project at work, rather than allowing hopelessness to take over or an erosion of self-esteem. This helps you weather rejection better. You do not devalue yourself, rather you feel, *This really hurts, but at the deepest level, I'm still a worthy person.*

Of course, if you are rejected because you have genuine character flaws (or annoying personality traits), you need to work to correct them. These flaws undermine self-esteem and lovability and cut you off from reality. Self-esteem is a matter of using your mind properly and choosing and pursuing values that you rationally judge are important to you.

Learn to Understand Yourself Through Introspection

Introspection means looking inward at the contents and processes of your own mind and identifying what you're thinking and feeling.[4] Why does it matter whether or not you understand yourself? First, you need introspection for self-esteem. Introspecting enables you to monitor your own mental habits and processes and determine whether you're in focus or not—that is, whether you're actively thinking, mindlessly drifting, or deliberately unfocusing your mind (for example, using defenses). Mental focus is necessary to be in control of your life.

Second, you need to understand your emotions, otherwise you'll feel moved by mysterious "forces" (subconscious ideas) that you can neither comprehend nor control. Nor is it attractive to your romantic partner if you have no idea why you respond to him or her as you do. (We discuss this issue further in Chapter 8; see also Chapter 4.)

> *An important point: Don't expect your partner to understand you if you do not understand yourself.*

Demanding that your partner spend hours upon hours probing your subconscious when you have no idea what's in there creates an impossible burden. If you expect this from your partner, consider consulting a therapist to help learn about yourself.

We noted in Chapter 4 that every emotion is caused by a specific type of subconscious evaluation or appraisal. Here are some examples:

- Happiness is the emotion stemming from the appraisal that you've achieved, or are making progress toward, your most important goals and values (for example, romantic love).
- Satisfaction is a narrower, less intense form of happiness, usually stemming from gaining or holding a particular value.
- Love results from a highly positive evaluation of another person based on their desirable qualities.
- Hope stems from the appraisal that a desired value will be achieved.
- Sadness is due to the perceived loss of a value.
- Depression is a more extreme form of sadness, which may involve a painful loss or the conviction that one is no good, that life is no good, and that things will never get better.[5]
- Anxiety stems from your appraisal that there's a threat to your values, often involving uncertainty; frequently, this threat is of a psychological nature, such as a perceived threat to your self-esteem.
- Fear is your response to the perception of imminent danger, usually a physical threat, or of your perception of the imminent loss of an important value.
- Anger is your response to a perceived injustice or the violation of some important moral standard by another. (You can also be angry at yourself for the same reasons.)
- Guilt stems from believing that you acted against your own moral standards or values.
- Hatred, a feeling of extreme animosity or hostility toward another person, stems from evaluating that person as in some way bad or evil or is a profound threat to one's illusion of self-esteem.[6] (Hatred of others can also be a

displacement of hatred toward yourself—here you urgently need counseling.)

- Envy involves resentment of, and/or the desire for, objects or qualities possessed by another. Jealousy is similar in meaning. In the best sense of these terms, they refer simply to wishing that one had what another has. In the worst sense, they refer to wanting the destruction of another person's values (including virtues of character), virtues, and values which one lacks. (*If I can't have X, then nobody should have it.*)[7]

Once you identify the emotions you're feeling, you can proceed to identify their specific causes. If a strong emotion is based on mistaken ideas or values, you can proceed to change it by consciously correcting the wrong ideas each time you feel that emotion. You can also work to change any future actions or events that precipitated your emotion. Eventually, the emotion will change. Since emotions are automatic, changing them can take some time and may require professional counseling.

Paul had some counseling sessions and discovered that his anxiety attacks stemmed from subconsciously held mistaken ideas. His fear that he would fail in business was not based on facts but on hidden worries that he might end up like his father who had failed. When he realized that business success and failure have causes that can often be controlled, to a considerable extent, by gaining the needed skills, his anxiety disappeared.[8] (A business failure resulting from a major economic recession, despite one's best plans, is nothing to be ashamed of. One simply has to move on the best one can).

Changing old thinking habits, challenging old ideas, and replacing them with healthier ones takes motivation, the learning of new skills, effort, and practice.

Emotions vary not only in type but also in intensity—from mild anxiety to severe panic attacks, from mildly sad to seriously depressed, from mildly happy to exuberant. Hormones aside, the intensity of your emotions depends on the importance of the value at stake. If you are feeling a powerful emotion, the intensity indicates: *This is really important to me.* If you sense that your emotion is too intense for the situation, ask yourself: *What mistaken interpretation am I making here?* Did you blow your top when your partner was ten minutes late? You initially may be thinking, *If my partner is late, it means the whole evening will be ruined* or *My partner doesn't care about me.* Then do a reality-check: *Is this really true? Is anger the appropriate response even if it is true?*

In other instances, your emotional reaction may be too mild considering the facts of the situation; this could be due to emotional repression or subconscious value conflicts. Your beloved spouse admits to having an affair and you seem to feel nothing. Are you repressing your feelings? When you learn to analyze your own emotional responses and to think more clearly and rationally about their causes, you achieve a harmony between your thoughts and your feelings.

A third benefit gained from introspection is understanding and controlling your moods. A mood is an enduring emotional state. A chronically sullen, anxious, or hostile partner is unromantic—not very lovable. Sometimes moods may be partly or wholly out of your control (for instance, those caused by hormones, a thyroid problem, or by an adverse medication reaction). Most bad moods, however, are caused by your subconscious ideas; you can introspect to understand and regulate them.

Your bad moods may sometimes be the cause of your partner's bad mood. For example, you may hate your job and come home to your partner in a cranky, sarcastic mood every night, which puts your partner in an equally negative mood. Once you clarify the cause of your mood and explain it to your partner, you can come up with a better strategy to deal with the work problem (be more assertive with your boss, be better at avoiding your boss, or change jobs).

Instead of chronically complaining or moping, work to solve your problems and shift your focus to what is going well in your life. If you can't do it alone, get help. You may legitimately be in a bad mood because of something your romantic partner did or didn't do. If so, clearly name to yourself which of your partner's words or actions are the source of your moodiness so that the two of you can take steps to remedy the situation.

The chances for romantic happiness are better if both partners are typically in a good mood. Having a genuinely pleasant, benevolent demeanor makes you obviously more lovable and more joyful to be around.

It is important to approach introspecting with the attitude that it's exciting and fascinating to come to understand yourself. What is the worst thing you can discover? That you have mistaken ideas or poor thinking methods—and these can be corrected.[9] Many individuals don't know how to introspect effectively and efficiently, but at least they make honest attempts to understand their emotions and they make some headway. Even keeping a journal when one experiences unsettling emotions or talking things through with a trusted friend (or, if needed, a therapist) helps with self-understanding.

When a person does something irrational, thoughtless, or immoral in relation to a romantic partner (or any friend or acquaintance) and is asked, "Why did you do that?" a very common answer is, "I don't know." Often, the real meaning of such statements is "I don't want to know," which means: *I don't want to introspect, because I do not want to face up to what I find.* Such evasion not only puts you out of control of your actions, it undermines any romantic potential. If you don't know why you act as you do (and thus can't trust yourself), how can any partner trust you? Introspection is essential for making yourself lovable.

A final point about introspection: It is extremely important to be objective about yourself. Living in a subjective fantasy world or playing a role to gain the illusion of self-esteem is self-destructive and destroys romance.

Acknowledging your flaws is the first step toward self-improvement.

Many people have some psychological problems that they would rather not have. Consider Kirsten's emotionally crippling problem, which was destroying her chances of romantic happiness. Kristen writes:

> I'm an attractive twenty-year-old woman with an active dating life—except for one problem. Every time I become involved with an attractive guy, I always feel that I'm not good enough for him. I assume he'll probably dump me for a prettier girl. To protect myself from being hurt, I drive men away by being distant and unpleasant. My problem with men is ruining my life! Please, I need help before I'm alone for the rest of it.

Kirsten is drowning in self-doubt; she does not feel psychologically or physically attractive. She is not convinced that she is lovable and has developed a self-sabotaging coping strategy of being distant by being unpleasant. She lacks self-esteem and mental health. Cognitive therapy, however, has been very successful in helping individuals correct such "stinking thinking" and self-sabotaging behavior. Kirsten can use this therapy to learn healthier, rational strategies to find a partner.[10]

What might Kirsten's problems stem from? Perhaps her parents were hypercritical and she unthinkingly accepted their appraisal of her as not being smart enough or pretty enough by their standards. Perhaps she was teased by her classmates for being "ugly." Perhaps her father dumped her mother for a "prettier and smarter" woman and totally abandoned Kirsten. To recover from this, she will need to identify and challenge wrong conclusions that she may have drawn about herself.

Mental health is important and psychological problems can be resolved. If you seek professional help, put in the effort and do the introspective work; you need not remain a mystery to yourself. You'll acquire the ability to remove the barriers to your happiness and will make yourself more lovable.[11]

An important point must be made here:

> *Your romantic partner cannot also be your therapist.*

The roles are totally different. Your partner can be understanding and supportive but cannot be responsible for your mental health. If you are riddled with self-doubts, fears, and anxieties, don't ask your partner to put you together again. That is your job, along with the help of a professional.

Congratulations on finishing this chapter. You now have some ideas on how to achieve or enhance your own self-esteem and how to feel happier! Self-esteem is vital to your romantic happiness—so you are well on your way to making yourself more lovable. You've learned how to identify and avoid faking self-esteem and how to detect and avoid defensive maneuvers. You have a deeper understanding of how to introspect, an understanding you can now build on.

You can identify at least some mental health problems and begin working to correct them. Perhaps, most importantly, you have grasped that self-esteem is something you can achieve and enjoy for yourself.

In our next chapter, we will help you become more passionate about your life, more attuned to your personal appearance, and more skilled at communicating.

Exercises

1. Since self-esteem relies on your power to think, ask yourself the following questions. For each question, try to give a specific example, positive or negative.

- Do I take facts seriously (not evading or pretending they are other than they are)—even when I don't like them?
- Do I exert mental effort to gain knowledge or do I drift along solely on the emotions of the moment?
- Do I think for myself or do I blindly follow others out of passivity or fear of disapproval?
- Do I think about the long-range consequences of my actions, not just what's here and now?

- Do I make firm decisions about my life or do I drift aimlessly?
- Do I choose my own values rather than copying what others seek, without thought?
- Do I take rational action to achieve my values—do I refuse to give up in the face of fear or doubt or guilt?
- Do I take conscious pride in the achievements I have honestly earned?
- Do I work on bettering my moral character? (See Chapter 5.)
- Do I work to understand myself through introspection?

2. Do you have any of the following defensive maneuvers that you would like to fix? You can learn to change any self-defeating coping strategies. The first step is your willingness to identify them. Again, in each case, give one specific example, positive or negative.

   a. *Defense Mechanisms*: Do I chronically shift the blame to others? Do I minimize or deny my problems? Do I evade facts that make me feel uncomfortable?

   b. *Defense Values*: Do I use potentially healthy, rational values as a substitute for self-esteem (for example: money, looks, intelligence, nice clothes, expensive cars)? Do I feel I need to achieve social status in order to have self-esteem? Do I need sexual conquests to feel good about myself? Do I set rational aspirations that I don't act upon? Do I seek the approval of others as a substitute for earning self-respect? Do I try to get self-esteem by putting others down?

   c. *Defensive Actions*: Do I blur my thinking by using alcohol or illicit drugs or by misusing prescription drugs?

If you are using your mind in self-defeating ways, there are many wonderful resources. We recommend the Cognitive Therapy workbook *Mind Over Mood: Change How You Feel by Changing the Way You Think* by Dennis Greenberger and Christine Padesky, and *Changing for Good: A Revolutionary Six-Stage Program for Overcoming Bad Habits and Moving Your Life Positively Forward* by James O. Prochaska, John Norcross, and Carlo DiClemente. You can improve your self!

3. It's well worth grasping the meaning of your own emotions. Using introspection, you may be surprised at how much better you understand yourself. Think of a specific time when you felt the emotions listed below. Search your subconscious for the ideas, beliefs, and values that caused the emotion.

    a. First remind yourself what each emotion stands for.

      (Refer to the list in the chapter.)

    b. Then give your example.

    c. Identify some reasons for your feeling that way.

- Hope stems from the expectation that I will achieve something I value. I am hopeful that by learning better communication skills, my husband and I will feel more connected to one another and cherish one another more.
- Anger means I'm experiencing something as "not fair." I felt angry because my girlfriend was ignoring me and paying a lot of attention to Ray at the holiday party. I felt she was doing this intentionally to hurt me.

Look for examples of these other emotions:

- Love
- Hope
- Sadness
- Anxiety
- Anger
- Guilt
- Envy
- Happiness

Notes

1. Ayn Rand, *Atlas Shrugged* (New York: Signet, 1957), p. 936. In discussing self-esteem, Ayn Rand states:

> To live, man must hold three things as the supreme and ruling values of his life: Reason—Purpose—Self-esteem. Reason, as his only tool of knowledge—Purpose, as his choice of the happiness which that tool must proceed to achieve—Self-esteem, as his inviolate certainty that his mind is competent to think and his person is worthy of happiness, which means: is worthy of living. These three values imply and require all of man's

virtues, and all his virtues pertain to the relation of existence and consciousness: rationality, independence, integrity, honesty, justice, productiveness, pride.

2. John Gottman and Nan Silver, *Why Marriages Succeed or Fail. . . and How You Can Make Yours Last* (New York: Simon & Schuster [A Fireside Book], 1994). For more information on types of defensiveness that couples engage in, such as denying responsibility, making excuses, whining, yes-butting, cross-complaining (husband: "You do x!" wife: "Well, you do y!"), and defensive body language (a false smile, folding your arms across your chest), see pp. 84–93.

3. The authors learned about the concept of defense values from Dr. Allan Blumenthal.

4. Edwin A. Locke, *The Art of Introspection* and *Special Topics in Introspection* (CDs available at www.aynrandbookstore.com).

5. Seriously depressed individuals are at risk for suicide—getting professional help is very important, since depression is highly treatable. For an excellent resource for suicidal individuals and their families, see Thomas Ellis and Cory Newman, *Choosing to Live: How to Defeat Suicide Through Cognitive Therapy* (California: New Harbinger Publications, Inc., 1996).

6. Hate (and love) can apply more broadly to categories of things such as sardines and bungee jumping, but in this usage, we focus only on people.

7. Ayn Rand, *Return of the Primitive: The Anti-Industrial Revolution* (New York: A Meridian Book, 1999), p. 130–131. Expanded edition of *The New Left: The Anti-Industrial Revolution,* 2nd rev. ed. (New York: Signet, 1963). Ayn Rand elaborates:

> Hatred of the good for being the good means hatred of that which one regards as good by one's own (conscious or subconscious) judgment. It means hatred of a person for possessing a value or virtue one regards as desirable.
>
> If a child wants to get good grades in school, but is unable or unwilling to achieve them and begins to hate the children who do, that is hatred of the good. If a man regards intelligence as a value, but is troubled by self-doubt and begins to hate the men he judges to be intelligent, that is hatred of the good. . . . The primary factor and distinguishing characteristic is an emotional mechanism set in reverse: a response of hatred, not toward human vices, but toward human virtues.
>
> To be exact, the emotional mechanism is not set in reverse, but is set one way: its exponents do not experience love for evil men; their emotional range is limited to hatred or indifference.

It is impossible to experience love, which is a response to values, when one's automatized response to values is hatred.

8. Edwin A. Locke, *Stress and Coping: An Inductive Approach* (CDs available at www.aynrandbookstore.com). Some books that offer principles and methods to cope with psychological problems are: Edmond Bourne, *The Anxiety and Phobia Workbook* (California: New Harbinger Publications, 1995); David D. Burns, *The Feeling Good Handbook* (New York: William Morrow & Co., 1989); James O. Prochaska, John C. Norcross, and Carlo DiClemente, *Changing for Good* (New York: Avon Books, 1994).

9. There is one exception to this point: thoroughly evil people, such as killers and dictators, will find thoroughly evil thoughts and values if they introspect honestly. However, such people virtually never introspect, because if they fully and honestly faced their own evil, they would commit suicide. Their entire existence is based on not letting themselves know their own evil. People who are contemplating but have not committed unforgivably evil deeds, however, can save themselves before it's too late by seeking professional help.

10. Cognitive therapy is based on the fact that the way we think affects the way we feel; therefore, by learning how to correct erroneous ideas, we can eliminate unhealthy negative emotions such as depression. For example, if a young man habitually catastrophizes ("I'll never find a partner!"), causing him to feel despondent, with a cognitive therapist he can learn how to think more objectively, in line with the facts, and develop new relationship skills. His emotions and mood will significantly improve. In this case the young man becomes hopeful, skilled, and action-oriented in finding a partner. Although cognitive therapy, originated by Dr. Aaron Beck, was developed for treating depression, it has been very successful in treating a wide range of mental health problems. Cognitive therapists help you identify your negative emotions, help you correct distorted thinking and the distorted core beliefs ("I'm unlovable," "I'm a failure") that cause them, and help you learn lifetime skills for thinking more clearly and for relating better to others. Cognitive therapy self-help books offer some useful principles, skills, and exercises. These can be used in conjunction with therapy or on their own if the situation is less serious. Highly recommended is the book by Dennis Greenberger and Christine A. Padesky, *Mind Over Mood: A Cognitive Therapy Treatment Manual for Clients* (New York: The Guilford Press, 1995). Also helpful is the book by Matthew McKay and Patrick Fanning, *Prisoners of Belief* (Oakland: New Harbinger Publications, 1991).

11. For mental health professionals, there are many training

opportunities by excellent cognitive therapists, such as the following, which you may find through Google: Christine Padesky, "Transforming Personality," sponsored by Cognitive Workshops, Dec. 1–2, 1999, Boston, Massachusetts; Cory Newman, "Bipolar Disorder: A Cognitive Therapy Approach," presented as part of the Master Therapists Series, University of Connecticut Health Center, Dec. 6, 2002; Christianne Esposito's presentation "Evaluating and Treating Depression and Suicidal Behavior in Adolescence," sponsored by the Rhode Island Psychological Association, April 30, 2004. For individuals seeking more information about therapists in your area trained in Cognitive Therapy methods, and to learn more about Cognitive Therapy, the website http://www.academyofct.org offers a wealth of information.

• CHAPTER 7 •

Values, Appearance, and Communication

*M*aking yourself lovable requires holding strong values, caring about your appearance, and knowing how to communicate.

It's not romantic, exciting, or fulfilling to be in a relationship with a dull partner, someone who has no strong interests or values and doesn't care to develop any. Such a person does not make life interesting. How can you feel romantically attracted to an empty, superficial person?

Who would want to date (or marry) an unkempt, smelly person who lives in grimy sweats, rarely showers, and seldom brushes his teeth or combs his hair? Looks do matter.

> *When you fall in love, you don't fall in love*
> *with a disembodied spirit, but*
> *with a whole person, mind and body.*

And who wants a partner who nags, yells, sulks, or never listens to you? Good loving and good romance require good, positive communication.

Become a Passionate Valuer

What does it mean to become a passionate valuer? In her private journals, Ayn Rand wrote the following:

> Most people lack [the capacity for] reverence and "taking things seriously." They do not hold anything to be very serious or profound. There is nothing that is sacred or immensely important to them. There is nothing—no idea, object, work, or person—that can inspire them with a profound, intense, and all-absorbing passion that reaches to the roots of their souls. They do not know how to value or desire. They cannot give themselves entirely to anything. There is nothing absolute about them.[1]

The capacity to be passionate about your life requires learning how to make yourself into a passionate valuer. But first you must identify the ways in which you kill your own capacity to enjoy life. Here are three major self-destructive habits:

The most pervasive killer of joy is altruism (self-sacrifice).

Your moral code is your psychological motor. To the extent that you have an anti-self moral code, you will suffer. To be a valuer, you must care about your self and your life. When Dr. Kenner asks clients, "What do you love in life?" many respond with a long, painful pause. Then they say, "I don't know. I never asked myself that question. I've been so busy living for everyone else that I never focused on myself. It feels selfish to do that." They are right; valuing is rationally selfish— and it is a healthy process. Living by the code of self-sacrifice destroys your capacity to value, because under that code, only other people's values count. What type of person will be attracted to you if you have no serious values? As we noted in Chapter 2, the selfless person is a magnet for the "me-only" narcissist who knows a good victim when he sees one.

A second joy-killer is mental passivity. When you let your mind rust, you become a dull, shallow person with no serious interests or goals. Some people passively copy what others value or make choices based on unanalyzed feelings. For example, Benson reveals: "My dad went to college and became an accountant; he told me to do the same, so that's what I ended up doing. I don't like it, but it's a living." Benson is taking a passive approach to his life. What if he does the same in romance—falling into a marriage without knowing what he wants? Only thinking purposefully about what you want, followed by action, will bring vitality to your life.

The third joy-killer is living in fear or with chronic anxiety. Say you were profoundly hurt by a failed love relationship and you promised yourself: *I'll never let anyone get that close to me again; the pain is too great.* You may have falsely concluded that suffering is the essence of life and that all attempts to achieve values and your own happiness are doomed. By withdrawing from life and living in fear of being rejected, you lower the risk of future failure or hurt, but you pay a terrible price. To live without taking reasonable psychological risks (pursuing personal goals and values), without learning how to cope well with setbacks, puts you in an emotional vacuum. Living means pursuing values. Pursuing values is the essence of life. Take steps, even if only small ones at first, to go after what you want.

What does life have to offer you? The variety of choices (in a free country) is awe-inspiring. Below are some of the areas in which one can pursue values.

- *Romantic love.* What this book is about.
- *A career or job.* Is your job or career something you love, or did you choose it for other reasons, such as conformity, fear, or duty? The ideal job is one about which you say, "This job is so great, I can't believe they pay me to do it." Not everyone can find such a job, especially in bad economic times, but it's worth the effort, even if it means changing careers.
- *Art.* Novels, plays, films, sculpture, painting, architecture, poetry, music, dancing, TV. There is so much to learn, admire, enjoy, love, and aspire to in the realm of the arts. For example, determine what type of literature you love; study the works of artists whose subject matter you find intriguing; take dance lessons and decide on your favorite dance step.

In admiring or enjoying a work of art, you feel, in Ayn Rand's words, "This is what life means to me."[2]

- *Home.* Make your home warm and inviting, tailored to your aesthetic taste and needs. Don't make it a vehicle for showing off, but do make it your own, a reflection of your standards and desires, not those of others.
- *Friendships.* Choose friends whom you value and who value you; don't acquire them by chance. Terminate friendships that cause boredom or pain and don't spend a minute longer with people who make you unhappy.
- *Family.* Note which relatives you would choose as friends regardless of family ties and make time to enjoy the pleasure of their company. They are gems. Limit your time with family members you don't enjoy. Don't fake a love you don't feel for abusive relatives. Doing so would be unjust and you would be devaluing yourself. There is no duty in life to re-traumatize yourself by pretending that an unloving or cruel family member was otherwise. Don't toss away precious hours you could enjoy with those dear to you.
- *Children.* Being a parent is an awesome, time-consuming, long-term responsibility. Do not choose this role out of duty or conformity. Remember that it costs not only time and effort, but also a lot of money to raise and educate a child. Plan long-range by saving money and by locating your home in a good school district. Make time for parenting—and for romance. Thus you maintain parenting as a value rather than letting it turn into an unwanted duty or allowing it to undermine your romantic relationship.
- *Hobbies.* Find fun activities you can spend your free time on. Some can be solitary, like reading or painting; others can be social, like tennis or dancing. If you can afford them, treat yourself to lessons with a professional to give yourself a growing sense of accomplishment. It is a special bonus if some hobbies can be shared with your partner.

- *Personal niceties.* There are personal indulgences you may engage in, such as writing in a journal, taking an early morning walk, playing with a beloved pet, enjoying baths, and so on. Treat yourself as being worthy of pleasure.

You'll want good preparation, prioritizing, and time management to coordinate your values. This way, values will continue to bring you pleasure and not become just obligations.

> *Imagine being eighty years old, looking at old photo albums with your kids or grandkids. What adventures, achievements, and experiences would you like to share with them?*

What obstacles do you have to overcome? Set personal goals for yourself and rank them according to what you value most. Then fit them into a reasonable schedule so that you will have time for work, hobbies, friends—and romance! Don't abandon yourself by sacrificing your life for others,[3] or indulging in short-term, shallow pleasures, such as excessive drinking and gambling. When you look back, have something to be proud of.[4]

Care About Your Appearance

Your looks matter! They convey your attitude towards yourself.

> *You can make two errors when it comes to your looks.*
> *You can believe that looks are everything*
> *and spend your life in front of a mirror trying to look*
> *just right. Or you can disregard or deliberately*
> *ignore your appearance, or even*
> *intentionally make yourself look unappealing.*

You are neither a body without a mind nor a mind without a body. But both of those errors say something about your evaluation of yourself. And potential partners don't fall in love with a mindless body or a disembodied mind. They fall in love with you—an integrated person with a body directed by your mind. How you take care of yourself and present yourself physically says a lot to a prospective romantic partner as well as to a long-term partner. It speaks to self-esteem and self-valuing.

We've all had the experience of seeing people dressed in dumpy clothes with unattractive hairstyles. We may think, *If only they made the most of their appearance—how nice they could look!* If you've been to a high school reunion and seen what some formerly attractive classmates let happen to their looks, you may have recoiled in shock thinking, *I can't believe they've let themselves go like that!*

Try an experiment: Take a careful look at yourself in a mirror. If your ideal romantic partner were to meet you now, what would be his or her first impression? What would your posture, clothes, and grooming reveal about you? What sort of person would you like to attract? Would changes in your appearance make this more likely? Ask a trusted friend for feedback.

Looks aren't everything, but they do matter. Of course, avoid comparing yourself unfavorably to fashion models. Enjoy doing the best with what you've got. Weight, physical fitness, grooming, how we dress, and how we carry ourselves are within our control.

> *Our looks convey our attitude toward ourselves.*

You have only one body for life, so you might as well take good care of it. Exercising regularly, eating well, and dressing nicely reflect how you feel about yourself and your life. If you pay attention to your health and appearance, you'll like yourself more and you'll have more esthetic appeal to others.

The former slim prom queen who is now obese shocks us because it reflects her lack of pride in her appearance. Serious psychological issues may underlie such a lack of self-care. For example, a sexually abused woman may label herself as "damaged goods" and then keep on the extra pounds to avoid looking sexually attractive. Or someone who accepts the belief that the body is shameful might mistakenly conclude that plain looks convey a superior moral status. Sometimes individuals are just too depressed, tired, or busy to make an effort to look better—it's too much work to shave, wear clean clothes, or put on makeup. Or ignoring one's looks may happen as a result of a failed romance; after being hurt, some just give up. Some feel that they would be caving into cultural pressure if they improved their looks. Others feel too meek and humble to make the most of their looks, fearing they'll be seen as vain. They fail to understand that looking nice is not the same as being obsessed with looks. If you suspect psychological baggage is holding you back, you might consider professional counseling.

There are aspects of your appearance you can't change such as your height, being covered in freckles, or some changes due to aging. You simply need to accept things that you cannot change and work to change things that are within your control. Certain aspects of one's appearance are changeable with the help of technology. Plastic surgery, cosmetic procedures, and even drugstore products, like at-home hair dye kits and teeth whiteners, are available if you want to and can afford to use them. It is perfectly healthy to use technology to reasonably enhance your appearance.

When looking for your soul mate, you want a partner you are attracted to both physically and mentally. You will spend most of your time with this person; why would you want to be with someone whose appearance displeases you?

Does this mean you can never let your hair down and have a casual day? Of course not. But if you don't value yourself enough to care how you look, you're not making yourself fully lovable and you are announcing your lack of self-value in a revealingly public manner.

When you value your appearance, you can enjoy stylizing yourself without being vain or compulsive. By "stylizing" we mean creating a unique, integrated way of dressing, grooming, wearing makeup, and body shaping that reflects and defines how you enjoy seeing yourself. When you value yourself, stylizing becomes not a dreaded duty but a treat. We spend a lot of time stylizing other aspects of our lives: we carefully decorate our homes; choose the make, year and model of our cars; design our gardens for maximum eye-appeal; we even enjoy decorating food with nice garnishes. In the same way, you can have fun stylizing yourself and making yourself more attractive.

Learn How to Communicate

> *Many people lack the communication skills needed to maintain a thriving romantic relationship. If you don't communicate effectively, you make yourself less lovable and you undermine romance.*

The following letter to Dr. Kenner's radio show illustrates this:

> *I'm engaged to Max. My problem is our communication. In a nutshell, it stinks. I try to communicate my needs, desires, fears, etc., in a respectful and non-threatening way. He perceives everything as a personal attack, shuts down, and then turns it into a guilt trip for me. There is never resolution without his putting on the verbal boxing gloves, and then I'm left emotionally wounded. What should I do?—Emily*

Emily needs to grasp that without a personality makeover, Max is not the right person for her.

What are the signs that someone isn't communicating well? The most obvious is that the person is unwilling to listen or refuses to make any effort to understand you. Some of the most common methods used to avoid dealing with problems in communication include: sarcasm, swearing, verbally attacking you then playing it off as a joke, giving lectures or unsolicited advice, not being fully focused on you, bossing you around, nagging, whining, screaming, being unjustifiably critical, talking incessantly, interrupting you when you speak, denouncing your values, using the silent treatment, walking out on you, or being indifferent to you. Obviously, such actions seriously undermine romantic attraction.

Consider these guidelines for effective, active listening that apply to both partners:

• Listen attentively and politely, with full focus, for clear understanding. If you're tired or distracted, let your partner know that this isn't the best time to discuss anything important. Such consideration sends the message that you value your partner.

However, sometimes you need to listen even when you're tired, because your partner may be in great need at that moment.

- Periodically summarize what you've heard, in your own words, when necessary for clarification. Make sure that you really understand what your partner is saying, for example, "So you are saying that . . . " or "Did I hear you correctly that . . .?"

- Listen for issues that seem tied to strong emotions. Ask what the important value involved is, for example, "The most upsetting aspect of this for you seems to be. . ."; "Is that what's making you so sad (or angry, or anxious)?"

Give suggestions only if it is clear that your partner wants them. Often your partner simply wants to feel understood.

Another major skill in effective communication is speaking assertively. Let's say that Paul and Sara are discussing an upcoming holiday, and Sara is assuming they will spend it at one or both of their parents' homes. Paul, however, has some suggestions for alternative ways to spend this time. He prefers a private getaway for the two of them in the Bahamas or even just going to a restaurant by themselves for a cozy holiday dinner. Actually, neither of them enjoys spending a hectic day racing between their two dysfunctional families.

Here are two wrong approaches to communicating that Paul might use. Talking aggressively, he might say: "Why the heck do we have to spend the day with those jerks? You always feel you need to please your family. I'm not wasting my time with your crazy relatives. I don't care what you do."

This aggressive approach is referred to as "finger-pointing language" or "you-language," since the essence of it is an attack on the character of the listener. (We will elaborate on this in Chapter 23.) Paul might also give Sara the silent treatment (or act annoyingly in some unrelated way). Sara would know that something is wrong, but she wouldn't know what it is. This is a passive (or a passive-aggressive) approach to communication. Both this approach and the aggressive communication style undermine any chance of having a good relationship.

Paul however has assertiveness skills; he can remain loving to Sara while revealing his own wants. Here's what he might say about the holiday plans: "Honey, considering all the frustration we go through with our parents on these holiday get-togethers, I wonder why we need to go through the same fiascos again this year. Let's put our heads together and come up with some alternatives. I've thought about visiting with our parents before the holiday and then going on that vacation in the Bahamas we've always dreamed about. The family is growing and it makes sense to make our visits more personal, rather than just a hectic holiday event."

Sara may initially say, "I'd love to go to the Bahamas, but I could never do that—they would be so hurt and insulted." If Paul gives her time to think about his suggestion, perhaps with a reminder that she has a right to be happy on holidays, later she may be more amenable to pursuing something other than the chaotic family meal.

Active listening and assertive speaking are skills that are indispensable for good communication, for self-respect, and for a loving relationship. You'll want these skills in all aspects of your life with your partner, including your sexual relationship (see Parts V and VI). Communicating well lets you and your partner know what's important to the other, while avoiding misunderstandings and allowing your lives together to run smoothly.

Communicating well helps you learn each other's vulnerable areas so that you don't unintentionally hurt one another. It also helps you make plans for your future together: vacations, career plans, buying and maintaining a house, having children (or not). Communicating well about day-to-day living preferences and how you'll divide up household responsibilities helps avoid typical tensions and resentments. Communicating well is indispensable for making yourself lovable and making your love relationship work—so indispensable that we'll come back to this topic in Part VI and talk about it in much more detail.

There are numerous books on the market that give couples practice in communication skills, and most therapists are well trained to teach these.[5] It's a mistake to think either that you're born with these skills or that you're hopeless. They are learnable skills. Partners can have fun learning them together.

Making yourself lovable is an essential and exciting investment in your romantic happiness.

Exercises

1. How can you start to improve your passion for life? Spend a few moments thinking about each category below and write one idea under each that would make you feel more passionate about your life.

Romantic love. For example, "I want to remember something fun I did for my wife when we first dated and do something similar to bring the spark back" or "I want to join an Internet dating service this week."

_____

_____

A career or a job. What type of job or what change in your current job would give you more of the feeling: *This job is so great that I can't believe they pay me to do it.*

_____

_____

Art. How can you bring more art into your life? Think about the choices among novels, plays, films, sculpture, painting, architecture, poetry, music, dancing, and more.

_____

_____

Home. Make your home warm and inviting, tailored to your aesthetic taste and needs. For example, "I want to buy a new bedspread and curtains to freshen up our bedroom" or "I want to clean the den; it stresses me out every day!"

_____

_____

Friendships. Choose your friends; don't acquire them by chance. Choose people you value and who value you. For example, introduce yourself to your interesting new coworker at the office and become acquainted.

_____

_____

Family. Play favorites. Make time to enjoy the pleasure you get from their company.

_____

_____

Children. Have children *only* if you value the process of raising them. For example, "I would love for us to start a family in two years" or "I am happy without children."

_____

_____

Hobbies. For example, "I would like to try camping with my partner. That could be a lot of fun."

_____

_____

Personal niceties. These are joyful personal activities you may want to indulge in. For example, "I want to get up half an hour early each day and take a walk in my garden or jog around the neighborhood before going to work. I'd love that!"

_____

_____

2. Name one way to improve your personal appearance. For example, "I want to exercise more."

_____

_____

What would be the next step toward reaching that goal? For example, "I will join the local gym or take a daily walk."

_____

_____

Notes

1. Ayn Rand, *The Journals of Ayn Rand*, ed. David Harriman (New York: Dutton, 1997), p. 28.

2. For an analysis of the role of art in human life, see Ayn Rand, "Art and Sense of Life," *The Romantic Manifesto* (New York: Signet, 1971), p. 35. The fuller text version is as follows:

> The emotion involved in art is not an emotion in the ordinary meaning of the term. It is experienced more as a "sense" or a "feel," but it has two characteristics pertaining to emotions: it is automatically immediate and it has an intense, profoundly personal (yet undefined) value-meaning to the individual experiencing it. The value involved is life, and the words naming the emotion are: "This is what life means to me."
>
> Regardless of the nature or content of an artist's metaphysical views, what an art work expresses, fundamentally, under all of its lesser aspects is: "This is life as I see it." The essential meaning of a viewer's or reader's response, under all of its lesser elements, is: "This is (or is not) life as I see it."

3. It is not a sacrifice to care for your children, if you choose to have them, because raising children is an important value to you. It is a sacrifice if you have children out of duty, to please others, when you really want to spend most of your time with your partner, on your career, or engaging in other activities.

4. Dr. Edwin A. Locke, an internationally renowned expert on goal setting, has two excellent talks: "Setting Goals to Improve Your Life and Happiness," part 1 and part 2 (available on CDs from www.aynrandbookstore.com).

5. Some books which give couples communication principles and skills are: Matthew McKay, Patrick Fanning, and Kim Paleg, *Couple Skills: Making Your Relationship Work* (Oakland: New Harbinger Publications, 1994); Jesse S. Nirenberg, *Getting Through to People* (New Jersey: Prentice-Hall, 1963). For mental health professionals, the authors recommend Frank M. Dattilio and Christine A. Padesky's book *Cognitive Therapy with Couples* (Florida: Professional Resource Exchange, 1990).

Part III: Finding Your Soul Mate

She looked as if this were her place, her moment and her world, she looked as if enjoyment were her natural state, her face was the living form of an active, living intelligence... what he felt was the sheer pleasure of the sight, the purest esthetic pleasure he had ever experienced.

—Ayn Rand, *Atlas Shrugged*

CHAPTER 8

Achieving Harmony Between Reason and Emotion

F inding the right romantic soul mate requires, not just an emotional bond, but a harmony between one's reasoned judgment and one's feelings.

Let's assume you're reasonably well off in the lovability department—that is, you possess most of the qualities discussed in previous chapters, such as moral virtue, self-esteem, passionate valuing, and more. Assume further that you've met someone who possesses similar qualities. Does that mean you've found the right romantic partner? Absolutely not. Love needs a solid foundation, but that foundation is not the whole story.

> *Romantic love is personal and individual.*
> *Someone who excites one person may leave*
> *another person indifferent or completely turned off.*

What you are looking for is a romantic soul mate: someone who will treasure you for what you value most in yourself, a person who has at least most of the qualities you cherish and enjoy on a daily basis, with whom you share fundamental values, who makes you feel visible. Your soul mate is a person you are strongly attracted to, intellectually, emotionally, and sexually. This is true not only at the level of your conscious judgment, though that is critically important, but also at the deepest level of your subconscious—as revealed by your emotional responses. You experience it as, "This is the perfect partner for me." But you will not necessarily experience these emotional responses, valid or not, after just one meeting.

Your first impression of any person is always intuitive— it is an automatic, emotional response to various cues, some of which you may not even be aware of at the time. Beyond what a person says, many cues are non-verbal, including tone of voice, facial expression(s), laughter, eye contact, and body language. Intuitive reactions are, of course, very personal. If a man says to a woman he just met, "Hey, you're a cute babe," one woman would be repulsed, thinking subconsciously that the comment implied she was a brainless sex object. Another might be flattered, seeing it as a compliment to her attractiveness. Others might think the remark was humorous or perhaps trite and superficial—and so on. The same personal reactions also occur in response to non-verbal cues.

Your intuitive first reactions, however, may get you into trouble if you let your initial gut response color everything else, overlooking characteristics that could cause serious problems down the road. Or you may ignore positive characteristics that could reverse an indifferent or even a somewhat negative first impression.

Your initial emotional response, whether positive, negative, or indifferent, needs to be validated (or invalidated) consciously by gaining more knowledge. This takes time. Get to know a person gradually, in layers. Attentively observe how the person acts in different situations (especially, but not solely, how the person acts toward you). Ask questions and listen closely to what the person says.

This needs to be accompanied by careful introspection, because you may value certain attributes of the person and dislike others or because the person may act inconsistently. You'll want to resolve any contradictory impressions you have of your potential partner and tie all your knowledge together to get a concise, clear picture of their character and personality.

Conflicts may also arise within your own psychology, such as indecision about whether you're ready for commitment or concern that this partner may discover your insecurities. Don't rush; take the time to explore and resolve such personal confusions.

What about the question: "Can there be love at first sight?" Strong attraction, yes, but love at first sight would necessarily be superficial because not enough can be known about a person at a first look or meeting. Again, first impressions can be very revealing (body language, demeanor, the content of what is said), but these impressions are not necessarily conclusive, even if very positive. However, they might be conclusive if they are very negative, such as when a person endorses values you find offensive; you know you do not need to learn anything more.

A few fortunate individuals have a first impression of a partner that turns out to be accurate; they are a perfect match. But even these individuals should not commit to a permanent attachment on the spot. "Attraction at first sight" is fine, but nothing can replace the need to gain more knowledge about your potential partner.

> *What people call "love at first sight" is often the result of infatuation. Infatuation refers to a strong, immediate, emotional attraction based on a small number of qualities, sometimes only one, such as looks.*

Consider poor Foster. He met Juliana when she waited on him at a bar. He discovered that this gorgeous, seductive woman, with long, silky hair, blue eyes, and a beautiful smile, was an aspiring Hollywood actress. Foster courted her ardently. She was short of money, so he convinced her to move in with him. He brought her flowers, cooked the meals, bought new clothing for her, and loaned her his car. He was ecstatic when she agreed to have sex with him, but her sexual response was mechanical, lacking in intimacy. In the back of his mind Foster knew something was missing in their relationship.

Juliana came home one day beaming; she had gotten her first small role in a movie. The following day Juliana ditched him for an up-and-coming young actor; she left him a curt "Dear John" note on the table. Foster was crushed. He had idolized her. As he thought about it more, however, he realized that he had never felt "at home" with her or loved by her. Behind Juliana's good looks there was no real self; she was a narcissist who used Foster to get money and attention but she never showed a personal interest in him. Clearly, he should have gotten to know her as a real individual. Intoxicated by her beauty, he gave her an unlimited benefit of the doubt about everything else.

Even when we keenly observe and accurately evaluate a potential partner's behavior, a person may be adept at temporarily camouflaging bad character traits. Juliana was a good actress, in this sense, although Foster was pretty easy to dupe. But it is impossible to fake one's own character indefinitely. The longer you know someone, the more likely you will be able to see that person's real, whole self.

As we noted, negative assessments often require less analysis than positive ones. Rejection upon first meeting is totally warranted if the other person reveals qualities that you clearly see as antithetical to your own. Consider a first date who is vulgar, mindless, and rude and expresses ideas that are deeply offensive to you. In such an instance, you do not need to waste your time looking for deeper layers. (Some people like the idea of trying to save seemingly hopeless cases, but we strongly advise against doing this. You cannot make another person over in your own image or to your specifications.)

> *The ideal goal is a harmony between your emotional response and your rational appraisal. If there is any conflict between the two, it will feel like a red flag.*

Treat all red flags as a signal to clarify and resolve any confusion and doubts you may have before making decisions about something as important as marriage. If you consider your partner to be a fine person and yet feel nothing emotionally, this will not work romantically. Nor will it work if you feel a strong emotional response yet conclude consciously that the person is of low character or a poor match for you. You want a strong emotional bond that agrees fully with your rational judgment of the person.

What do you need to learn in order to achieve a harmony between reason and emotion? Find out in the next three chapters.

Exercises

1. Think of a time in your life where you were romantically infatuated with another person. What qualities were you responding to subconsciously?

_____

_____

2. Use the example from Exercise 1 (or a different one) to describe a time when an infatuation turned out to be the wrong partner for you. What did you learn that made you realize that this person would not be a good match for you?

_____

_____

3. Have you ever been in a romance that worked for some years but then soured? What changed? Did you miss anything at the beginning?

_____

_____

• CHAPTER 9 •

Choosing the Right Partner I

*R*omantic compatibility involves reasonable similarity with respect to: sense of life, values, interests, and personality, but partners need not be (and should not be) identical mirror images of one another.

Selecting Your Partner

Almost everyone has some vision of the ideal romantic partner. These ideals vary widely from person to person and may be vague or detailed, deep or superficial, constant or ever-changing, realistic or unrealistic. In the next two chapters we present ten factors that we believe can help you choose the right partner.

- Sense of life—your deepest subconscious values and approach to life
- Values—what is fundamentally important to you
- Interests and tastes
- Personality
- Habits
- Attitude toward money
- Appearance, fitness, and health

- Leisure and lifestyle
- Visibility
- Deal-breakers and trade-offs

In this chapter, we will cover the first four factors.

Sense of Life

Ayn Rand defines "sense of life" as "an emotional, subconsciously integrated appraisal of man and of existence.[1] She notes, "a sense of life always retains a profoundly personal quality; it reflects a man's deepest values; it is experienced by him as a sense of his own identity."[2] Your sense of life is the deepest level of your self and affects the choices you make in life. But what does this have to do with love? Ayn Rand goes on to say:

> Love is a response to values. It is with a person's sense of life that one falls in love—with that essential sum, that fundamental stand or way of facing existence, which is the essence of a personality. One falls in love with the embodiment of the values that formed a person's character, which are reflected in his widest goals or smallest gestures, which create the style of his soul—the individual style of a unique, unrepeatable, irreplaceable consciousness. It is one's own sense of life that acts as the selector, and responds to what it recognizes as one's own basic values in the person of another.[3]

You experience an attraction or repulsion to another person's sense of life as an emotion that is much deeper than infatuation; you feel a deep, strong connection.

It is based on a subconscious appraisal of the person's perceived essence, not of one, often superficial, trait (for example, recall Foster's infatuation with Juliana's looks in Chapter 8). Your initial response to another person—mistaken or not—may be based on a sense-of-life response.

Let's consider two examples. Bryan met Suzanne at a friend's outing. He was immediately attracted to her and not just because he found her physically appealing. She did not try to be the center of attention. She dressed tastefully. She seemed interested in conversations about ideas rather than idle gossip. It didn't bother her when people disagreed with her views. When Bryan talked with her, she looked at him directly; he saw no hint of fear, only curiosity about what he had to say. Bryan, an independent thinker with genuine self-esteem, felt an emotional bond with Suzanne; he felt he might have met his soul mate. Unlike Foster, however, Bryan remained cautious. He knew he needed to get to know her better.

Consider a contrasting example. Mary met Daniel on a blind date. Although Daniel was financially well off, he wore an old tee shirt and his hair was dirty and unkempt. Mary asked him what he did for a living and he replied, "computers and stuff." She asked him why he liked his work; he didn't know, except that it was "fun sometimes and scary other times." She asked what he wanted in life; he had no long-range goals. She asked what books he liked; he didn't read books, he watched TV and played video games.

Instead of looking at her, he looked at the ceiling or at other people in the restaurant. Mary was an attractive, successful, and ambitious lawyer who loved reading and developing her mind. She couldn't stand Daniel and felt totally invisible to him. Being with Daniel, she felt as though he was from an alien universe. His sense of life was opposite to hers.

Values

Your potential partner's sense of life reflects his or her deepest values and it is important that you try to identify those values consciously. Some view life as an exciting adventure and—using their best judgment—look for values to pursue that give their lives meaning. Others view life as a frightening burden and fear that achieving great values is hopeless. Some have no personal values and live only for others.

You will want to know if your partner's philosophy matches your own and whether that philosophy is a healthy one: pro-happiness, pro-long-range achievement in the real world. People's professed philosophy and values may not be their real ones and may even be in conflict with the values that govern their daily choices and actions.

> *To discover a potential partner's actual values, don't just listen to what this person says; also look at their choices, actions, and responses over time.*

Observe what a potential romantic partner responds to emotionally, and why. For example, do they show passion, indifference, or contempt for certain events, objects, activities, or individuals? Notice what makes them happy, excited, or angry Observe how they make difficult choices—with careful thinking, by weighing the pros and cons, or going by emotions only.

Look at what a potential partner likes or doesn't like in the arts—greatness, mediocrity, or depravity? Ask what this person aspires to and observe if there's any action taken toward these goals. Note how this person views his or her work—is this person passionate about it or is it just a job? Do they resent the responsibility of earning a living? See whom this person chooses for friends—admirable individuals or people who are empty or just no good?

Romantic partners don't have to—and should not—share all values. It would be boring to marry a near replica of yourself. You want your soul mate to be another self, but only in a fundamental sense, not in every detail. The key is to share enough important values to form an unshakable bond and to feel psychologically visible to one another. This allows for non-fundamental differences that make your partner a unique and interesting individual.

> *Belonging to the same religion, sharing the same secular philosophy, being of the same race or nationality, sharing the same social background— none of these guarantees romantic compatibility.*

You can share the same religion or secular philosophy, be of the same race and nationality, or come from the same social background and still be different in enough fundamental ways, including sense of life, to make a successful romantic relationship impossible.

Your aspirations for the future need to be compatible. For

example, it is important for partners to be comfortable with each other's level of ambition. This does not mean both need to have the same level of ambition, but their ambitions should not conflict. One partner may need to work long hours or move frequently to get ahead. The other partner must be on board with this for the relationship to work.

An important value to discover is whether you and a potential partner want to have children or not, and if you do, how many. This choice dramatically affects your future together. A discrepancy in values here is often a deal-breaker. Explore this value honestly and openly. Even if you initially agree, one partner may have a change of mind later and this can become a source of conflict. If a partner has children from a previous relationship, it is very important to learn how that might affect your daily life together and your long-range goals.[4]

Interests and Tastes

Interests are a type of value referring to specific activities you enjoy. One partner might enjoy hiking, surfing, swimming, bicycling, and movies, and the other might enjoy gardening, reading, cooking, tennis, and opera. Partners rarely share all interests, but it is important that they share some or they will spend less time together and may drift apart emotionally.

Interests also include activities of the intellect. Although most communication between partners is about personal matters, as it should be, most people like to talk about other matters too. If their intellectual interests are very different, or if one partner is interested in intellectual issues and the other not at all, this can create distance between them. Some couples compartmentalize their lives: they talk to friends about what interests them and discuss only personal matters with their partners. This can work but sometimes it leads to feeling less visible with one another.

Tastes are a type of value referring to personal preferences in such areas as art, music, food, clothes, and your home. Differences in tastes can be stimulating as long as they do not become a source of destructive conflict.

Darcy and Mark met at work and had become each other's confidante. After dating a few months, they decided to move in together. But their differences in personal interests and tastes became a significant sore spot in their relationship. Darcy loved dancing. Mark feared making a fool of himself on the dance floor. He recoiled when Darcy suggested taking dance lessons together. Mark was a sports guy. As spring approached and Mark started frequenting the golf course, Darcy felt the distance grow between them. Mark pressured Darcy to join him; she staunchly refused. Both felt abandoned by each other. Due to the growing resentment, even small differences in their tastes flared into major arguments. Although they both had lovable qualities, their differences in interests and tastes brought out the worst in them as a couple.

Personality

Personality refers to ways of acting that are habitual. Often the first thing that strikes us about another person is whether that person is nice.

> By "nice," we don't mean the syrupy, selfless, sweet type of person who has no independent values and never judges anyone. We mean the generally friendly person who is considerate, pleasant, tactful, and shows good will.

The opposite is a person who's just not nice, someone who's unfriendly, impolite, inconsiderate, grumpy, gratuitously critical, tactless, or otherwise shows ill will. Genuinely nice people create a positive emotional climate, and this helps romance thrive.

A trait related to genuine niceness is personal warmth. By warmth we mean friendly affection from your partner. Warmth is essential for romance to flourish. Coldness can be temporary, as a result of anger at your partner for some particular action, but romance is impossible if it is a constant presence in your relationship. *How* your partner shows warmth and affection is also important. Whether it's through small gifts, loving words, hugs, frequent phone calls, and smiles and kisses, or through all of these ways and more, you'll want to make sure that you enjoy each other's affection and manner of showing it (see Chapters 13 and 19 for more details, including the importance of touching).

Another important personality trait is genuineness. Is the person trying to play a role or are they just themselves? Role-playing stems from insecurity and its goal is to make an impression, usually for the purpose of boosting the illusion of self-esteem.

> *People who are genuine are far more likely*
> *to have authentic love relationships*
> *than those who are always playing a role.*

Another valuable personality trait is openness. This applies especially to emotional openness and the willingness to share one's deepest values and feelings with the other. If one partner refuses to do this out of fear or is unable to do it (due to poor introspective skills), then the other partner necessarily feels cut off from the deepest layers of the "closed" partner's soul. This severely limits emotional intimacy and closeness and undermines visibility. (Openness does not mean your partner should act as your therapist.)

Another important trait is conscientiousness—for example, being responsible about one's money, work, promises, chosen obligations, and health.

The above traits are a boon to every romantic relationship. However, we can all be categorized by other personality traits as well, traits that can properly be a matter of personal preference. Some partners enjoy more humor; some less (for more on humor see Chapter 15). Some prefer a gregarious partner; others prefer a more introspective, quiet one. Some like a person who enjoys spontaneity; others prefer planners. If partners are not well matched or at least accepting of differences, such legitimate differences can result in chronic tension, painful arguments, and a conflict-ridden relationship, even among partners who are good people. Partners sometimes mistakenly treat such optional personality traits as moral issues. Such differences may be legitimate reasons for not wanting one another as soul mates, but they don't make a person morally wrong.

Compatible personalities are crucial. Being compatible does not mean being identical—it means that the partners do not constantly clash but make each other happy on a daily basis. Nor is it the case that opposites necessarily attract; this may be true of some traits but not others. An introverted man might enjoy the way an extroverted woman brings him out of his shell, while an extroverted man might feel at peace with a quiet, self-contained woman. On the other hand, many people prefer partners with similar personalities. People who are adventurous, for example, usually prefer partners who are the same.

The important issue here is whether you feel at home psychologically with your partner's personality or whether there is constant friction or hurt.

Do you feel relaxed, in sync, on the same wavelength, or tense, at odds, alienated? Do you enjoy being around your partner, or do you feel relieved to be alone or prefer the company of others? Do your partner's habitual ways of acting make you happy, secure, and yet excited, or anxious, angry, and depressed? These questions, which can be answered by introspection, will help you identify if you have found your personality soul mate.

Personality clashes that are bothersome during the dating process, when both parties are allegedly on their best behavior, often worsen with time.

Take personality clashes seriously. Though personalities are relatively stable, they are changeable, but because they are automatized in the subconscious, change requires considerable conscious work, time, and sometimes even professional help. For example, Rudy was a rather intense person. He would become very tense when he and Sheryl got ready to travel, especially when it came to deciding when to leave for the airport. He wanted to leave very early and drive fast— just in case of bad traffic. Sheryl, in contrast, was more relaxed though still conscientious. To relieve travel stress, they agreed to let Sheryl decide what time to leave for the airport and also do the driving. As a result, they were both more relaxed. This is a good example of creative problem solving.

You now understand four important factors—sense of life, values, interests and tastes, and personality—that will help you choose the right partner. In the next chapter, we will give you more guidance to help you choose well.

Exercises

1. How would you describe the sense of life of the best partner you have ever had? Start with the emotional tone of the relationship, and relate how your sense of life and that of your partner created it.

_____

_____

2. What values do you most want in a partner?

_____

_____

3. Do you and your partner have different interests and tastes? What are those differences and how do you deal with them?

_____

_____

4. How would you describe your partner's personality? Does it cause you problems? Is there a resolution?

_____

_____

Notes

1 Ayn Rand, "Philosophy and Sense of Life," The Romantic Manifesto (New York: Signet, 1971). p. 25.

2. Ibid., p. 31.

3. Ibid., p. 32.

4. For a comprehensive list of books on step-parenting see:
  http://www.saafamilies.org/education/catalog/amazon.htm
  http://www.saafamilies.org/education/reviews/index.htm
  http://ecommerce.4w.com/stepfam/booksandtapes.htm#200900

CHAPTER 10

Choosing the Right Partner II

We covered in Chapter 9 four factors out of our list of ten that are relevant to compatibility between partners. Now let's consider the last six.

- Habits
- Attitude toward money
- Appearance, fitness and health
- Leisure and lifestyle
- Visibility
- Deal-breakers and trade-offs

Habits

Like personalities, habits are consistent ways of acting but they refer to particular actions rather than consistent styles. Examples of habits are smoking, drinking coffee each morning, being late, and so on.

Some seemingly innocuous habits can be a source of real annoyance to a partner, such as leaving the toilet seat up, ignoring crumbs dropped on the floor, throwing dirty clothes about, or driving recklessly. Both partners have to decide how dangerous or important negative habits are, and they should make a serious effort to change those that are a real source of friction. Bad habits can be changed more easily than bad personality traits (for example, impoliteness, tactlessness) because, although habits function automatically, they are more limited in scope than traits. Changing habits, however, still requires a deliberate, conscious focus.

> *Positive habits, such as courteous manners and being considerate, make a relationship run smoothly.*

Other positive habits include voluntarily helping out around the house, leaving love notes and cards to surprise your partner, frequently exchanging hugs and kisses, and dressing nicely, even around the house. By making it a goal, you and your partner can acquire such habits, even if lacking them initially.

Time management is frequently a source of tension. Is one partner habitually late, even when being on time is objectively important? Or is one obsessed with time management, compulsively rushing through life and having no fun? The first shows a lack of integrity. The second is a psychological problem. It is important for partners to work together when making plans and arrangements and take into account both partners' wants and desires. Time management should be made compatible with other good habits in your relationship.

Attitude Toward Money

It is claimed that sex and money are the two most frequent sources of marital conflict. (We discuss sex in Part V.)

> *Learn about your partner's attitude toward money issues before making a long-term commitment.*

Certainly there is no future in marrying a gold-digger— someone who wants only your money. It's also a mistake to marry a wild spender who thinks only about today but not tomorrow when the bills come due. Barring these types, money conflicts do occur among decent, responsible people, and strong differences of opinion can arise about spending priorities, even when there is agreement on the amount to be spent. Partners will argue over whether to spend money on a new car, a house down payment, a nice vacation or eating out—or whether to put it into savings.

Another source of friction may appear when one partner makes considerably more money than the other. The higher-income earner may feel entitled to make all the major financial decisions and the one who earns less may feel like a second-class citizen. The big money-maker could also be a cheapskate, spending much less than can readily be afforded, making the other feel devalued. Determining who will manage the bill-paying and investments (possibly both partners), how much money to budget in different spending categories, whether to have joint or separate savings accounts, and whether to have a prenuptial agreement (especially if one partner is wealthier than the other) are questions to explore when seriously considering a long-term partnership or marriage.[1]

Wall Street Journal reporter Jeff Opdyke advises couples planning on marriage to discuss, ahead of time, the following nine financial issues.[2] It is better to deal with these questions beforehand rather than end up with painful or bitter conflicts later on.

1. What are your financial assets and liabilities?
2. What is your debt situation and debt history?
3. What is your money-earning and spending history?
4. Is a pre-nuptial agreement needed to protect both of your interests?
5. What are your financial aspirations for the future? What would you like to do with the money you earn?
6. What are your career aspirations? Do both parties plan to work? What if you have children?
7. How would financial responsibilities be divided between you?
8. Will you have multiple checkbooks or one?
9. What money-management skills do you possess?

We would add to this list:

10. If one spouse makes more money than the other, how will spending decisions be managed?

Lack of honesty with respect to money issues is a common complaint among romantic partners. It is no more appropriate to lie about money than it is to lie about sex or any other aspect of a relationship. Assuming that both partners are of good character, thoroughly discussing and agreeing on how to handle important money issues beforehand will build trust and mutual respect.

Appearance, Fitness and Health

Taking pride in one's appearance is important in romance, as we discussed in Chapter 7. Infatuation aside, you want a partner whose looks you enjoy. Preferences in looks are very personal. A woman who delights one man might leave others indifferent or even turned off, and the same goes for women evaluating men. Romance will not work if your partner physically turns you off. Ideally, you want to view your partner as the most beautiful or attractive partner in the world—that is, attractive to you personally.

> *An interesting phenomenon often occurs regarding looks: when you ardently love your partner's soul, your partner seems more physically beautiful to you.*

This phenomenon has its limits, however. It will not overcome the effects of a partner's chronic neglect of his or her looks. Almost anyone would be turned off by a partner who is grossly overweight or has deliberately unkempt hair or a greasy, ungroomed beard, or who dresses like a slob.

Fitness, which is obviously good for your health, affects appearance. Being fit makes you look and feel better, whether you do it by means of sports, going to the gym, dieting, or some other activity. You may enjoy engaging in fitness activities together, though this isn't always feasible. Denise was seventy pounds overweight, and it showed in her stomach and in her face. She hated her double chin and her pudgy belly. Her boyfriend, Russ, was afraid to offend her but he didn't enjoy looking at her during sex. She sensed this and insisted that the lights always be turned off, and she tried to make sure his hand never touched the rolls of fat on her stomach. Denise felt extremely self-conscious and completely unsexy during their lovemaking.

Russ had to fantasize that he was with someone more attractive, and Denise sensed this from the sexy magazines and erotica that he kept in his desk drawer. As time went on, she started bathing less frequently and letting herself go, hoping to be a turnoff to Russ so she wouldn't have to go through the humiliating experience of exposing her hefty body to him. This relationship was in deep trouble.

But one day Denise was watching a fitness show on television. The health professional was persuasive and encouraging, particularly when she talked about her own period of being overweight. The professional discussed how and why she changed her thinking and behavior. Denise felt that rare moment of hope and commitment; she decided to make this change for herself. With Russ's loving support, she joined a local gym and went to a nutritionist. It took her twelve months to lose the extra seventy pounds, but she discovered a perseverance that she didn't know she was capable of. She loved her new, shapely, toned body, and Russ found her increasingly sexy. Feeling better about herself had major effects on her life. She enjoyed wearing more feminine clothes at work and sexier clothes when going out with Russ. Now she wanted to keep the lights on while making love and enjoyed feeling Russ's hands on her body. And she encouraged Russ to take up bike riding with her, which made for delightful getaways on the weekends. Fitness helped save their romantic relationship.

A related issue is health. Does a potential partner have any health problems that would frustrate you or become intolerable to live with on a daily basis? For example, does he or she have allergies to cats or an inability to join you on the ski slopes because of knee problems, a heart problem, debilitating migraines, or a chronic disease? You yourself may have health problems, and you would want to make sure that your partner is accepting of them. Some people don't mind having a partner with even serious physical limitations, but for others, even minor but chronic limitations become a major source of frustration.

Another important health issue is the refusal of a partner to take a medical condition seriously, such as high blood pressure.

> *Individuals who do not value their own lives enough*
> *to take steps to keep healthy condemn*
> *their partners to chronic worry.*

Who enjoys the prospect of living with someone who is at high risk health-wise yet refuses to take reasonable action to significantly reduce that risk? It's like living with someone committing slow suicide.

The same principle holds for partners with mental health problems. This can be a serious problem, because often people with mental health problems deny or do not realize how serious their problem is (for example, depression). Outside help from the family doctor may be needed to convince the person to seek therapy.

Leisure and Lifestyle

Spending leisure time together in compatible activities is a wonderful way to strengthen your love. Whether it's dining out, reading in bed together, going to the movies, attending concerts, playing sports, listening to music, or going on vacations—taking time to deliberately bask in the enjoyment of one another's company is ultimately one of the most rewarding things you can both do. Even if you have different tastes, there are ways to make both of you happy. (Resolving conflicts is discussed in detail in Part VI.) Some activities you can do with friends, but it is important that you and your partner do not routinely go your separate ways.

Partners need compatible lifestyles. If one person is a homebody and the other wants to be out every night, if one loves to cook and the other prefers to routinely eat out, if one takes part in strenuous physical activities and the other consistently seeks intellectual ones—disagreement and conflict often result. A certain amount of compromise is possible, but if disputes arise weekly or even daily, a long-term relationship becomes very difficult.

Visibility

Since romantic love is based on the visibility principle (as we explained in Chapter 1), it is absolutely critical that each partner feels visible to one another.

You should feel especially visible for what is most important to you, and ideally you'll want to feel visible as a whole person, not just for a few narrow traits.

- Emotional visibility means understanding and empathizing with each other's emotions.
- Philosophy-of-life visibility means understanding and acknowledging your partner's deepest values and sense of life.
- Intellectual visibility means showing respect for your partner's mind. It's helpful if partners possess roughly the same degree of mental ability and education. If there's a huge discrepancy, it will be difficult to have interesting conversations about topics that you both enjoy.
- Sexual visibility means appreciating your partner's body and his or her ability to give and receive sexual pleasure. It means feeling more masculine or feminine in one another's presence.

All the factors we've discussed in this and the previous chapters affect visibility. If you feel invisible to your partner in any way that is of crucial significance to you, this issue needs to be addressed. Feeling invisible implies that you are not important to or perhaps not well matched with your partner.

Deal-breakers and Trade-offs

It is unlikely that even an ideal romantic partner will be what you want in every detail.

Anyone who wants to establish a long-term relationship is faced with the question: What's essential in a partner for my happiness?

Choosing someone as a potential soul mate is very personal undertaking but we can suggest some guidelines. You can start by *eliminating* certain potential candidates.

Newspaper love columns are filled with letters beginning, "My partner is a wonderful person except for one thing. . ." Almost inevitably this one thing turns out to be something very important, such as drug abuse, infidelity, making parents more important than the partner, neglect, being a cheapskate, being a control freak, or psychological or physical abuse. Any type of abuse is most certainly a deal-breaker. Remember that every person is a whole, not a series of disconnected parts. Any serious, uncorrected flaw will almost inevitably undermine other qualities that are good.

We recommend that you:

• Eliminate anyone with poor moral character, for example, someone who is dishonest or lacks integrity. No matter what other qualities he or she possesses, and no matter how good that person makes you feel in the short run, such a person will bring you nothing but heartache and disappointment in the end.

• Be cautious regarding people with significant psychological or mental health problems (for example, severe repression, significant chronic anxiety problems, recurrent depression, addictions such as substance abuse or gambling), especially if such individuals are not yet under treatment, have no motivation to fix their problems, or don't take their problems seriously. Don't make a partner's *untreated* problems your lifetime career. A romantic partner can be supportive, but should not be a live-in therapist.

• Eliminate anyone whom you do not respond to emotionally, including sexually; love, after all, is an emotion. (If the problem is solely sexual due simply to lack of knowledge or poor technique, it can be remedied. See Chapter 19.) Notice how your partner treats you. For example, if the person is stingy with praise but generous with criticism, dump him or her.

• Eliminate anyone whom you consciously know is a poor match for you on the deepest value level (for example, one partner is unquestioningly religious and a homebody and the other is uncompromisingly pro-reason, anti-mysticism, and adventurous; one is openly anti-intellectual and the other loves reading and learning and discussing new ideas).

• Eliminate anyone in whose presence you feel constant friction, annoyance, resentment, anxiety, or self-doubt due to differences in values, personality, habits, tastes, interests, and so on. If you feel like this during the dating process, the problems will get worse. Be aware of the warning signs of an abusive partner or a controlling personality—a person who tries to control you through fear and destroy you by attacking your self-esteem.

> *Of those remaining in your potential love pool, pay special attention to anyone who makes you feel fully visible and is a joy to be with—assuming it is not false flattery.*

Then decide if you can ignore any habits, tastes, and personality traits you don't care for. Are these trade-offs minor or fundamental to you? Are they likely to grow or diminish in importance? If the qualities you value clearly outweigh those you don't value, then further consideration is needed. This may take time to process, because things that bother you a little at first may bother you more later. This is another reason not to rush into a permanent relationship.

Some final points: Too many individuals settle for less than they want because they are desperate to have a relationship or a spouse, then spend years or decades regretting their decision. Take the time to discover what you long for in a partner. On the other side of this coin, do not hold to unreasonable standards requiring your partner to be exactly what you want in every last detail.

Decide what's most important and then decide if you're willing to make allowances for the smaller things. And avoid spending years pining for what you can't get. If your dream partner is brilliant, highly educated, incredibly attractive, and a high-level professional and you are none of these things, find a more suitable match. Never wish for something you can't have. It will only make you miserable. Finally, marrying to rescue your partner from their psychological problems or flaws almost never works. It's best to let your partner work on their problems first.

Exercises

1. What habits really annoy you in potential or actual romantic partners?

_____

_____

2. Have you had conflicts with a partner about money? Were they resolved?

_____

_____

3. What do you want an ideal partner to look like (be realistic)?

_____

_____

4. What is your ideal lifestyle? Has this caused you relationship conflicts?

_____

_____

5. Do you feel visible to your partner or date? What makes you feel visible or invisible?

_____

_____

6. What have been deal-breakers for you in past relationships?

_____

_____

Notes

1. No matter who manages the money, both partners should be fully informed about family financial matters.

2. Jeff D. Opdyke, "Love & Money: Nine questions partners should ask each other before getting married," _Wall Street Journal_, March 27, 2006, pp. R-1, R-3. See also podcast: WSJ.com/Free.

CHAPTER 11

Choosing the Right Partner III

C hoosing a potential lifetime partner involves much thought and evaluation. In the last two chapters, we identified ten factors that will help you find a soul mate. Judging whether someone is the right one is no easy task. Here are some final tips to help you.

Judging Others: Words versus Actions

Everything we have discussed so far involves judging a potential partner. Just how do you go about judging someone? What one says is important, but to fully assess a person's character, values, and personality, observe not only what they say but also how they act in different situations.

> *If there is a contradiction between words and actions, treat the actions as representing the real person.*

Actions reveal your partner's actual operating values or philosophy. If a person claims to be honest but lies, then that person is a liar. Partners cannot hide their real selves indefinitely. No matter how many times a person says he or she loves you, watch what this person actually does to show it.

Usually when words contradict actions, the words are more alluring than the actions. But sometimes the actions—which represent the person's subconscious philosophy—are more admirable than the words. Consider a man who has good character and acts in ways that show he values his partner but who fears putting his feelings into words and comes out with inappropriate humor or passionless chatter. This, of course, is a psychological flaw needing correction, but the problem is not with the man's basic values; rather, the problem is his not knowing how to express his feelings verbally and the fear and awkwardness that result.

How long does it take to thoroughly get to know a person? That depends on the person. Sometimes you gain enough key information to make a reasonably informed negative judgment within minutes— for example, if the person has obvious traits that you despise. But for a person you choose to continue seeing, it can take many months of interaction to learn everything you need to know.

A useful, though not foolproof, guideline is to know the person for at least a year before getting married. Some can be sure in less than a year; others need several years to know a person really well. There may be red flags you want to investigate. For example: He seems to drink a lot when they go out but claims he's never had an alcohol problem. Check on this from other sources: friends, family, co-workers. Or she's been caught lying once or twice.

What does this mean about her character? Your partner cannot camouflage their true character for long unless you're unobservant and gullible or if you have the misfortune to be dating a highly skilled con artist—although even they give themselves away eventually. For example, they may ask you for loans, which is a big red flag in itself, and then never pay you back.

> *Romance is potentially a lifetime value, so avoid letting temporary passion rush you into making a poor choice.*

Look at Your Love Trajectory

As your relationship develops, notice whether it becomes more positive, more negative, or stays the same. With a great partner, love gradually grows in depth and intensity, and there will be no contradictory evidence showing that it's not a good match. Your love trajectory—the course your relationship takes—should move in a positive direction, but if, in contrast, the trajectory moves downward, it means you and your partner are discovering more and more things that you don't like about one another.

Such relationships are doomed, barring some major turnaround. If the trajectory stays flat, this is also a red flag. Usually this happens because there is no real passion and partners are staying together out of inertia or convenience. Unless partners simply want friendship, this is a dangerous trap, because such quasi-romantic, unsatisfying relationships can go on for many years without either partner actively searching for a true romantic soul mate.

Other types of trajectories are possible. There is the roller coaster, which involves frequent major shifts, like strong passion followed by a big fight, then making up, followed by another fight, and so on. Such relationships are unstable and have a grim future unless the source of the blow-ups can be identified and resolved. You do not want constant anxiety, fear, and tears.

A number of factors can cause the course of a relationship to change, such as developing new ways of relating, handling conflict better, changing your perspective on your partner's attributes, or rethinking what you want. Even a great relationship can have some ups and downs. If the causes of the downs are resolved, then the upward trajectory can resume.

Some of the rockiness may be caused by inner conflict over making a long-term commitment to someone rather than personality characteristics of the partner. The process of meshing together the many aspects of your life with those of another unique individual is not easy, but so long as communication remains strong (honest, tactful, and respectful), partners can often resolve such problems and strengthen their love.

How Do You Know If Your Partner Is "The Right One" for You?

We've made many suggestions about finding the right partner. This doesn't mean you should make a checklist of important attributes and then rate everyone you date by it and choose the one with the highest score. This is far too mechanical.

It's best to spend time getting to know a person and to keep track of both your own rational judgment of and your emotional responses to that person.

> *Identify what you do and do not like about the person and why. Introspect to identify the causes of your reactions.*

It sometimes helps to put your private thoughts into words, and keeping a personal journal is helpful in translating feelings into clear thoughts and tracking your love trajectory over time.

Using key attributes we discussed earlier, such as sense of life, visibility, interests, attitude toward money, lifestyle preferences, and fitness (Chapters 9 and 10), compare your present companion to people you have dated before. What are you getting now that you missed before? Are you missing something now that you got before? If none of the people you've met satisfy enough of your requirements, keep looking.

If you recently found a potential soul mate, review the last few chapters to see whether there is anything important that you've overlooked. Is your partner lacking something you really want? Can your partner be trusted? Does your partner have traits that grate on you and can any of them be viewed as trade-offs in view of better qualities? Are there potential sources of conflict between you that need discussion?

> *Does your best judgment mesh with your emotional response to your partner or are there still red flags?*

If necessary, keep learning more. At the end of a year, if you are seriously dating, see how it all fits together. Don't take any big steps until you are fully satisfied that this is the right person for you.

What If the Partner You Want Doesn't Want You?

One essential principle to remember in the dating world is that you cannot force a mind.[1] You can't force someone you like to like you, no matter how strong your desires. That person is judging your appropriateness for his or her happiness just as you are doing. Rational dating properly includes mutually judging one another. Because love is so individual, finding the right match is not easy, and rejection and disappointments are likely, if not inevitable, before you find the right partner.

If you are rejected by a partner you like, you can ask for honest feedback. Use your own judgment in evaluating the feedback. For example, if your ex-partner attacks a good quality, such as telling you that you are too intelligent, then you know what to do—find a more intelligent partner! Anyone who is too insecure to appreciate your mind is not for you.

In contrast, if your ex-partner makes a valid criticism and points out that you are dishonest, unhealthily overweight, domineering, narcissistic, drink too much, or some other legitimate complaint, then acknowledge to yourself that you are less lovable than you could be and take steps to correct such problems as soon as possible. Honest feedback after one unsuccessful date may be more difficult to get, but if you're baffled as to why you are repeatedly rejected, you might try to find out by just asking.

Rejection comes in all forms: from subtle to shocking. You may feel rejected the first time you meet someone when you see signs of disappointment in the person's face. You may have been stood up. You may have been dumped at the end of a long-term relationship or been divorced several times. Some hurt is unavoidable, but knowing that you are, in principle, lovable is the antidote (see Chapters 5–7 to learn if you need to improve yourself). When you have the right perspective on your own life and on the goal of finding your soul mate, rejection hurts less.

> *What you say to yourself when you're rejected is critical. Your inner thoughts are based on your fundamental ideas about yourself, romance, and life in general.*

Everyone you date gives you more opportunity to fine-tune your knowledge of what you want to avoid and what you want in yourself and in a partner. If you discover flaws that make you less lovable, work on correcting them as you're looking for another soul mate.

Put the past behind you. Don't wallow in self-pity or self-doubt or fantasies about what could have been. Don't pursue the unimportant or the unattainable in your search for a soul mate. If you have been rejected by someone you truly know and love, or if you have broken off a long relationship, give yourself reasonable time to grieve the loss, just as you would if a loved one had passed away. Healthy mourning involves re-investing in your own life; in this case, it means motivating yourself to look for a better match.

> *Finding the right person is hard work. Expect that most individuals you meet will not be the right one. The rewards of finding your soul mate are worth your effort.*

Even if you fear further rejection, never lie about yourself or withhold important information when you believe that your relationship has a future (such as withholding that you have a disease, a criminal record, or children from a former relationship). Hiding relevant information from a potential soul mate is a significant breach of trust and damaging to your own self-respect. Even if you know you might be rejected, it is better to get the rejection over with as soon as possible, since there would be no future in that relationship. The idea that "What they don't know won't hurt them" is wrong; it will hurt them—and you too!

How to Search for Potential Partners

Just as with any important goal in life, don't be passive when searching for a partner. True, somebody might just come along, but there's no guarantee of this. It is better to be proactive. Proactive doesn't mean desperate. Desperation will tempt you to move too fast and disappointment is likely.

There are many ways to meet people: through friends and acquaintances, through work, through organizations you belong to, during singles activities, through professional dating or matchmaking services, or through the personals ads in magazines, newspapers, or online. The Internet has proven to be a tremendous boon to people looking for romantic partners; it is replacing some conventional dating services. There are dozens of Internet-based companies that provide you with a questionnaire and then match you with people who fit your profile. Many thousands of people use these sites, so you can meet a wider range of potential partners.

There are books that offer particulars about dating online, such as *The Complete Idiot's Guide to Online Dating and Relating*.[2] However, don't be deluded into thinking you can really know someone just from communicating through a website or e-mail. You cannot get a complete, accurate impression of someone unless you see them face to face over a long period of time. The person you meet online may turn out to be very different from the one you meet in the flesh.

There are safe ways to meet potential partners in person so that your privacy and safety are protected: meet in a public location, carry a cell phone, don't give your date any personal information such as your address, and let friends or family know where you plan to go on your date. If you find yourself trusting the person on this first encounter, you can set up future meetings and gradually give out more personal information.

Finding the right romantic partner may seem like a daunting task, but it is much less daunting when you know what to look for and how to look for it. This can help you get what you want and avoid painful errors.

Once you have found the person you believe is your soul mate, however, the story is not over—it is only beginning. You will want to know how to preserve and strengthen your relationship, and most people have no idea how to do this. Most make one major, often fatal, mistake. In the next chapter, we discuss this mistake, how you can avoid it, and explain how you can make your romance thrive and endure.

Exercises

1. Think of a time when you misjudged another because you relied too much on their words and too little on their actions.

_____

_____

2. Have you experienced a love trajectory? In which direction did it go? Why?

_____

_____

3. Have you ever concluded that Mr. or Ms. X was "the right one" (or maybe "the wrong one") and later realized you were mistaken? What changed your mind?

_____

_____

4. Have you been rejected in romance? How did you handle it?

_____

_____

5. If you haven't found a romantic partner, what can you do in the next week to search for one?

_____

_____

Notes

1. Leonard Peikoff, "The Initiation of Physical Force as Evil," _Objectivism: The Philosophy of Ayn Rand_ (New York: Dutton, 1991), p. 310:
> [T]here are only two basic methods by which one can deal with a dispute. The methods are reason or force; seeking to persuade others to share one's ideas voluntarily—or coercing others into doing what one wishes regardless of their ideas. Objectivism countenances only the method of persuasion.

[Note: In self-defense against the initiation of force by individual criminals or criminal nations, it is, of course, appropriate to use force.]

2. Joe Schwartz, _The Complete Idiot's Guide to Online Dating and Relating_ (Indiana: QUE (Macmillan], 2000).

Part IV: Making Your Romantic Relationship Thrive

*Concern for the welfare of those one loves
is a rational part of one's selfish interests.*
—Ayn Rand, *The Virtue of Selfishness*

CHAPTER 12

How to Cherish Your Partner I

Once you have found your soul mate, how do you keep the relationship thriving over many years? We believe you can avoid the fading or loss of romance and passion by thinking, planning, and acting to keep and sustain them.

> *The main reason for fading romance (aside from a poor match or partners moving in incompatible directions) is letting the love relationship "go on automatic," letting it be carried along solely by emotion.*

Letting the course of the relationship go on automatic is the fatal error that we alluded to in the previous chapter. It may seem paradoxical that you can't sustain love simply by being in love, but this is precisely our point. Emotions, despite their built-in urges or action tendencies, are the passive part of one's psychology. They occur automatically as a result of subconscious appraisals (as noted in Chapters 4 and 8).

It is true that love involves a built-in urge to act—to talk with your partner, to protect, touch, hold, and comfort each other. But this isn't enough. Urges don't guarantee action, and tendencies usually only last for a short time. A felt tendency can't tell you if it should be acted upon or which action is proper.

Emotions alone are insufficient to make the thousands of decisions and guide all the actions that have to be made over many years in order to sustain a passionate, intimate romantic relationship.

Consider John, who is madly in love with his new wife, Mandy. They are initially passionate lovers, but after a few months John gets wrapped up in some difficult work projects and takes his worries home. He ignores Mandy and sits down to have a beer. At dinner he complains about his job problems and she complains about hers. After dinner John does the dishes while she pays some bills. Finally, they go to bed and John is suddenly aroused by seeing Mandy undress. He tries to make love but gets the brush off. Mandy isn't in the mood because there has been no love-related communication since John got home. Annoyed, John goes to sleep. The same thing happens several days in a row. A barrier starts to grow, and John and Mandy find themselves increasingly aggravated by little things that the other does or doesn't do. The marriage slowly deteriorates because both are functioning on automatic. Their initial emotion of love does not carry them through the ins and outs of daily living. How should they fix this?

Love can be sustained only by an active mental process— the process of thinking.

Thinking is conscious and volitional. You must think about and plan what actions are needed to make your relationship with your loved one prosper in both the short and the long run—and then take the requisite action. One executive put the issue this way: "I simply decided to start treating my wife as if she were my most important client. That might not sound overly romantic, but I recognized the way I was wired and this approach has worked exceptionally well for me."[1] What this individual did was to consciously make his wife important.

Think of your love relationship as a garden full of rare and valuable flowers—the most important treasure in your life. Growing a garden isn't possible by just loving it; it has to be cultivated. If you start a garden and then neglect it, the plants will slowly wither and die. Cultivating a garden is an ongoing process requiring continuous thought and action. The same is true of love.

In these next chapters, we'll describe several categories of actions to take (or avoid) to prevent your passion from fading and to ensure that your relationship grows deeper, stronger, and more passionate over time. Everything we discuss in Part IV applies to both partners.

Show That You Value Your Partner

How do you value one another? We focus on seven ways to help you both feel truly cherished:

1. Work to understand your partner.
2. Encourage your partner to pursue his or her values.
3. Communicate constantly.
4. Show concern for your partner's welfare.
5. Show generosity.
6. Make decisions together.
7. Respect your partner's need for private time.

We will cover the first two points in this chapter.

Work to Understand Your Partner

> *Even though you may already understand a lot about your partner, knowing him or her is a continuous learning process that takes years.*

Here are some aspects of your partner you'll want to find out about.

- What are your partner's intellectual interests? What does your partner like to discuss, learn, read, and think about?
- What hobbies and sports does your partner enjoy and why?
- What types of art or recreational pursuits does your partner

like and why? (Asking why helps you and your partner define some of your core values.)

- What are your partner's favorite and least favorite foods and drinks?
- What is your partner's personal style? Do you know his or her favorite color, styles of clothing, and decorating preferences?
- What does your loved one consider an ideal romantic evening?
- What about a romantic weekend getaway?
- What types of vacations does your partner like: resorts, sightseeing overseas, or camping in the wilderness? Find out why.
- Does your loved one like surprises (surprise parties, spontaneous weekend trips) or prefer to look forward to jointly planned events?
- What types of small gifts does your partner most enjoy?
- What is your partner's psychology? Are there sensitive areas that set your partner off? Are there words, actions, or gestures that affect your loved one deeply—positively or negatively?
- What does your partner's job or career mean to him or her personally? In what ways is it important? Knowing why a job or career is important is valuable to both of you, ensuring visibility.
- How does you partner view family and specific family members? How important is the extended family?
- What is your loved one's self-concept? How does your partner see himself or herself? Does this contradict how you see your partner? (If so, this could be a source of conflict.)
- How much private time does your partner need and when? (See Chapter 14 for more information on private time.)

As you learn more about one another, it becomes easier to nourish your relationship. Each day ask yourself: *What can I do today to make my partner feel loved?* Avoid the error of assuming that what makes you feel loved is exactly what makes your partner feel loved.

In *The Five Love Languages,* author Gary Chapman recommends that each couple know one another's most important love languages.[2] One category of love language includes positive encouragement, ("I know you can do it!"), giving recognition ("Great work!"), and showing appreciation ("Thanks for doing the dishes!"). We recommend that you show sincere appreciation to your partner every day. These positive gestures are great visibility enhancers.

A second category is spending meaningful time together, giving full attention to one another. How you spend your time is a volitional choice. Quality time says to your partner: "You're important to me!"

A third is giving gifts. We do not recommend buying expensive gifts, even if affordable, except for special occasions, and especially not for the purpose of making up after an argument or for neglect or poor treatment. (To fix that you need to change your whole pattern of behavior). Small, thoughtful gifts as a symbol of your love are ideal. If you've discussed this (see list above), you'll know what types of gifts your partner values. On a special occasion, buy something that your loved one truly wants but would never buy. But usually just a card, flowers, candy, or love note on the pillow is the perfect gift.

A fourth is voluntarily helping with the cooking, dishes, laundry, child care, shopping, yard work, and repairs. This of course makes your partner feel supported—and less tired! Again, find out what kind of help is most wanted and appreciated.

A fifth is touching your partner. Touching is a very important form of communication; it expresses and promotes intimacy. Where does your partner like to be touched? How does your partner like to be touched, such as holding hands, giving back rubs, giving light kisses on the neck, cheek, lips, or hand? (We cover sex in Part V.)

These five types of actions—showing encouragement and appreciation, spending quality time together, giving gifts, helping out, touching—are not exhaustive and are not mutually exclusive. But they are all ways of making your partner feel loved and visible. Most partners will appreciate all five categories. However, different people may place different degrees of importance on them. Find out what your partner's love languages are—including ones you discover on your own.

If you neglect trying to understand your partner, it conveys that you don't think your loved one is important. Your partner feels invisible and not connected to you on the deepest level, and this undermines your romantic relationship—including your sex life. For example, if you don't understand your partner, even when you do take actions that demonstrate love, they might be the wrong actions.

Consider Linda's story. She was upset for weeks because her husband sent a male stripper to her place of work for her birthday. Beyond feeling humiliated in front of her co-workers, she hated the idea of a male stripper. Her husband, Martin, didn't understand why she was so upset when he was only trying to give her a "nice surprise." The clueless husband hadn't bothered to find out what his wife would actually value as a present.

> *Before giving a surprise, make sure your partner likes surprises, including the type you plan to give.*

Working to understand your partner is well worth the effort. And to help your partner better understand you, you need to first understand yourself. If you don't know what you want and value, it makes it much harder for your partner to understand you.

Encourage Your Partner to Pursue His or Her Values

The principle of self-sacrifice destroys relationships (as we noted in Chapter 2). You do not want your partner to ever give up important values (assuming they are not irrational values, such as taking illicit drugs, being abusive, or having an affair). In an earlier example, Joanie used guilt to stop her husband from golfing. Later Bob retuned the guilt, getting her to give up her theater tickets. Their relationship would have been healthier if Joanie had encouraged Bob to enjoy golf and Bob had supported Joanie's enjoyment of the theater! Neither partner should ask the other to give up valued activities or valued friends (assuming the friends are not unpleasant or dishonest people). This principle applies to all important values held by your partner, but especially the most essential ones such as a career. Encouraging your partner to act to achieve important values, but also helping your loved one to maintain the proper attitude toward those values, is part of living up to this principle.

Consider this example from the life of novelist-philosopher Ayn Rand. There was a period during the writing of her best-selling novel *The Fountainhead* when she felt profoundly discouraged about the state of the culture as it was and found herself unable to write:

> It seemed as if I would never regain the energy to move one step further toward "things as they ought to be." Frank [her husband] talked to me for hours, that night. He convinced me of why one cannot give up the world to those one despises. By the time he finished, my discouragement was gone; it never came back in so intense a form. . . . Frank was the fuel. He gave me, in the hours of my own days, the reality of that sense of life which created *The Fountainhead*, and he helped me to maintain it over a long span of years when there was nothing around us but a gray desert of people and events that evoked nothing but contempt and revulsion.[3]

Charles and Mary Ann Sures, who were close friends of Ayn Rand and her husband, identified the meaning of these events:

> What does this say about their relationship? This is a tribute written by a woman who is deeply in love with her husband, and about a husband who is deeply in love with his wife. You see, Frank understood Ayn. He knew what she valued, he knew what to say to her to restore her view of life and gave her the motivation—the fuel—to move forward. And he didn't give up; he spoke for hours until he convinced her. And equally important, she respected his understanding of her—she knew she could turn to him for encouragement. Is there anything more important in a marriage than understanding each other's values and encouraging each other to pursue them; than helping each other maintain that basic [benevolent, joyful] outlook on life that they hold in common?[4]

We should note that Ayn Rand reciprocated. She encouraged her husband to start a new career as an artist, helped him find a suitable art school, and took a great personal interest in his work and progress. They both took great joy in his painting.

Contrast this with an example from an advice column. A recently remarried man stated that he wanted to take a trip with his twelve-year-old daughter from his first marriage in order to bond with her before she became a teenager enmeshed in school and peer relationships. His wife adamantly opposed this idea, even though she didn't object to his taking an equally long vacation with his fishing buddies. Her objection to his vacationing with his daughter was based on jealousy and insecurity, which she allowed to undermine an important value of her husband's. If she truly loved him, she would not only permit but also encourage him to take the trip because it was important to him. This would have strengthened their relationship.

You do not need to personally value everything that your partner or spouse values in order to encourage action. For example, he might enjoy watching action movies and playing golf and she might enjoy reading mystery novels and hiking. This isn't a problem as long as each shows respect for the other's values. (This assumes that the values are rational.) Of course, if you have no values in common, the question arises: Why are you partners at all? You can't make your partner into something he or she isn't. You can't remake your loved one into your image. You need to find the right person for you—as we noted in Part III.

One last important point: What if your partner or spouse is constantly pursuing important values, with your encouragement, but none of the choices includes you? For example, you're a chronic golf widow or a girls' nights out widower or you're ignored in favor of your partner's career. If this happens, you need to ask your partner: "How important am I to you? Am I a top value or way down on your list?" If it turns out that you're not a top value, then is this the right partner for you? The ultimate proof of how important you are to your partner is how your partner acts toward you on a daily basis—not just what words are expressed. With a loving partner, there will be many loving words as well as consistency between word and deed.

Exercises

1. How well do you know yourself and your partner? Copy the table below so each partner can fill it out privately. Under the categories below, write your values, interests, and preferences and then write what you know of your partner's.

Mine/My partner's:

- Intellectual interests
- Hobbies and sports
- Art and recreational pursuits
- Favorite foods/drinks
- Personal style
- Ideal romantic evening
- Vacation type
- Surprises or jointly planned events
- Small gifts
- Sensitive areas: words, actions, gestures that affect your loved one deeply (positively or negatively)
- Career importance
- Family
- Self-concept

Now compare notes. What did each of you learn about yourself and your partner that you did not know before?

_____

_____

2. Love languages

- Offering positive encouragement, giving recognition, showing appreciation
- Spending quality time together
- Giving thoughtful gifts
- Helping out
- Touching

What are your preferred love languages, in order of preference?

_____

_____

What are your partner's?

_____

_____

Can you think of any love languages not on that list?

_____

_____

Do you have any differences that are a source of conflict?

_____

_____

Notes

1. Sue Shellenbarger, "Readers' Marriage Tips: Hard Hats, Boat Rides, Purring and Prayers," *Wall Street Journal,* December 22, 1999, p. B1.

2. Gary Chapman, *The Five Love Languages: How to Express Heartfelt Commitment to Your Mate* (Chicago: Northfield Publishing, 1995).

3. Original source of quote: Ayn Rand, "Introduction to the Twenty-fifth Anniversary Edition," *The Fountainhead* (New York: Signet, 1971), pp. vi-vii. Reprinted in: Mary Ann Sures and Charles Sures, *Facets of Ayn Rand* (California: Ayn Rand Institute Press, 2001), pp. 113–115.

4. Ibid., *Facets of Ayn Rand,* p. 115.

CHAPTER 13

How to Cherish Your Partner II

How does one actually go about understanding one's partner? Mainly through talking and everyday observation. Partners also communicate by touching and—for the more eloquent ones—by writing romantic letters or poems. Of course, saying that partners should communicate is not an original idea—it's in virtually every book on love ever written. But it is amazing how many couples have problems in this realm.

Many partners don't make communication a conscious priority. Some feel their loved one should just know what they're thinking. Communication can be undermined by fear. And partners may lack communication skills.

Communicate Constantly

First, why is communication not a conscious priority? Most partners feel that because they're settled in a relationship, they no longer need to talk as much about their feelings toward one another. They focus on everyday practical matters, yes, but expressions of tenderness, concern, and interest in one another's lives go untended. They go on automatic and don't talk unless their subconscious mind happens to feed them something.

It is precisely because they are in love that partners need to communicate—in order to maintain and deepen that love.

Second, partners often assume their loved one is, or should be, a mind reader, and then become annoyed when their partner doesn't know what they are thinking or feeling.

Third, conversation can be threatening. Partners sometimes believe that their loved ones won't understand what they are saying or that it will be ignored or rejected. Maybe they are afraid or embarrassed about disclosing what they want or how they feel. Giving in to the fear and keeping silent will undermine their closeness and cause them to feel less visible and more distant from one another. Partners need encouragement before and during communication, and positive feedback afterward.

Fourth, many partners lack communication skills; for example, they may not be very articulate and thus struggle to express what they think or feel. Communication skills can be learned, as we've noted in Chapter 7; see also Part VI.

Listening is an important part of communicating. Many people find it very difficult not to interrupt before their partner has finished expressing a complete thought.

Listening well, giving your partner your full attention, and summarizing what you heard when necessary sends the message: you are important.

Observe how your partner acts in different situations. How one acts is a form of communication, inadvertent or not, and it can reveal valuable clues to your partner's values and deepest feelings. For example, does your partner withdraw in the face of conflict? Is your partner easily angered or depressed by criticism? Does your lover get excited when you dress (or undress) in a certain way? Do your partner's moods change in predictable or unpredictable ways in response to people or events?

Such observations set the stage for ongoing communication. Let's say you notice that your partner becomes highly anxious when company is expected for dinner. Through talking, listening, and asking questions, you discover that your partner fears you might tell inappropriate jokes. By promising not to, you can lessen the fear and make the whole evening more enjoyable.

> *Terms of endearment or special nicknames are important. They are very personal and intimate—only for the two of you. Using such loving terms daily helps keep tenderness alive.*

Using nicknames that have personal meaning and appeal to both of you endears you further to one another, so never use sarcastic or mean ones.

Some tips on speaking: No one wants a partner who chatters incessantly about nothing in particular. This drives one crazy and leads to tuning out. And if the jabbering consists of criticism, the tuning out occurs even faster. Tell your partner about things that happened to you during the day, being aware of what events might be most interesting. Talk about things you have read or heard, memories of your childhood, ideas for future vacations, recent experiences, news items, personal longings, ideas about morality, interesting relatives, your children, new movies or books. The possibilities are endless; be creative.

Revealing things about yourself, your likes and dislikes, attitudes, and values, can be very effective. Tell your partner what you like, such as, "Boy, do I appreciate it when I come home late and smell dinner cooking—thanks!" or "I love the way you look in that suit." If you don't like something your partner does, communicate this in a positive way—for example, "Sweetheart, I enjoy making love with you most when you've just showered and your breath is fresh."

Sharing information and problems, including fears, is another important part of communication: "Honey, I worry sometimes that my business will fail, and I'll leave you and the kids with nothing." This underscores a key issue that comes up in many marriages: finances (discussed also in Chapters 10 and 14). In the past, men typically took charge of finances and didn't want their wives to worry about them, leaving their wives in the financial dark. This traditional view is not necessarily based on bad motives on the man's part; it may stem from his protective attitude toward his wife. However well intentioned, it's a poor idea. Consider the case of Molly, a sixty-two-year-old housewife. She and her husband Bill were living the high life together until one day Bill died of a heart attack. Molly was shocked to discover that they'd been living on borrowed money and that Bill had left her penniless. She had had no clue about their financial situation. She had to go to work, at minimum wage, just to make ends meet. In this case, Bill's motives were not to protect his wife from financial responsibilities but to protect her from his deceit. Protecting a loved one from basic knowledge needed to live, especially finances, is not a benefit. It leaves the "protected" partner feeling psychologically dependent on the knowledgeable one for basic needs and is often used as a means of control, rather than as an expression of love.

> *It is important to tell your partner that you love them and express why. This keeps the relationship from going stale.*

There is no limit to the number of times or ways you can say, "I love you," provided you genuinely feel it and provided you routinely *back it up* with actions consistent with your feelings of love. Don't fall into the trap of the tough-guy actor whose movie wife complains that he never says he loves her, and he replies gruffly, "Well, I married ya', din' I?" And don't fall into the trap of repeatedly saying, "I love you," in a rote, mechanical manner, without ever giving any reasons. Author Susan Jeffers recommends this romantic way of expressing what your partner means to you: "Thank you for being in my life."[1] We can add to this comments such as "I love it when you do that" or "I love it when you say that."

Telling your partner why you love them is especially important as you are falling in love and around the time of the marriage proposal—but don't stop there. Partners want to know what qualities their loved one values in them to know if they are the same qualities they value in themselves. For example, if you tell a woman you fell in love with her because she's cute and that's it, nothing else, she probably isn't going to feel flattered.

> *A woman of substance surely wants to hear something profound about why she is loved—something specific about her character, mind, values, and way of approaching her career and life. This principle applies to both partners.*

Telling your partner why you fell in love should not be a one-time occurrence, and it would become meaningless if you went through the same list every day. Better to point out specific qualities that you've observed from time to time:

- "You look especially handsome (beautiful) tonight. I love that color on you."
- "I admire the total honesty you showed when talking to the Smiths. That's a quality I've always cherished in you."
- "I love the way you encouraged me to pursue my career when I was having real doubts about my ability to do it."

Understanding another person is not always easy. You come to understand your partner in layers; you see the obvious aspects first and gradually come to understand the deeper layers. This takes mental work. For example, you notice that your partner gets upset when you're away on business, but you might not discover until much later that this is tied to fears of abandonment stemming from a traumatic childhood or a former cheating spouse. Your partner might not even be aware of such a fear if not much time has been spent introspecting. If you keep listening, observing, and talking, you will gradually come to know your partner more intimately, and assuming no surprising negatives are uncovered, you will feel much closer as a result.

> *To keep your relationship and the conversation interesting over a period of years, stay mentally active and alert. Together, learn and discover new things, acquire new tastes, study new ideas, and choose new values.*

If you shut your mind off, you'll become a bore, and no one will enjoy talking with you—not even your mother. Vegetables are good to eat, but they aren't any fun to converse with. Recall Part II: If you want to be loved, work to make yourself lovable.

In addition, to maintain that feeling of togetherness over a period of years, you will want a plan to deal with the temptation of having an affair. This requires a commitment to communicate on a difficult topic. Some partners will, from time to time, meet someone attractive or intriguing outside the marriage or partnership. Most partners feel that such attractions should be kept private. Why? First, they fear their partner's response: Will he get angry (or leave me) when I tell him I've been flirting with Jay at work? Will she have a nervous breakdown when she learns that I've gone to the gym early just to talk with Cheri? Second, some love the forbidden feelings and don't want to spoil the pleasure. Such partners rationalize: What my partner doesn't know won't hurt. Why expose the cherished secret and risk losing the exciting and sexy feelings of an extra-marital romance? Third, thoughts of adultery generate chronic guilt that a partner will try to suppress. Unfortunately, the result of suppressing rather than confronting these thoughts and desires often makes them stronger—and may eventually lead to later regretted actions, landing partners in divorce court.

What can you do to help safeguard your relationship against cheating? First, hold on to your moral character. Second, remind yourself of all the reasons why you love your partner and what the relationship means to you. Make these reasons objective by expressing them in words to your partner.

Columnist Sue Shellenbarger gives another suggestion in her article, "Honey, I'm Thinking of Having An Affair."[2] She advises that you talk openly with your partner about being attracted to someone else while your relationship is still on firm ground. Agree, in writing if necessary, that if either of you feels sexually attracted to someone else, you will bring it out in the open right away. Also discuss in advance what situations put you at risk (a business trip with a sexy co-worker, a holiday party with an open bar).[3]

The benefits of such open communication are:

- It promotes honesty and integrity—you are not attempting to live a double life. You are not faking an attraction to your partner while secretly fantasizing about having an affair with Cheri or Jay.

- It enhances trust and communicates how much you value your partner: "Boy, if she could share *that* with me, I can really trust her. She must value me more than Jay."

- It helps you and your partner communicate about the possible reasons for an extra-marital attraction and thus allows you to address a problem. ("I want us to spend more time together." "It bothers me to see you drinking every night." "I miss the way you used to look and dress; you were so sexy.")

- It defuses the secretiveness and forbidden fruit aspect of the contemplated affair, which often decreases its appeal. You are no longer Romeo secretly meeting Juliet at the gym, trying to hide it from your wife. Your wife now knows.

- You are allowing yourself to face all the facts without evasion. You will be motivated to look at the situation with more scrutiny and deal with the wider consequences of the attraction (a possible divorce). You can make choices such as changing what gym you go to or what time you go so you don't continue to tempt yourself.

Notice how important it is to communicate constantly—even on difficult topics.

What if your partner just doesn't talk or want to listen, even after repeated attempts to communicate? What if you feel as though you're talking to a wall—that nothing you say will get a response? Several factors could be at work here. First, your partner could be ignoring you out of anger or resentment, perhaps over frustration about love-making or spending. He or she may be acting in a passive-aggressive manner, to get even about something.[4] Refusing to talk is one way; there are others, such as refusing to do any yard work or help out with the kids. If you suspect this, ask, "Hon, is there something I'm doing that's upsetting you? I feel a distance between us."

It may be the manner and tone in which you ask or tell your partner something. You may be too unassertive or hesitant in expressing yourself, so your partner doesn't think you mean what you say. Make sure to be clear and resolute in expressing yourself, especially about something important to you. Or you may make your wants clear but in such an obnoxious, insensitive manner that the content of what you say is overwhelmed by your overbearing style.

Your partner could have narcissistic tendencies perhaps, such as holding the premise that you are supposed to listen but not vice versa—a one-way-street relationship.[5] Such a partner will never make an ideal soul mate—for anyone.

Partners also fail to communicate because they are trying to hide their true or deepest selves. They may fear something about themselves, or perhaps they have no authentic selves.

Your partner may not talk much simply due to shyness. You can do a lot to bring your partner out of his or her shell by being warm, open, and encouraging.

Another reason that your partner doesn't make communication a conscious priority is that he or she may not consider you important— translation: your partner does not really love you, a painful discovery.

> *As noted earlier, the best proof of whether a person loves you is how that person acts towards you on a daily basis.*

Suppose your partner spends so much time at work you virtually never see him or her. Then it would be appropriate to ask, "Honey, if I'm so unimportant relative to work, why did you want to marry me?"

As to time spent on one's career, there are no rules about how many hours one should or shouldn't work—and this can change from day to day, week to week, month to month, or job to job. Every couple has their own personal needs and unique context regarding the amount of time spent together. For example, if a partner has been called up for active duty in the military, then obviously the context is important and long periods of time without one another may be unavoidable.

> *What is essential is that partners take the time to show their love for one another as often as is feasible.*

Finally, a partner's refusal to listen or respond—especially the silent treatment—may be an attempt to control you by deliberately causing you to feel intimidated, helpless, upset, and even desperate. It's a cruel way for a partner to act and must not be tolerated for long; either both communicate or there is no relationship.

The bottom line in communication is that romantic partners need to let each other know, in word and deed, that they fully value, understand, and accept each other and that they are all each other needs and wants as a lover.

Exercises

1. Name one good aspect of your communication style:

_____

2. Name one to three aspects you would like to improve:

_____

_____

3. What is one step you might take today to improve them?

_____

_____

Notes

1. Susan Jeffers, *Lasting Love* (Santa Monica, CA: Jeffers Press, 2005) p. 166.

2. Sue Shellenbarger, "'Honey, I'm Thinking of Having An Affair': Therapists Advise Confessing Temptation," *Wall Street Journal*, October 26, 2006, p. D1.

3. Ibid.

4. A passive-aggressive person is one who takes out his or her anger in a passive way that is indirectly aggressive (an irritating but camouflaged means of expressing anger); for example, always "forgetting" to make the bed or put the toilet seat down, being chronically late, continually calling you and insisting on talking at times when you've asked not to be interrupted, such as in a business meeting or while attending a class.

5. For the telltale signs of a narcissistic personality, see the symptoms described in Chapter 2.

• CHAPTER 14 •

How to Cherish Your Partner III

*I*n the last two chapters we covered three principles to help you feel cherished by one another. They are:

- •Work to understand your partner.
- •Encourage your partner to pursue his or her values.
- •Communicate constantly.

We now turn to four more categories:

- •Show concern for your partner's welfare.
- •Show generosity.
- •Make decisions together.
- •Respect your partner's need for private time

Show Concern for Your Partner's Welfare

If you're in love, you will take great interest in your partner's personal well-being. Showing mutual concern deepens your feeling of being valued by one another and it's important to preserve each other's dignity while doing so. If one partner is regularly away on business trips, you might install a security system. Partners could take a self-defense class together and always carry cell phones.

> *Showing concern for your partner's physical health, in a way that's not belittling or paternalistic, is important. This takes tact and—in some cases—subtlety.*

You and your partner should get regular check-ups, including age- and sex-appropriate tests. If a partner is resistant, a gentle reminder may do the trick. In other cases, a more direct approach may be needed ("Honey, it would mean a lot to me if you got your annual check-up").

A healthy diet and lifestyle are important, such as eating well, getting sufficient exercise and rest, and taking daily vitamin supplements. Setting an example for your partner and giving your reasons for your own choices tactfully communicates your concern.

> *You fall in love with the whole person—body and soul (mind) together. So it is legitimate to care how your partner looks and how you look to your partner.*

If you have an overweight partner, carefully encourage a change to a healthy diet and exercise without bullying, belittling, or threatening. Show gentle and supportive appreciation when your partner takes any step in the direction of better health.

Know that overeating can have psychological implications. It's often used to relieve feelings of anxiety and stress, and sometimes to avoid intimacy. Resolving such problems may require the help of professionals.

If psychological problems are hurting the relationship, encourage counseling. Encourage your loved one to take any medication in accordance with the doctor's orders and to report any side effects. Beware the fine line between being concerned with your partner's welfare and being a pest. Make it clear that you care deeply about your partner and hate to see your loved one in ill health because it affects you personally.

Show Generosity

> *Generosity is a sign of love, benevolence, and good will.*
> *Generosity is shown in many forms, for example*
> *money, time, and action.*

Being a cheapskate is unromantic, because it implies that saving every last cent is more important than your partner's enjoyment. Then again, showing off your wealth is unromantic, because it reveals insecurity. Being generous simply means doing a bit more than is necessary or expected.

If your partner admires an affordable art book or a nice piece of jewelry but doesn't buy it, consider it for a birthday, anniversary, or holiday gift.

> *Giving small, thoughtful gifts at unexpected*
> *times is another way to show your love.*

Don't give thoughtless, impersonal gifts—they're almost worse than no gift at all.

Remembering your partner's birthday, your anniversary and special holidays sends a strong "you're important" message. Forgetting them can be very hurtful.

You can also be generous with your time. Cook a special meal for your partner, make your partner a romantic card, write a tender e-mail that expresses your love accurately, or take the kids for the day and let your partner have the day off. You might also offer to run errands or do chores if your partner is busy with a work project, give a massage, or even take a day off from work for a romantic activity.

Generosity sometimes involves sharing one's belongings. There may be particular objects you don't want to share (such as your toothbrush or comb), but there are many things you can share with pleasure, such as favorite books, clothes (sweaters, tee-shirts, caps), cars, food, laptop computers, and cameras. Of course, partners shouldn't take unfair advantage of one another by monopolizing something the other person needs, such as a computer.

Make Decisions Together

> *A romantic relationship is ideally*
> *a partnership of equals.*

Decisions that affect both partners should be made jointly, which is another way of enhancing mutual visibility. Joint decisions include: financial planning, buying property or other expensive items, vacation planning, choosing furniture and décor, dining out, moving to another location, and child-rearing practices.

Consider a negative case. Katie complains that her boyfriend Chuck is full of surprises that are intended to please her, such as vacation getaways. It's a disaster because he never bothers to ask her what she actually wants. Imagine telling your partner on Wednesday that you've arranged for a vacation to Alaska next week, when, in fact, your partner has no desire to go to Alaska and has a busy work schedule. The same applies to many smaller, everyday decisions. Joint decision-making is a sign of love and respect. Of course, you can agree to delegate certain decisions to each other according to your respective skills and interests.

Respect Your Partner's Need for Private Time

People are individuals first and partners second.

> *No matter how wonderful living with a romantic partner*
> *is, it necessarily will take some attention away from*
> *yourself. Sometimes people need time to do things alone.*

Partners need some freedom to do things in their own way, such as how they cook meals, what time they go to bed, how (and if) they make the bed, when and what they eat, what time they get up and shower, what TV shows they watch (if any), when they go out and for what purpose (shopping, etc.). They need to be free of concerns about always checking what their partner would want. Having some time alone reinforces your sense of being an individual.

Feeling a sense of relief when your partner goes on a trip does not necessarily mean you don't love that person. Maybe you need some private time, just as your partner does occasionally. (If you always want your partner to leave town, that is a different matter!) In a thriving relationship, you will always be glad to see your partner come home. You will be happy you had time to yourself and will feel reinvigorated romantically. Obviously, we don't condone sneakiness, irrationality, or any type of dishonesty during those times you're on your own.

You are now better equipped to answer the question: How do my partner and I show that we value one another? We've reviewed seven key ways to help you feel truly cherished by each other. Next we'll explore how to prevent your passion from fading and how to strengthen your emotional intimacy by creating a positive emotional climate in your relationship.

Exercises

1. One way my partner has shown concern for me:
(Example: My husband bought me an emergency kit for my car.)

_____

_____

One way I've shown concern for my partner:

_____

_____

2. I was generous toward my partner when:
(Example: I bought my wife a spa visit that she had wanted.)

_____

_____

My partner was generous toward me when:

_____

_____

3. We make decisions together in the following areas (circle any that apply):
Financial planning
Buying expensive items (a car, a home)

Vacation planning
Choosing home furniture and décor
Dining out
Where to live
Child rearing
I wish we made joint decisions in the following area(s):

_____

_____

(Consider tactfully letting your partner know about these over the next week.)

    4. Do you feel the need for private time? If so, how much? How much private time would you be willing to give your partner?

_____

_____

---• CHAPTER 15 •---
Creating a Positive Emotional Climate

reating a comfortable emotional climate in your relationship should never be left to chance. But how do you create it? Here are five steps to achieving this goal:
- Build a positive mood.
- Take joy in each other's achievements.
- Grow together.
- Show playfulness and humor.
- Help protect one another against stress.

Build a Positive Mood

Moods are enduring emotional states. A positive mood is essential for a romantic relationship to survive. Research by John Gottman has shown that successful romantic relationships are dominated by positive communications.[1] Creating a positive mood by having a feeling of goodwill toward your partner permeates your time together. If resentments and issues lurk behind everything, establishing a caring climate will be impossible. You will need to introspect and seek professional help, if necessary, to resolve your issues. Hidden issues (psychological disorders aside) typically center around one of two things (or both): My partner doesn't understand me, or my partner doesn't value me. Establishing a positive relationship environment presupposes everything we have discussed in the previous chapters.

Maintain the positive climate daily—not just in terms of important issues but also in many small ways. As a song from the 1950s says: "Little things mean a lot."

Small gestures like a hug and wishing your partner a good day at work and later asking how the day went may seem simple, but they make both of you feel valued by the other.

Many couples take each other for granted, fail to value each other in day-to-day living, and end up extinguishing the spark in their relationship.

To create and maintain a positive mood you must take control over your own moods. Since emotions are caused by thoughts, you can help control your moods by focusing on the good parts of your life and the positive aspects of your partner or spouse. How do you do this? Train your mind to focus on genuinely positive daily events, understand their source, and underscore their importance. Contrast this with making exhaustive lists of the upsetting things that happen to you each day (as many chronic worriers do). The former mindset will create a positive climate in the relationship, but the latter will not.

We don't mean to ignore negatives. On the contrary, take every action possible to resolve problems that undermine your happiness. If your partner avoids you because you're in a bad mood every night after work, think about how you can improve your mood, either alone or together.

If your partner occasionally comes home in a bad mood for some reason, learn to read the mood and help raise your partner's spirits. Your partner might want some sympathetic listening and support, or perhaps just some alone time to decompress. As you both learn to understand one another better, you will be become more effective at helping improve each other's mood.

Though you can help, you're not ultimately responsible for improving your partner's moods. Each person is primarily responsible for his or her own mood.

By controlling your own mood and not letting your partner's bad mood become contagious, you can better manage a temporary bout of the blues.

If you or your partner suffers from anxiety or depression, seek professional help. Therapy, medication, or a combination of both may be beneficial.[2]

Take Joy in Each Other's Achievements

Competition is an essential element of sports and capitalism, but it has no place in a romantic relationship. You must never feel that you have to beat your partner at anything except in pure fun, such as a good-natured game of Scrabble. Sometimes partners unwisely compete over who makes the most money or progresses faster in their career. Take joy in your partner's achievements and have enough self-esteem not to feel inferior, resentful, or jealous when your partner achieves something significant.

Your own worth and character can never be enhanced or diminished by your partner's achievements (or failures). Your self-esteem comes from your own choices and actions.

Grow Together

To sustain a positive emotional climate, both partners need to have an attitude that encourages personal growth. When couples don't grow together, they often grow apart—and end up unhappily married or divorced. Couples are in danger if there are significant differences in the way they grow their lives—for example, one may grow in intellectual ability, character, or self-esteem, and the other may not. If one is ambitious, expanding his or her life and making it interesting, while the other stagnates or grows at a much slower rate, the discrepancy often leads to the breaking of the loving bond, leaving the couple mismatched even if they initially were well matched. Partners need to grow together, intellectually and emotionally, for a relationship to thrive.

Of course, partners can grow in different directions in terms of values and interests. This is not necessarily fatal to the relationship—it depends on whether they have enough left in common. But when both partners grow together in the same direction they are more likely to be fulfilled and happy with one another.

Show Playfulness and Humor

It is important to take your life, character, and values (career, romance, ideas, friends, hobbies, leisure activities) seriously. If you do not, they slip away and life becomes increasingly empty and meaningless, because nothing is truly important. This is why a sense of humor is *not* a primary virtue.

That said, a healthy playfulness and humor are delightful add-ons to a relationship. They help reinforce the premise that life is fun and joyous. Learn what your partner considers funny. There can be a substantial difference of opinion in this realm. Make clear what you dislike so you won't be exposed to it.

> *Humorous repartee and good-natured teasing can be a lot of fun when partners are in sync.*

Never use humor in anger or as a disguised form of aggression, such as sarcasm, or to score points with an audience. Imagine telling an embarrassing story about your partner at a dinner party. Sometimes your partner might enjoy the story being told and sometimes not, depending on the content of the story, the audience, and your partner's psychology. Out of respect, always ask permission before you tell a funny story about your partner. Agree beforehand on what you can share in public.

Help Protect One Another Against Stress

Stress is an integral part of most people's lives today. Perhaps the most common cause is time pressure, although money is often an important factor as well. For many couples there's too much to do and too little time—or too many bills and too little cash. Partners can help each other in times of stress.

•Be a good listener, not an unwelcome advice-giver—which only adds to the stress.

•Provide serenity and a restful environment for each other.

•Make your home a sane universe, where everyone is treated with understanding, benevolence, and goodwill.

•Give your partner moral support and encouragement.

•Help your partner find solutions to practical problems—*if* help is requested.

Consider Sandra who felt overwhelmed by stress. Although her job was intellectually challenging, her boss was bad-tempered and critical. He never praised good work and constantly blamed subordinates for bad results, most of which were due to his own poor leadership. The hours were long and unrelenting, often including weekends. Sandra went home every day in a tense and resentful mood. After this went on for some months, she asked for help. Her partner Scott suggested she seriously consider quitting her job, taking a rest for a while, and then searching for something better. He showed her how their budget could be adjusted to compensate for her lost salary. Sandra took his advice and her stress diminished dramatically. She subsequently found a better job—with much less stress.

Another important point: Do not be the cause of your partner's stress. This not only undermines the relationship, it undermines the health of both partners. Continual conflict is unhealthy and makes both partners unhappy. Use the techniques in Part VI to help reduce conflict.

You no longer need to leave the climate of your relationship outside your control. You and your partner can actively work to create a comfortable, positive ambiance as the norm in your relationship. You now have five ways to do this.

In our next chapter, we explore actions you can take to prevent your passion from fading.

Exercises

1. Observe yourself with your partner today (or this week) and notice what you do to help create a positive emotional climate in your relationship. Jot down what you notice.

_____

_____

2. In what ways do you support your partner's achievements? Write down two of your partner's achievements and note how you responded to them. Examples: My wife got promoted at work. We went out to her favorite restaurant to celebrate. (Or: I felt jealous and I ignored her accomplishment.)

_____

_____

3. Do you feel you and your partner are:
   •Growing together?
   •Growing at different rates?
   •Growing apart?
If you are growing together, note two ways in which you are doing so:

_____

_____

If you are growing apart, or at different rates, jot down two ideas that can help you grow together. (Example: My wife and I are spending more time with our friends than with each other. Perhaps we can reverse that trend by taking dance lessons together.)

_____

_____

4. List some ways you show playfulness and good-natured humor in your relationship:

_____

_____

5. In what ways do you offer support when your partner is stressed?

_____

_____

If you are not supportive, what would you consider doing differently?

_____

_____

Notes

1. John Gottman, *Why Marriages Succeed or Fail: And How* You *Can Make Yours Last* (New York: Fireside, 1994).

2. We highly recommend the book by Dennis Greenberger and Christine A. Padesky, *Mind Over Mood: A Cognitive Therapy Treatment Manual for Clients* (New York: The Guilford Press: 1995). We also recommend the following books: Edmond Bourne, *The Anxiety and Phobia Workbook* (California: New Harbinger Publications, 1995); David D. Burns, *The Feeling Good Handbook* (New York: William Morrow & Co: 1989); James O. Prochaska, John C. Norcross, and Carlo DiClemente, *Changing for Good* (New York: Avon Books: 1994).

CHAPTER 16

Love Destroyers and How to Fix Them

*W*hat destroys love—and how can you prevent it? Several problems can undermine love. Many people are aware of them, yet don't know how important they are to fix—or how to fix them. In this chapter we explain how to do the following:

- Correct bad manners and bad habits.
- Replace anger with positives.
- Replace repression with the ability to feel and express emotions.
- Replace white lies with the truth.
- Don't let relatives or children undermine your relationship.
- Don't let money issues undermine love.

Correct Bad Manners and Bad Habits

Bad manners and habits are a turn-off. Correcting them should not be a sacrifice because a rational person wouldn't value them. When repeated often enough, the message is: "I don't value you." Correcting them will make you a more lovable partner—and a better person.

Such corrections are signs of respect and of genuinely valuing one another. If some bad habit bothers you, such as clothes left scattered all over the floor or chewing with the mouth open, be sure to speak up in a benevolent way.

Breaking bad habits is often difficult because they are actions you take automatically, without conscious planning or reflection. To break them, become more aware of them and learn to catch yourself before acting.

Replace Anger with Positives

A successful romantic relationship requires a warm, loving atmosphere. Anger is a big romance destroyer.

You cannot simultaneously be warm and angry toward a person. Occasional anger is not uncommon, but it cannot be the prevailing mood of a happy relationship. Anger comes in many forms (belittlement, sarcasm, insults, criticism). One of the most common forms is resentment—for real or imagined slights or injustices. Partners who hold grudges for days, weeks, months, or even years without expressing them keep their loved ones in a state of bewilderment. Eventually, the victim of anger withdraws emotionally from the relationship, which leads to more resentment and a downward love trajectory.

A difficult problem for those who hold justified resentments is what and how to forgive. By forgive we do not mean that you should forget the unjust act. You may never erase what happened from your memory, but you may be able to put the injustice into the fuller context of your total relationship history and what your partner did subsequent to hurting you—that is, how well your partner repaired the damage.

Forgiveness also means moving forward; do not hold a past injustice against your partner as a chronic, grating irritant (provided you've sufficiently resolved the problem). But be aware that many hurtful partners use this moving on argument to avoid taking responsibility for their actions. For example, "Can't you just put my affairs in the past and move on?"[1] It is impossible to move on until your partner has openly and sufficiently addressed the damage done to your satisfaction (assuming you have reasonable standards); only then are you emotionally ready to move on. You do not have a duty to forgive and you're not a "good" person if you betray your true feelings and fake forgiveness. Contrast this to conventional moral advice, which is based in the doctrine of altruism.

The doctrine of altruism would say that you should forgive almost anything—regardless of the harm done to you and regardless of any remedial steps taken on the part of the hurtful partner. Any doctrine that preaches such self-immolation is not a moral doctrine.

A romantic relationship is a mutually beneficial trade, not charity or self-denial. In deciding whether to forgive, consider the following:

- How serious or characteristic was the offense? Adultery or driving while drunk are extremely serious transgressions, as opposed to forgetting to pick up milk on the way home from work. Sometimes the problem is not one big event but a series of disappointments that form a pattern over years, such as forgetting your birthday and anniversary every year, neglecting you, or constantly criticizing you.
- Is the problem reversible? Adultery and serious injury due to drunk driving aren't reversible. Forgetting the milk is: You can get back in your car and go get it. Patterns of neglect may or may not be easily changeable.
- Was a proper, sincere apology given, assuming that an apology is sufficient? (For example, "Honey, I'm so sorry I made fun of you in front of our guests. I was trying to score points for myself. I promise I'll never do it again.") Any meaningful apology has to be backed up by subsequent behavior that is consistent with it.
- Is there evidence (especially for more serious offenses or long-term patterns) that the person has really changed? The more serious the offense or the more long-term the problem, the longer it takes to know if the partner has genuinely reformed. Don't forgive too soon. Many people are repeat offenders.

No one else can make the decision to forgive for you. Nor are there any formulas, only guiding principles, such as those just listed, and often a great deal of thought. Take the case of adultery. For many individuals, such an act is unforgivable and the hurt partner immediately terminates the relationship. To others it might signal that something is very wrong with the relationship and the response would be to uncover the causes and decide whether the partnership can or should be repaired. Various considerations would come into play here.

How good is your current relationship? Are you both still committed to it? Is the adultery a long-term pattern or a one-time event? Is your partner willing to do what's necessary to rebuild trust over time? Are the factors that caused your partner to commit adultery changeable? How deeply hurt are you emotionally? Finally, if you conclude that you cannot forgive, realize that you will not be able to have a warm and loving relationship; such a realization is often a prelude to separation or divorce.

Not all anger is justified. A partner might characteristically blame others for everything that goes wrong. Never accept unearned guilt for someone else's unjustified anger. Suppose that your partner berates you for, among other things, bringing home the wrong groceries, even though your partner never made clear what was needed. The problem belongs to your partner, not to you. Be aware that major habit and personality changes in adults are rare, especially without dedicated effort.

Nor should the intensity of anger be out of proportion to the current cause. Your partner should not go ballistic if you forget to bring home the milk (assuming this isn't a long-standing, passive-aggressive pattern on your part). Often when a partner overreacts, it is due to a series of actions causing resentments in the past that were never openly resolved. Such resentments are held and stored subconsciously—ready to explode like an over-inflated balloon with only a small provocation. Outbursts against a partner can also be the result of displacing anger caused by outside events (such as a failure at work) onto a partner—which is obviously unjust.

Anger issues must be fully resolved and then replaced by positives such as love, communication, admiration, gratitude, and caring if romance is to thrive.

Some ways to express anger safely and rationally are to use active listening and assertive language (see Chapters 7 and 13 and Part VI). When your partner treats you unfairly and you feel the anger boiling within and you are aware you're about to counter-attack, it's best to:

1. Summarize what you heard your partner say and check to see if what you heard was accurate. Avoid adding comments of your own at this point. The goal is to let both of you digest what was said and clear up misunderstandings. For example, suppose Aaron complains to his wife Jayne in general terms that they have been spending too much money. Jayne might ask: "Are you upset with me for buying those new clothes? Is that what's bothering you?" Aaron could then clarify what he meant. He might say, "Yes, that bothers me a lot," or he may say, "Oh no! I love your new outfits. I'm upset that I spent so much on landscaping." Many arguments are based on what we think our partner meant, and often it's not accurate. Active listening helps clear up such misunderstandings.

2. Take some time to privately sort out your feelings and thoughts. Let's say Aaron is extremely upset with Jayne's purchases— too angry to effectively talk with her at that moment. He could buy himself some cool-down time by saying, "Jayne, I'm too angry right now to talk about this sensibly. I'm taking some time to sort out my thoughts and feelings. Let's touch base later today and talk about it." By handling his anger this way, Aaron avoids giving Jayne the silent treatment or playing mind games (walking away in a huff without letting her know why he's leaving and without giving any indication of when he'll return). Instead Aaron openly lets Jayne know that he's too upset to talk at this time and that he's committed to figuring out why he feels so angry and what action would help resolve the issue.

3. Alternatively, Aaron might express himself immediately *without attacking Jayne's character*. Instead of Aaron contemptuously fuming to her, "You're reckless with money! You make me furious!" which attacks Jayne's character and invites a counter-attack from her ("You're even more reckless!"), Aaron can say, "I'm very upset. We both agreed on a fair budget and we need that money for the rent

this month." It's a skill to express your anger openly and assertively. Your body language and tone of voice need to be consistent with your assertive language. With practice, you can communicate your anger accurately without subtly attacking your partner's character. An assertive response typically invites remorse from your partner. Jayne might say, "Aaron, you're right. We worked hard to come up with a fair budget. I saw those outfits and loved them. I know that our jobs are not as secure as they used to be and I forgot about the rent. I'd like to keep one of the outfits as my birthday gift, if that's okay with you. I will return the rest. I want us both to feel comfortable financially. I'm sorry to have upset you so."

4. Another effective way to argue is to do so on paper. If you are prone to angry outbursts, try writing a note to your partner, being careful to limit your frustration to the current issue. Keep the note short—a paragraph or two. Here's what Aaron might write: "I'm angry that you spent money on clothes when we need that money to pay for the rent. We agreed to keep to our budget." He could leave the note on the kitchen table. Jayne may then respond on paper: "I feel so bad that I ignored our budget. I bought the outfits on a whim. I will return them tomorrow." Sometimes writing down your thoughts allows you the time to express yourselves assertively and helps break a pattern of face-to-face, heated, destructive arguments.

> *Unjust anger can be resolved only by addressing and eliminating the causes and by then focusing on the positive qualities (if there are enough) that you cherish in your partner.*

Replace Repression with the Ability to Feel and Express Emotions

Another big romance destroyer is emotional repression. Repression is a psychological defense mechanism that prevents painful emotions from entering into conscious awareness, through a standing order to your subconscious: *Don't feel.* Obviously, this mechanism works in the narrow sense that it is possible to not let yourself feel emotions. The result, however, is a deadening of your psychological vibrancy.

> *The mechanism of repression is a Trojan horse. It seems to benefit you, but in the end it works against you.*

Why? Because the standing order "Don't feel" cannot discriminate between positive and negative emotions; it can only block emotional responsiveness as such. Thus, a repressed person becomes an emotional cripple who cannot fully experience feelings and therefore does not show much emotion at all.

A repressed lover's lack of passion will undermine the entire emotional tone of the relationship. Who wants to make love to a robot? Repression can be difficult to cure and usually requires the help of a trained professional. The roots of repression often lie in an unhappy childhood full of pain, during which the child (usually subconsciously) decides to block off the psychological pain by refusing to feel anything. This helps the child get through the painful times, but not without cost.[2]

Some people are passionless for other reasons. They may be shallow individuals with no independent, deeply held values at all. Such people are not promising as romantic partners, as discussed in Chapters 7 and 9.

Replace White Lies with the Truth

White lies are usually told in order to protect the listener from bad news or pain. If you tell white lies to your partner, it implies that your partner is incapable of facing reality and has to be protected from it, a degrading view of your partner. It's a serious problem if your partner does not want to face facts.

This does not mean you should be tactless in saying things that are gratuitously hurtful, such as "That was a stupid question." In such situations, it's not lying to say nothing. Unless your silence can be taken to incorrectly imply agreement with something important, saying nothing is often appropriate. For example, if your spouse asks, "Am I too fat?" you can first actively listen by reflecting their thoughts: "You're concerned about your weight?" This invites your partner to elaborate. Giving your partner an opportunity to think aloud may help motivate him or her to lose weight. But if your partner actually wants your input, tell the truth tactfully: "I think you'd feel and look better, and be healthier, if you lost some weight. Let me know if you'd like my help. I can stop bringing home all that junk food."

White lies breed distrust. If your partner lies to you, you will naturally wonder, *If my partner lied about this, what other things has he (or she) lied about?*

White lies are sometimes used in planning a surprise event. But many people do not like surprise events and feel hurt or duped by the white lies that are used to camouflage the surprise. Consider Sally's case. For a month, she saw her partner and her best friends furtively whispering to one another when they were around her. They seemed to shun her. When she asked what was up, they conjured various white lies. Sally felt isolated and she worried about her marriage. When she found out that they had been planning a surprise party, she was not relieved. The party didn't make up for that painful period; she had not enjoyed being tricked. She would have preferred having had some choice in who was invited and the pleasure of looking forward to and helping plan the event.[3]

Surprises do not have to involve white lies. For example, you can invite your best friends to meet you for dinner on a special occasion without telling your partner. Or you can surprise your partner with a small, thoughtful gift. Or you can have a hot bath ready when your partner comes home from a hard day. But here is a critical caveat: Be sure you know your partner's attitude toward surprises before you consider one and—more specifically—what kinds of surprises your partner likes and does not like. A surprise dinner with friends might not be appreciated whereas a surprise gift might delight your partner.

Don't Let Relatives or Children Undermine Your Relationship

Your loved one is your highest social value. That means your partner comes before anyone else—including your parents! Often relationships are undermined by the desire not to hurt the feelings of relatives who have unreasonable expectations or make unreasonable demands.

Putting your parents or relatives first devalues your partner, and also damages your self-esteem and independence.

> *Growing up means gaining independence from your parents and setting the terms for your own life.*

Your parents have no right to expect you to share all their values or spend all your free time with them. If their feelings are hurt by your desire for independence, the fault lies with their unreasonable expectations, not with you. Make it clear, tactfully and firmly, that your partner comes first.

This point applies even more strongly if one or more of the parents or in-laws are critical or abusive. Some experts recommend ignoring such abuse or discouraging your partner from standing up to an intrusive or disrespectful parent. We strongly disagree.

Parents and in-laws must not become a source of marital resentment. If one partner's parent constantly belittles the other partner or intrudes into the relationship (physically or emotionally), it's important to address the situation by speaking up, partner to partner and then partner to parent. Respectful boundaries must be set between partners and their parents.

> *Suppose, as the husband in this situation, your mother is critical or mean to your wife— if so, it is your job to protect her.*

Barry's wife Kaily tells him that when his mother drops in unannounced, interferes with the way she does things, and even criticizes her, she feels very uncomfortable. It's Barry's responsibility to talk to his mother and explain that he and Kaily understand she is trying to be helpful, but that they do things differently and would like her to stop, as they often feel criticized by her actions. Barry can then ask his mother to agree to planning visits together in advance.

> *If you allow constant parental abuse or intrusiveness, you are sanctioning it by your silence—which means you are choosing your parent(s) as a higher value than your partner. For romance to thrive, you need to protect your privacy and establish proper boundaries with your parents.*

Remember, you chose your partner; you did not choose your parents. You should not cater to an unreasonable or blatantly irrational parent. Your partner comes first and deserves your loving support.

Now consider children. Of course, children are beloved, irreplaceable values. Assuming you had children for the proper reason—you wanted the joy of raising them—then it is not a sacrifice to give up lower priority values, such as being in a time-consuming tennis tournament. (You've made a tragic and emotionally costly error if you had children out of duty or to please others.) Spending time with your children is typically a great source of pleasure. Nevertheless, partners need private time together on a regular basis. A romantic relationship should not be sacrificed on the altar of children. A note to a love columnist reported that five husbands among a circle of friends got divorced, all for the same reason. With each succeeding child, the husbands became increasingly less important to their wives until they felt totally abandoned. The husbands eventually turned to other women who treated them as important. The wives, ironically, had no idea why their marriages ended. One problem was obviously the breakdown in communication. But the core problem was that the husbands were no longer their wives' highest values.

Child-rearing, for most parents, is exhausting. The main caregiver may desperately need rest or alone time. The other partner can be a big help here, not only by voluntarily taking on some of the load, but also by finding ways to bring additional caregivers like sitters or grandparents into the picture.

Don't Let Money Issues Undermine Love

Money is a common source of conflict in many romantic relationships (as we noted in Chapter 10). Many households are burdened by considerable debt, often caused by the loss of a job or undisciplined spending. Sometimes money problems are due to overspending or spending behind a partner's back, both of which constitute a lack of character. (Spending more than you can afford is irrational.) Money conflicts can be a serious problem even in partnerships that are otherwise promising.

> *It is not the case that all the money has to be jointly managed, but a couple should always discuss important money matters together.*

Both partners should know how much money they have, where it is, how it's invested, what future income to expect and the details of their expenses and debts. It might be necessary to have an agreed-upon household budget. If problems arise, they should be discussed together before any decisions are made. A partner should share information about financial problems in his or her business, and both should fully understand all financial aspects of wills and other legal documents, such as leases or property titles. (If you do not have a will, be sure to write one.)

Often money problems are caused by unresolved psychological problems. A partner may have had a deprived childhood and desperately wants to make up for it by overspending or overworking. Such individuals may work a hundred hours a week in order to become rich, without enjoying the work or having time for their loved ones. Others may use money to show off as a way of gaining a false sense of self-esteem.

Ironically, the joke is on the big spenders. Self-esteem comes from how one uses one's mind—not from any given amount of wealth and not from showing off (see Chapter 6). Earning a good living by productively doing something one loves builds genuine self-esteem.

Many types of money issues need to be addressed in every romantic relationship. For example, how much money do we want to make and how should we spend it? There are trade-offs in making money, such as:

- What kind of work week do you want? What is the importance of money versus the importance of time?
- How important is money compared to one's enjoyment of the job? (The ideal is to get paid well for doing something you love.)
- Where and how often are you willing to move in pursuit of your career?
- How will you balance work with your partner and your children?

A good antidote to reckless spending is to ask the following questions before buying anything, especially the big-ticket items:

- What is the real reason I (or we) want this? Is it to show off or because it's a real value to me (and my family)?
- Would I even want this if no one other than my partner knew I had it?
- Did I choose it using my own judgment or just because others said it was desirable?
- Is this the best possible use for this money? Is there something that would be more valuable to us in the long run, like putting it in investments or savings?

Money conflicts can still occur even if time and self-esteem problems are absent. Partners can legitimately differ in their priorities. Communication and joint decision-making are essential here. Listen carefully to your partner's priorities and determine the reasons for them. What does the desired object mean to your partner?

Money problems also occur due to setbacks such as job loss, illness, unwise investments, or bad economic times. They can be painful and difficult to overcome, but the key is to agree on a recovery plan.

If conflicts still remain after your discussions, compromise may be appropriate. Be creative and work out a fair solution that will make you both happy. (See Part VI.) Both partners must be totally honorable in holding to agreements.

In financial matters, partners should encourage one another to balance the short-term and the long-term. Only a small percentage of people engage in long-term financial planning; yet everyone needs to do this and you should start at least thirty years before retirement. Today, more than ever, couples need to take charge of their own retirement planning.

> *When your loved one is your highest, most selfish, most important social value, you will want to treat him or her accordingly—and your loved one will want to treat you similarly.*

This means regularly asking yourself: *What can I do to make this relationship thrive?* The actions you take will sustain and enhance your emotions, your love, and your passion. Your love will grow and flourish. The ideas we've discussed do not exhaust the topic of how not to undermine love, but we have covered the key issues.

Exercises

1. What one bad habit or manner do I have that irks my partner?

_____

_____

What one bad habit (or bad manner) could my partner change that would really make me happy?

_____

_____

What would motivate me to change my bad habit/mannerism?

_____

_____

2. When do I typically experience anger and resentment toward my partner? (Example: When he comes home and expects to sit and relax for two hours rather than helping me around the house. When she talks about our private life to her friends and family.)

_____

_____

How do you respond? Circle any that apply:

     I emotionally withdraw.

     I use sarcasm.

     I insult my partner.

     I nag.

     I criticize.

     I yell or scream.

What is bothering me, at root, when I feel angry? (Example: I feel I don't matter to him anymore.)

_____

_____

Would I be willing to talk to my partner about the main cause of my anger and resentment?

_____

_____

3. Do I allow myself to experience and express my feelings or do I typically try to stop myself from experiencing strong feelings?

_____

_____

If I typically repress my feelings, would I be willing to get some help to learn how to feel more open in expressing my feelings?

_____

_____

4. When have I recently told a white lie to my partner?

(Example: My wife made a batch of cookies and asked if I like them. I said yes even though I didn't. Two weeks later she surprised me with another batch of the same cookies.)

_____

_____

How did I feel about this lie?

_____

_____

What prevented me from telling the truth?

_____

_____

How could I have handled that situation truthfully, tactfully—without lying? (Example: Rather than telling my partner that I purchased an expensive suit on sale—which I didn't—I could have told her that the purchase was important to me and that I would like it as my birthday gift—or I could have shopped at a store that offers good clothes at a discount.)

_____

_____

5. Which relatives or outsiders have I given the power to undermine our relationship? (Example: I let my parents visit whenever they want to. It robs us of our private time together.)

_____

_____

Do I tend to put the children's needs ahead of nourishing our relationship as a couple? (Example: I always put our kids needs ahead of us. We have never had a babysitter in five years of marriage.)

_____

_____

What one change would I be willing to try to prevent my relatives and our children from undermining our relationship?

_____

_____

6. Money issues: These are especially relevant if you're planning to marry or just married. What is my (and my partner's) saving/ spending history?

_____

_____

What are my financial aspirations? Are they similar to or different from my partner's?

_____

_____

Do we pool all our income, or do we keep some, or all, separate?

_____

_____

How does debt play a role in our relationship?

_____

_____

Do we have a plan on how to divide financial responsibilities? (For example, who earns what, who pays the bills, who monitors stocks and other financial assets, who looks for investment opportunities, if applicable?)

_____

Do we have a savings/retirement plan?

_____

Do we have a will?

_____

Notes

1. Janis Abrahms Spring with Michael Spring, *After the Affair: Healing the Pain and Rebuilding Trust When a Partner Has Been Unfaithful* (New York: HarperCollins, 1997).

2. An excellent discussion on repression can be found in Ayn Rand, "Art and Moral Treason," *The Romantic Manifesto* (New York: Signet, 1971):. The following is from that chapter (pp. 149–150):

> While the child is thus driven to fear, mistrust and repress his own emotions, he cannot avoid observing the hysterical violence of the adults' emotions unleashed against him in this and other issues. He concludes, subconsciously, that all emotions as such are dangerous, that they are the irrational, unpredictably destructive element in people, which can descend upon him at any moment in some terrifying way for some incomprehensible purpose. This is the brick before last in the wall of repression which he erects to bury his own emotions. The last is his desperate pride misdirected into a decision such as: "I'll never

let them hurt me again!" The way never to be hurt, he decides, is never to feel anything.

But an emotional repression cannot be complete; when all other emotions are stifled, a single one takes over: fear. (There are men who, when they grow up, are thrown into panic by a display of any strong emotion in others, negative or positive.)

3. For an elaboration on the insidious harm done by so-called well-meaning white lies, see Mary Ann Sures and Charles Sures, *Facets of Ayn Rand* (California: Ayn Rand Institute Press, 2001), pp. 84–86.

Part V: Enjoying Sex

*And that night we knew that to hold
the body of ... [a lover] in our arms is
neither ugly nor shameful, but the one
ecstasy granted to the race of men.*
—Ayn Rand, *Anthem*

• CHAPTER 17 •

Understanding What Sex Is and Why It's Good

Sex, in the most cherished sense, is your physical expression of deep attraction to what you admire and love in the character of your soul mate. Unfortunately, for most couples, this vibrant sensual attraction fades with time. How can you avoid this fate and instead nurture your sensual attraction to your partner?

You'll want to avoid two common pitfalls. Then you'll want to grasp the deepest meaning of romantic intimacy—and never lose your desire for it. Romantic sex is a profound union of your body and your mind.

First, the pitfalls: Two common misconceptions are guaranteed to undermine your sexual pleasure. They do so by minimizing (or denying) the fact that you're a whole person: mind and body.[1] The first misconception views ideal romantic love as separated from the physical: true love is "unsullied" by sex. The second misconception views sex as simply a physically pleasing bodily function, or sensation, while rejecting the role of a deep bond and detaching you from the person you're with.

You've probably heard of the first error. It usually goes by the name Platonic love. In this view, the body is low and corrupt, thus the highest form of romantic love is purely spiritual, something floating, ethereal. Platonic love, however, is not romantic love.[2] In a truly romantic relationship, you feel sexual desire and want sexual fulfillment. The Platonic notion of love allows you to feel admiration, but damns you for having a "degrading" sexual response. This view makes you feel ashamed of sexual feelings. The notion of Platonic love destroys romantic love.

Many people with a strong religious upbringing have been imbued, consciously or subconsciously, with the belief that sex is not a glorious union of mind and body but rather a duty or, at best, a guilty pleasure that one should not think or talk about. This causes problems in relationship after relationship.

Consider the case of Dirk and Susanna. Susanna had had a few healthy sexual experiences in good relationships before she met Dirk. Although her sexual history bothered him, he nonetheless asked her to marry him. Susanna loved Dirk passionately and was unrepressed in her enjoyment of sex with him, but the more she enjoyed it, the more disturbed he felt, finally accusing her of being a slut. Because of his upbringing, he believed that true love was spiritual and felt that Susanna's capacity for sexual pleasure proved that she was depraved. He divorced her over this issue and ruined his own happiness in the process—he lost a loving wife.

> *The Platonic view that sexual enjoyment is shameful or wrong is profoundly insulting and unjust. Your body— with its capacity for sexual pleasure—is neither good nor evil; it is a fact of your nature. You are born with it, and thus it's outside your realm of choice. To feel condemned for your sexual capacity is to make a mockery of morality.*

Choice enters in not with your capacity to experience pleasure, but with how, when, and with whom you express and enjoy your sexual capacity. These choices are determined by the judgment of your mind, not by your body.[3]

The second misconception is that sex is merely a primal urge or innate instinct that is unrelated to your mind, your values, or your character. Sex in this view is just physical. Thus, it hardly matters whom you have sex with as long as you get some positive physical sensations. There is no spiritual aspect, no connection to the mind.

Consider in how many ways the physical or materialistic view of sex is wrong.

- If sexual pleasure were nothing more than a physical sensation, you wouldn't need a partner. You would be happy with self-pleasuring. But this is not the case. To fully enjoy romantic sex, you need a partner, someone you deeply value. Masturbation or sex with someone who leaves you cold emotionally (such as a prostitute or one-night stand) may provide physical release, but such sexual experiences are impersonal and empty (and brief) compared to sex with someone you love.[4]

- If sex were purely physical, it wouldn't matter how you viewed yourself as a person. But to fully enjoy sex, you must feel worthy of sexual pleasure. A person who feels selfless, or who feels self-contempt, will not get the same pleasure from sex as one who feels worthy and has high self-esteem. A man or woman who uses sexual conquests as a substitute for self-esteem soon finds that sex only hides their anxiety and self-doubt for a short time. Sex cannot fill the void caused by a lack of self-value; it can only express the self-value that you already have.

- If sex were purely physical, it wouldn't matter what you think about sexual pleasure itself. But it does matter. To fully enjoy sex, you must believe that it is good. If you view sex as a guilty pleasure that must be hidden, not talked about, and thought of only with embarrassment, this will undermine your enjoyment. Dr. Lonnie Barbach, a noted clinical psychologist and expert in the field of female sexuality, observes that many of us have a "sex is good/bad" script in our minds: "We are told that sex is dirty—yet we are instructed to save it for someone we love."[5]

- If sex were disconnected from your mind, then mood and setting would not matter. However, to experience full enjoyment, both partners must be in the mood for sex and in a setting conducive to sexual pleasure.
- If the expression of sex were only a physical instinct, no experimentation or discovery would be required to fully enjoy it. But both partners benefit from learning what techniques work to arouse and give pleasure to one another. This requires thinking and communication.

Both errors, the purely spiritual and purely physical views of sex, make sex degrading—the spiritual view because it regards your body as sinful, and the physical view because it divorces sex from your consciousness—your knowledge, emotions, and character. The spiritual view leaves you feeling shame, guilt, and regret about the sex act, evading the fact that sex is fundamental to a romantic relationship.

The physical view trivializes sex and turns it into a meaningless animal act. It implies that sex is divorced from you and your partner's deepest values. It also implies that it doesn't matter who your partner is—but, of course, it does matter. Sex itself is not bad or meaningless, but the wrong views that many people hold about it are.

> *In contrast to the spiritual and physical views, our view of sex holds that more than any other pleasure, sex involves the integration of mind and body.*

There are pleasures that involve mainly the mind, such as intellectual achievements or contemplating a work of art, and ones that are primarily physical, such as a good workout, a massage, or a hot bath. More than any other pleasure, sex involves you as a whole person, combining both conscious and physical sensations.

Romantic sex is the most intense pleasure a human being can experience. The hero in Ayn Rand's novella *Anthem*, who has just discovered sexual pleasure, says: "And that night we knew that to hold the body of … [a lover] in our arms is neither ugly nor shameful, but the one ecstasy granted to the race of men."[6] As Ayn Rand put it, sex is "a celebration of … [one's] self and of existence."[7]

> *Sex is an intensely selfish pleasure and is based on both a deep emotional connection with your partner and a selfish desire to give your partner equal pleasure. We view sex, in the context noted above, as good. The pleasure of sex is properly viewed as an end in itself, not as the means to any other end.*

Sex is good because it is rationally pleasurable; it is part of your nature as a human being to enjoy life-affirming pleasure. Dr. Leonard Peikoff explains that sex "is a celebration of one's power to gain values and of the world in which one gains them."[8]

We are not advocating or condoning hedonism. Promiscuous or indiscriminate sex do not, in the end, bring much pleasure—and what little you do get is often followed by painful regrets, guilt, boredom and, possibly, sexually transmitted diseases, some of which are incurable. Use your mind to discover which pleasures are good for you and which are against your self-interest (like illicit drugs). Sexual pleasure with someone you value contributes enormously to the joy in your relationship and thus to your happiness with life.

If you have contradictory or confused views of sex, it is important to gain a healthy perspective and uproot damaging ideas learned in childhood, from your religious upbringing, or from bad experiences or flawed relationships. You don't have to accept your parents' views about love, sex, or any other issue if you judge them to be wrong.

What about sex before marriage? We have no problem with this provided one genuinely cares for the partner and practices safe sex. We obviously don't condone mindless sex divorced from any valuing of the partner. Why not? Because it won't have any personal meaning.

In summary, although the sexual capacity is given to you, knowing how to enjoy it, whom to enjoy it with, and whether it should be enjoyed or not is not self-evident. Such sexual knowledge is not instinctual or innate, as is evident with the widespread sexual problems so many people experience. You need more information about the nature of sex and how to enjoy it. There are hundreds of books and videos showing many ways to enjoy sex (positions, ways to pleasure one another). These can be helpful, but they are not the whole story—and in our view, not the most fundamental part of the story. Read more about sex in the next three chapters.

Exercises

1. Growing up, what ideas about your body and sex did you absorb from the people and influences around you? Those influences might have been from your parents, your siblings, your friends, your church, or religious training—or from watching movies or TV. Some of the ideas might have made sex sound intriguing and romantic, perhaps silly or unimportant, or even disgusting. Think about some of the influential observations or ideas you picked up in your youth pertaining to sex or body image.

From my parents: (Examples: My mom seemed embarrassed about sex. She would never let dad kiss her in public.

My dad was a womanizer. He would make lewd jokes to any woman he met. It made me feel that sex lacked dignity.

My parents had a wonderful relationship. They would cuddle in bed at night and would frequently hold hands when they went out.)

_____

_____

From my siblings: (Example: My sister would wear very revealing clothes—sometimes I admired her; other times I felt embarrassed. I think it's because I was afraid of allowing myself to feel sexual.)

_____

_____

From my friends: (Examples: In gym class, a good friend would go in the bathroom stall to change clothes because she was ashamed of her body. It made me feel that I should be ashamed of mine also. When I was at camp, I had two friends who talked incessantly and openly about sex. It made sex sound wild and fun—but also not very private.)

_____

_____

From my school, church or religious training: (Example: In my school, we had a special assembly on the importance of abstaining from sex until we were married. The presenters asserted [without proof] that premarital sex was sinful and that we would suffer permanent guilt were we to engage in such sex.)

From movies or television: (Examples: I loved watching the romantic and passionate scenes in movies.

TV sitcoms often portrayed sex as silly and unimportant.)

_____

_____

Other important sources:

_____

_____

2. From exploring the above: What two negative ideas seem to undermine your sex life now?

_____

_____

3. Do you sometimes feel that sex is not quite moral or good? If so, how does this affect your sexual pleasure?

_____

_____

4. Do you sometimes feel that sex is just a mindless bodily act? If so, does it make you feel that something is missing?

_____

_____

Notes

1. We elaborated on both errors in our historical overview in Chap. 1.

2. Allan Gotthelf, "Love and Philosophy: Aristotelian vs. Platonic." This lecture was first written in 1975 and has been revised since; it has been given on more than twenty-five occasions at colleges and universities and to private groups, nationally and internationally. (For more details, see Chapter 1, note 2.)

3. In *Atlas Shrugged* by Ayn Rand, there is an excellent elaboration on the connection between sexual desire and your mind, your values, and your self-esteem. Below is an excerpt explaining the relationship (New York:

Signet, 1992):

> [S]ex is not the cause, but an effect and an expression of a man's sense of his own value. . . . [A] man's sexual choice is the result and the sum of his fundamental convictions. Tell me what a man finds sexually attractive and I will tell you his entire philosophy of life. Show me the woman he sleeps with and I will tell you his valuation of himself. No matter what corruption he's taught about the virtue of selflessness, sex is the most profoundly selfish of all acts, an act which he cannot perform for any motive but his own enjoyment—just try to think of performing it in a spirit of selfless charity!—an act which is not possible in self-abasement, only in self-exaltation, only in the confidence of being desired and being worthy of desire. It is an act that forces him to stand naked in spirit, as well as in body, and to accept his real ego as his standard of value. He will always be attracted to the woman who reflects his deepest vision of himself. (p. 455)

4. Although masturbation cannot match sex with a valued partner, it is of value. Self-pleasuring can be a good way to discover what is physically and emotionally pleasing to you and to give you pleasure when a partner is simply not available. Sex therapists will often encourage an inhibited partner to engage in self-pleasuring as a means of sexual self-discovery—and then to share such knowledge with a loving partner (as a means of making sexual pleasure satisfying and less inhibited). The pleasure of masturbation can be enhanced when combined with fantasies of a real or idealized partner.

5. Lonnie Barbach, *For Each Other: Sharing Sexual Intimacy* (New York: New American Library, 1984), p. 24.

6. Ayn Rand, *Anthem* (New York: Signet, 1946), p. 95. The use of "we" and "our" in the quote is due to the hero's having been raised in a totally collectivist society and not knowing, at this point in the novella, of the existence of the words "I" and "my."

7. Ayn Rand, *The Voice of Reason: Essays in Objectivist Thought* (New York: NAL Books, 1989).

8. Leonard Peikoff, *Objectivism: The Philosophy of Ayn Rand* (New York: Dutton, 1991), p. 344. Chapter 9 on happiness has an excellent section on sex (pp. 343–348).

Creating Intimacy and Mood

*P*leasurable sex requires emotional intimacy and setting the right mood.

Now that we've affirmed that sex is important and morally good and includes both mind and body, in this and the next two chapters we will cover six key issues that are important for sexual pleasure, starting here with the first two.

- Emotional intimacy
- Mood
- Technique
- Afterplay and feedback
- Prioritizing
- Avoiding subverters of sexual pleasure

Emotional Intimacy

Emotional intimacy is the most fundamental prerequisite for sexual interest and arousal—and pleasure—in a successful, long-term relationship.

Emotional intimacy is a feeling of psychological closeness to your partner. What causes you to feel close to your partner? Here, everything we've said in previous chapters applies. Although it may feel instinctual, sexual attraction in a romance is not an uncaused primary but rather the result of the quality of the whole relationship.

Attraction and desire are greatest when you:
- Feel visible to your partner
- Selfishly value your partner and are selfishly valued in return
- Understand the causes of your love
- Work toward making yourself lovable
- Choose the right partner
- Feel understood and valued
- Communicate well
- Know and act on each other's love languages
- Feel that your partner is emotionally open and expressive in ways that create a positive emotional climate

> *We believe that many, if not most, "sex problems" are not, at root, sex problems but rather relationship problems.*

Typically, couples who enter therapy with "sexual problems" soon discover that underlying the tension or breakdown in the sexual relationship are a multitude of unresolved and often unidentified conflicts or resentments, as in the following case.

Allison and Jared were married for only a year when their relationship started to sour. Allison was a sweet, loving wife who was quietly attentive to Jared's needs. Jared thought the world of her, and yet something peculiar was happening to his sexual response to her—it was dying. Allison insisted on making his meals, doing all the housework, and taking care of their two dogs, even though he had enjoyed cooking as a bachelor. He tried to pitch in and help around the house, but she said it was easier to do everything herself. After a while, he became frustrated. He would try to plan romantic getaways, but she resisted, saying that they needed to save the money and she was happy staying at home. He wanted to sign up for dance lessons, but she showed no interest. She was the same sweet Allison he had fallen in love with, but her sweetness was now boring. Their sex life was no different. She was eager to please him but then did not want pleasure for herself. He had tried to be adventurous and daring in sex but was met with such a wall of resistance that he gave that up in their first married months. A lifetime of the missionary position with a passionless wife was not what he wanted. He turned to the Internet and started enjoying a fantasy sexual life.

Actually Allison was not the person without values that Jared was now seeing. Privately, she longed for intimacy, but when she told him that she would love him to give her a massage, he gave her a perfunctory two-minute back rub and never again offered her a massage. When she told him she felt sexy wearing long, soft velvet dresses, he instead bought her leather mini skirts and fishnet thigh-highs, which she hated. She felt uncomfortable in those clothes but failed to assert herself. He seemed to be deaf to any choices that were not his own. She would have loved a getaway to the mountains but not the golf weekend he suggested! She resisted dance classes, not because she disliked dancing, but because he was embarrassingly flirtatious when he was around other women. She would have welcomed his help around the house, especially with the dogs, but he swore so much every time they barked to go out that it was more peaceful when she took charge. If he was this way with the dogs, she couldn't imagine ever having children with him. He was sometimes a fun guy and a hard worker, so Allison blamed herself for their failed marriage and became the selfless wife—until she discovered, in horror, his Internet activities.

Then she told him that he had taken her for granted and she was sick of it. She accused him of never listening to her, which baffled Jared because he had never heard her express herself. She insisted they go to therapy to get to the bottom of his "sexual perversion." In therapy, his problem turned out to be their problem and it was not fundamentally sexual. Allison was shocked to discover that she had trained Jared to take her for granted; she had not been assertive enough in making her needs known. Jared was shocked to discover that he had never grasped nor genuinely tried to discover what she really wanted.

Consider how many of the principles discussed in previous chapters this couple violated. They failed to communicate. They did not really make an effort to understand one another. They hadn't learned each other's love languages. They didn't take each other's values seriously or treat one another as being important. They did not make joint decisions. And they hadn't attempted to set up a positive emotional climate. They felt invisible to one another. No wonder sex was no longer any fun.[1]

Apart from other relationship problems, partners rarely know how to develop a couple style of intimacy: a style of sexuality that is mutually satisfying.[2] Partners develop a couple style when they have clearly communicated what is arousing and pleasing, and together they come up with a variety of methods of sexual pleasuring that integrate both partners' needs and are not off-putting to either one. As partners learn each other's intimacy preferences, they come up with their own style.

If partners have not developed a couple style, one partner might be left feeling like a sex object. If either partner does treat the other as just a sex object, the relationship is not a good one.

A common mistake many women make is to view their male partner's passion and frequent advances as a purely physical urge, rather than as a desire for mutual intimacy.

Noted marriage and family therapist Michele Weiner Davis explains the issue:

> I am convinced that one of the grossest misunderstandings about sex is the belief many women have that men desire sex because they just want, or better yet, need a physical release. It's true that men (and some women) love an occasional quickie without much emotional hoopla. However, I've been privileged to hear men describe the way they really feel when their wives aren't interested. And if you've assumed that your husband wants sex just to "get off," what I've heard will undoubtedly surprise you.[3]

What these men experience, says Davis, is not being loved,

appreciated, or cared for, and a physical urge is often a loving, emotional desire for closeness. When the relationship is a good one, being sexually desired is a great compliment and should be taken as such. What the partner is saying is, "It is through you (and no one else) that I choose to take my pleasure, to celebrate my life, and to express my love." What greater compliment could one have from a romantic partner? In contrast, being rejected means, "I do not value closeness and intimacy with you—you are not that important to me."

The experience of shared sexual pleasure is important because it greatly strengthens the bond between partners, as long as there is a bond to strengthen.

> *Sex can reinforce romantic love but cannot create closeness from thin air; it is the expression of love, not its cause.*

Sex cannot create self-esteem that is lacking in one or both partners. As a celebration, sex expresses self-value, but it cannot fill the void of non-self-value.

On the other side of this coin, lack of sex or unsatisfying sex often undermines a romantic relationship by weakening the existing bond between partners. Sexual dissatisfaction can undermine feelings of closeness and intimacy and send the relationship on a downward spiral that spreads far beyond sex, especially when one or both partners' frustration and anger lead to progressively less sexual satisfaction for both.

People frequently blame their partner for a lack of intimacy, but it is not always the partner's fault. Some people truly fear intimacy. Having a fragile sense of self, they feel vulnerable to being hurt, ridiculed, or rejected. Such individuals are chronically anxious. Paradoxically, they may also cling to the partner—for security, not for intimacy—and make unreasonable, narcissistic demands.

Some reject intimacy because they fear valuing, wanting, or desiring. They may be emotionally repressed or feel guilty. Valuing, they fear, is too risky or too self-assertive. They may have spent their lives pleasing others or may have been hurt in the past, falsely concluding that it's safer not to pursue or have personal values.

Therapy can help individuals struggling with intimacy problems provided they are willing participants and find a good therapist.

Mood

Most people are aware that there is an important sex difference regarding mood. Men can become sexually aroused, sometimes within seconds, by a stimulant as slight as seeing their partner walk through the door. Women, in contrast, take longer to become aroused and require more of an emotional context. (There are exceptions, but this holds true for most couples.) This is not to say that men do not need a context for sex—but typically they can get in the mood much faster. How do you create that emotional context?

The first step is to have a close, intimate relationship. But even this doesn't mean that each of you will be in the mood for sex all the time or even at the same time. Your desire for sex may vary depending on many factors: your age, health (including medications you are taking), energy level, work demands, time pressure, personal mood, the time of day or month, or some specific event (for example, seeing a romantic movie).

When you are in a sexual mood, how can you invite your partner to join you? Find out what your partner likes—for example, their favorite time of day. What arouses your partner? A bubble bath and wine? Dancing in the living room? Cuddling and kissing? A sensuous massage? Watching romantic or erotic videos?

It helps create the mood if you make your partner feel sexually visible. In Chapter 13 we talked about the importance of partners expressing the reasons why they love one another. This applies to sex as well. Tell your loved one what you like about him or her sexually, including physical attributes you adore and the physical movements you enjoy. This includes letting your loved one know what sensual enhancers you would enjoy (being kissed on the neck or wearing a certain perfume), how to eliminate turn-offs (being tickled or kissing before brushing your teeth), and what special ways your partner can dress—and undress—that excite you.

Playfulness enhances sexual enjoyment.

Playfulness may involve good-natured teasing and mutually enjoyable games (tickling with feathers, blindfolding, strip poker). But do not make sex itself into something foolish or unserious. Do not undermine your joy with mockery or with a snicker. Sex is joyful and playful, but also serious, in the sense that it reflects an intense and intimate form of valuing your partner. It should not be trivialized by either of you.

However, what if you have a genuine complaint about something that turns you off sexually—how would you approach it positively? Try making a polite suggestion.

How do you increase the playfulness and joy in your sexual life and keep it from becoming stale? Think of new and creative ways to share sexual pleasure with one another.

> *Creativity isn't something that should be used only in business or home decorating. Use it in sex and keep the enjoyment alive over the years.*

Spend pleasurable time finding out what excites you and your partner.

A word of caution: some women might feel unduly pressured if they know that their partner is engaging in these preliminaries (for example, going out to a romantic restaurant, giving her a relaxing massage) with the sole goal of having sex afterwards. If she feels this type of pressure, she needs to suggest that these preliminaries might sometimes be done as pleasures in themselves, with no definite expectation of sex. Sex therapists suggest giving pleasure with a "non-demand" (for sex) agreement understood between you. If, for example, the woman feels that a massage inevitably leads to sex, she will avoid giving or receiving massages when she's not in the mood. With a "non-demand" agreement, the wonderful massages or warm moments of intimacy will increase, some leading to sex, others enjoyed for their own sake. The decision to have sex is thus left open, depending on the ultimate moods of both partners.

Whatever you do, take your time. You will both enjoy it more and be more aroused without time pressures.

A final issue: What if the relationship and sex are good but one partner still wants sex much more frequently than the other? Usually, though not always, this is the man. Here couples need to be creative and empathetic. If the woman is comfortable with this (without building resentment), she can help her partner achieve orgasm without intercourse. And, of course, he can use self-pleasuring. Finally, if the man treasures his partner, he will not pressure her to have sex every time he feels aroused.

Exercises

1. Do you feel emotional intimacy with your partner? If so, what do you think makes it possible? If not, what's missing?

_____

_____

2. Do you know how to help your partner get into a romantic mood? Does your partner know how to help get you into one? How? Do you both agree on the answers ?

_____

_____

Notes

1. This is not to deny that there can be sex problems even within good relationships. Michele Weiner Davis, in her excellent book *The Sex-Starved Marriage* (New York: Simon & Shuster, 2003), has written at length about couples who, for example, differ greatly in their desire for sex. Many of her examples reveal relationship problems, but not all. We recommend this book for those who want to delve into sexual conflicts more deeply.

2. Barry W. McCarthy, "Cognitive-Behavior Strategies and Techniques for Revitalizing Nonsexual Marriages." This workshop, sponsored by Rhode Island Psychological Association, in conjunction with the American Psychological Association, was given on Oct. 29, 2004. See also Barry McCarthy and Emily McCarthy, *Rekindling Desire* (New York: Harmony Books, 2003).

3. Davis, op. cit., pp. 56–57.

• CHAPTER 19 •

Technique, Afterplay and Feedback

Technique

*T*here are approaches to having sex that don't work in relationships. For example, one-way satisfaction or pleasure between partners (the man having an orgasm and the woman feeling used) doesn't work. A man may believe that because he enjoyed the experience, the woman must have enjoyed it also. He fails to grasp or understand her frustration or irritation. Or he may be keenly aware that it is one-sided, lacking mutual joy, but feels helpless in knowing what to do or how to talk about this openly and comfortably. And if the woman meekly replies, with an edge of resentment in her voice, "I didn't have an orgasm, but it's okay," her meekness will spell sexual dissatisfaction for both and relationship trouble for many years to come—if the relationship lasts.

To discover if your lovemaking technique is working, good questions for both partners to privately ask themselves after a sexual encounter are: *Was this enjoyable for me? Did I have a satisfying orgasm? Did we share a feeling of intimacy?* If the answers are *no*, it is important to understand what aspects can be improved and how to improve them.

For many women, sex feels like a chore when they don't achieve orgasm. Why is this pattern so common? One key is the fact that since most women cannot have vaginal orgasms, they seldom experience orgasms from traditional intercourse alone.

> *For women, physical stimulation*
> *comes mainly from the clitoris.*

The penis rarely makes the needed contact with the clitoris during regular intercourse to bring a woman to orgasm. Many women feel self-doubt, guilt, frustration, and annoyance, wondering why their partners don't pay attention to their needs and why they themselves are too embarrassed to explain what helps them achieve orgasm. Sometimes they may not know. When sex feels like a duty, resentment escalates and the result is often a sexually frustrating partnership.

In his book *The Great Sex Secret*, veteran sex educator Kim Marshall notes that women often lack sexual satisfaction because neither partner understands the essential role of clitoral stimulation in achieving orgasm. Marshall advises: "The key to long-term sexual happiness is having a strong love relationship and finding an effective, mutually satisfactory way to bring both the man and the woman to orgasm while they are together."[1] This does not mean partners have to have orgasms simultaneously or that they can't have occasional lovemaking sessions in which one or the other does not climax. But it does mean that they both need to know how to bring the woman to climax when she wants it. (Stimulating the man to help him climax is more obvious and better understood.)

Prior to or during lovemaking it helps if the man asks whether his partner wants clitoral stimulation and learns her preferred way of receiving it. (This includes: lubrication, degree of pressure, speed and direction of movement of the man's fingers, using the tongue or vibrators, and so on.) As to timing of orgasms there are several options. Marshall names three effective approaches:

1. Separate orgasms, with the woman having her climax before or after actual intercourse. Either or both partners can

stimulate the clitoris.

2. Simultaneous orgasms, with the woman touching herself during intercourse (with her hand or by using a vibrator) to achieve orgasm.

3. Simultaneous orgasms, with the man stimulating the woman's clitoris with his hand before and during intercourse.[2]

It is essential that partners openly communicate their preferences.

Once you both accept that sex is pleasure for two, let yourselves experiment with variations in technique and style. Find out what you each like and then ask for it in a mutually respectful way: "I'd really like to try X" or "It really feels good when you do Y." Partners need to banish embarrassment about sex. Remember—sexual pleasure is one of the great gifts of being human and it is both good and important in your lives together!

What about sex as you get older? As noted in the book *A Lifetime of Sex*,[3] geriatric specialist and director of a sexual dysfunction clinic Fran Kaiser, MD, stated in a medical journal that "There is no age at which sexual activity, thoughts, or desire end." Sex and couple therapist Barry McCarthy, PhD, presented "Guidelines for Sex over 60," in a workshop he gave, underscoring the importance of realistic expectations saying, "Sexuality is more likely to remain functional and satisfying when both the man and woman value a variable, flexible, pleasure-oriented sexual style rather than a performance-oriented, pass-fail intercourse approach."[4]

A final note on sexual technique: Many couples find that sex that is made predictable and routine becomes boring. For others, having regular, mutually satisfying sex is quite enjoyable. They have settled on a style and method that works well and they look forward to it.

If you find that sex is becoming too routine, experiment by adding some novelty to your romantic life. You can vary the location, time of day, how you dress and undress, and how you express your passion. Novelty can also be enhanced with sex toys (for example, vibrators that enhance clitoral stimulation), videos, games, and fantasies. Creativity pays off.

Afterplay and Feedback

Everyone knows about the need for foreplay in sex, but afterplay is important too. Cuddling for a while and exchanging loving words are usually a treasured form of afterplay. If you roll over and go to sleep right away or leave abruptly, your partner may feel as a result like a sex toy or object.

> *After sex it may be helpful to ask if your partner enjoyed it. This teaches you what your partner likes and dislikes so you'll know what and what not to repeat and how to make the next experience more pleasurable.*

Be sympathetic and caring; make it clear you want your partner to feel loved and sexually fulfilled. If your partner makes a reasonable suggestion, promise to act on it in the future. Feedback is important, because resentments about unfulfilled desires can lead to a downward trajectory in the relationship. Never be defensive or you will stop getting feedback.

Observe your own sexual pattern with your partner: How do you let your partner know what you like and don't like? What works well for each of you? How do you communicate during sex? Sex therapists emphasize the need to phrase feedback lovingly. For example, rather than saying, "I hate it when you do that!" it is far better to just gently move your partner's hand. Or you might say, "I prefer you touch me here—this feels really good."[5] Ask your partner what feels good. Do not assume that either of you are mind readers.

It is important to avoid deceiving your partner about your sexual enjoyment. For instance, do not fake orgasms. This is dishonest and a breach of trust. There may be times when you or your partner simply are not aroused enough to achieve orgasm.[6] On certain occasions a feeling of closeness and intimacy may be satisfying enough. However, if this is the pattern in your relationship, you should figure out how to increase your mutual pleasure.

What if, as is often the case, you learn that you and your partner do not like exactly the same methods or techniques? This is a common situation and we'd like to make three points here.

First, you may occasionally be willing to step out of your comfort zone and try experimenting with things your partner likes.

> *For a true egoist, there is great selfish pleasure in giving pleasure, because you treasure your partner.*

Finding different ways to give one another pleasure is an exciting part of your relationship. And when the relationship is trusting and passionate, partners are usually more willing to experiment.

Second, you can informally take turns doing the things each partner most prefers so that each partner is assured of enjoying pleasure. Taking turns should be done with good will, not with resentment. Resentment results when you or your partner thinks, "My desires are important and good, but yours are trivial and stupid."

Our third point is a qualification of the first. While it is benevolent and loving to fulfill your partner's desires, there may be certain techniques or acts that one partner strongly dislikes. In some cases a loved one may learn to like something he or she did not like at first (for example, oral sex, anal sex, sex games, sex toys, and various fantasies). But this is not true in all cases.

> *If your partner strongly dislikes some activity, you need to fully respect your partner's right to say "no."*

You should not pressure your partner to sacrifice on your behalf. However, if one partner is saying *no* to almost everything new, there are two key questions:

1. Would this partner be willing to suggest creative variations in sex that are potentially enjoyable?

2. Are the frequent *no's* a consequence of relationship issues that need to be brought out into the open?

We are not condoning prudishness or excessive modesty, which can seriously undermine sexual pleasure. The more inhibited partner would benefit from understanding any anxiety and fears related to intimacy—and can learn more about the tenderness, joy, and closeness achieved by having a good sexual relationship. The less inhibited partner needs to be supportive and encouraging. For example, if a woman is embarrassed about being seen naked by her partner (which will undermine her own sexual pleasure as well as her partner's), she can make the effort to overcome this by first turning the lights out and placing a lit candle in the next room, then in the corner of the bedroom, then next to the bed, then accompanied by a dim light in the next room and so on. The less inhibited partner must be patient and should gently encourage progress and show appreciation at every improvement.[7]

Exercises

1. Do you and your partner like the quality of your lovemaking? If so, what makes it work for both of you? If not, what would each of you like to change to improve it?

_____

_____

2. For women: Do you let your partner know specifically what works to help you achieve an orgasm? Do you feel comfortable bringing up the issue of clitoral stimulation? If not, what would be the next step you could take to open up communication for both of you? (We recommend both partners read _The Great Sex Secret_ by Kim Marshall.)

_____

_____

3. For men: Do you let your partner know what feels best to you? Do you invite conversation on what works best to stimulate your partner's clitoris?

_____

_____

4. For both: Do you know your partner's favorite technique/positions? Does your partner know yours? Do you discuss new, creative ideas?

_____

_____

5. For both: Do you and your partner give each other feedback after sex? If you do, what have you learned from one another that has helped improve your sexual lives together?

_____

_____

Notes

1. Kim Marshall, *The Great Sex Secret: What Satisfied Women and Men Know that No One Talks About* (Illinois, Sourcebooks Casablanca, 2007), p. 4.

2. Ibid, chap. 6: "Three Approaches to Mutual Satisfaction," pp. 107–129.

3. Stephen C. George, K. Winston Caine, and the editors of Men's Health Books™, *A Lifetime of Sex: The Ultimate Manual on Sex, Women, and Relationships for Every Stage of a Man's Life* (Pennsylvania, Rodale Press, Inc., 1998).

4. Barry W. McCarthy, "Cognitive-Behavior Strategies and Techniques for Revitalizing Nonsexual Marriages." This workshop, sponsored by Rhode Island Psychological Association, in conjunction with the American Psychological Association, was given on Oct. 29, 2004. Also cited in Barry and Emily McCarthy, *Rekindling Desire: A Step-by-Step Program to Help Low-Sex and No-Sex Marriages* (New York: Brunner-Routledge, 2003), p. 4.

5. In an interview on Dr. Kenner's radio show, Dr. Judy Kuriansky, sex therapist, author, and radio-talk-show host, elaborated on these suggestions.

6. Michele Weiner Davis, *The Sex-Starved Marriage* (New York: Simon & Schuster, 2003), chap. 3.

7. For women, see Lonnie Barbach, *For Yourself: The Fulfillment of Female Sexuality* (New York: Doubleday & Co., 1975). For men, the following book may be of help: Stephen C. George, et al., *A Lifetime of Sex: The Ultimate Manual on Sex, Women, and Relationships for Every Stage of a Man's Life*. For clinicians, the following book is recommended: Helen Singer Kaplan, *The New Sex Therapy: Active Treatment of Sexual Dysfunctions* (New York: Brunner/Mazel, 1974).

CHAPTER 20

Prioritizing Sex and Overcoming Subverters of Sexual Pleasure

Prioritizing Sex

*M*ost couples make precious little time for amorous moments. Making a relationship work and keeping the romance alive takes motivation, time, planning, and communication. Even small misunderstandings can destroy a romantic moment, and accumulated, festering misunderstandings can destroy your romance. When you are juggling dual-career work schedules, kids, paying bills, in-law visits, checking e-mail, doing laundry and dishes, getting daily exercise—how do you find spare time for romance?

Notice a problem with the way this last sentence was phrased. "Spare time"? What ranking was romance assigned? Where did it come in terms of priorities? After everything else. How can partners manage all the details of a relationship and still keep their romance vibrant?

> *It is true that active, productive people have to make time for sex, but sex shouldn't be relegated to the category of a spare time activity.*

Sex is an important part of romantic partners' lives together. Of course, crises can and do cause long intervals between sexual encounters, but many couples allow such temporary interruptions to become normal.

Young couples sometimes ask, "Is it true that sexual attraction normally fades as time goes on?" And many do let other aspects of their lives take priority over intimacy, but they don't have to. It is a choice. In the most successful romantic partnerships, sexual intimacy is made a conscious priority.

> *Ideally, sexual attraction is enhanced with time, especially as emotional intimacy deepens.*

What practical steps can you take to make sure that sex is a priority and not a duty? Start by always promoting strong *emotional* intimacy and visibility. Find ways to reduce fatigue. Discover the best ways to create a romantic mood. Set aside private time. Make sure you and your partner both experience pleasure so that sex will be something to look forward to. Share fantasies if both of you feel safe doing so.

To make sex a priority, you need a body that is able to cooperate. Some factors are more controllable. You cannot control your actual age, but you can have some influence on how well your body functions as you get older. Regular exercise, a healthy diet, stress reduction, and getting enough sleep are all important to your physical and emotional well-being. Men whose arousal is impeded have the benefit of potency-enhancing drugs. It is well known that testosterone is important for male sexual arousal but in much smaller amounts it also plays a role in female sexual arousal. Some drugs, such as antidepressants and birth control pills, undermine testosterone production. A medical specialist can help sort this out. Although alcohol in small amounts can reduce inhibitions, it is a depressant that can undermine sexual function when consumed in excess.

Overcoming Subverters of Sexual Pleasure

A number of factors undermine sexual arousal and enjoyment. Here we will discuss four: anger, fatigue, too much "other" focus, and children.

Anger

We noted in Chapter 16 that anger and resentment are romance destroyers—so obviously, they are sex destroyers too. In a *Newsweek* cover story, "No Sex, Please, We're Married," one woman said, "I get angry because he doesn't help around the house enough or with the kids. He sees the groceries sitting on the counter. Why doesn't he take them out of the bag and put them away? How can I get sexy when I'm ticked off all the time?"[1] Observe that "helping" is one of this woman's love languages (see Chapter 12).[2] It is important to have a mutually agreed upon division of labor regarding household chores, career and financial issues, and parenting responsibilities. This sets the proper context for a healthy sex life. When each partner feels that the other is fair and supportive, romance is much more likely to flourish.

Sex expert Michele Weiner Davis has noted that men who feel rejected sexually often express their hurt as anger.[3] This tends to drive their partners away, which intensifies their anger. To prevent this downward spiral, men need to be good at introspection (looking inward) and women need to see beneath the anger to understand the rejection. Cutting off communication guarantees that the issues causing anger will remain unresolved.

Nagging is another way of expressing anger, more often used by women. Nagging invites resistance and resentment, undermining your partner's desire to have sex with you. And likely your partner will just tune you out. If you and your partner have unresolved problems, there are better ways to resolve them. (See Part VI for details.)

Fatigue

Modern life is often hectic, especially for couples with children and even more so for dual-career couples with children. It is nearly impossible to become sexually aroused when you are exhausted. The *Newsweek* article on sex and marriage told the story of Maddie, who had enjoyed sex with her husband, Roger, but her increasingly busy life—children, career, and so on—left her too tired for sex. In an effort to be romantic, Roger would typically light a candle in the bedroom, but Maddie told *Newsweek*, "I would see it and say, 'Oh, God, not that candle. . . . It was just the feeling that I had to give something I didn't have."[4]

Sex was low on Maddie's priority list and had become a duty, an unwanted obligation. Having sex out of self-sacrificial duty when you're tired is guaranteed to take the joy out of sex. At the same time, letting sex fade away due to fatigue can undermine a relationship. Partners sometimes allow their work to take over their lives, forgetting that they will have no energy for affection or lovemaking at the end of very long days. Sex is too important a pleasure and too crucial for promoting intimacy to be put on the back burner.

> *If you show indifference to your partner's sexual pleasure, you are showing indifference to your partner.*

If either of you suffers from fatigue, discuss ways to ease the burden. Is there an agreed-upon division of labor for housework and childcare? Would hiring a babysitter help? Can you arrange for take-out every Friday night to reduce the workload? Are the children old enough to pitch in more around the house? Can you just say *no* to some of those volunteer activities you feel obligated to do? Find time to rest and be alone with each other when you are least fatigued. Find places to get away together. These don't need to be elaborate or expensive getaways. Sometimes a surprise lunch date or an overnight at a bed-and-breakfast helps tired couples reconnect and re-energize their romance. It is often easier to recharge away from home where all the chores are temptations that threaten to distract your focus from one another.

Make sure to keep yourself in good physical condition. If you are out of shape, you will tire more easily. And before deciding to have another child, ask yourselves if you can handle the additional work involved and still have time for romance. Couples often have the fantasy that it is wonderful to have a large family. For many, however, the reality is often overwhelming.

Too Much "Other" Focus

Loving couples selfishly want to give their partners as much pleasure as possible. However, there are two ways that focusing too much on your partner can undermine sexual pleasure. One way is to let your mind anxiously wander, worrying, *What is my partner thinking about me?*[5] This is usually due to self-doubt. The following examples of pleasure-blocking, anxiety-provoking thoughts do not enhance sexual intimacy:

- Will I climax too soon? Too late?
- Does she think I'm big enough for her?
- Does my partner think my breasts are too big or small?
- Is his/her hand that's stimulating me getting tired?
- Does what I'm doing look foolish?
- Am I making too much noise? Or too little?
- Am I too fat? Too skinny? Too unmuscular?

A related error is to focus solely on your partner's pleasure. As noted sex therapist Dr. Helen Singer Kaplan explains, a self-sacrificial approach to sex destroys pleasure:

> [T]he compulsion to please, to perform, or to serve, not to disappoint, can be a severe source of disruptive emotion. A man's thought "I must have a rapid erection and hold it for a long time or she won't be pleased" or a woman's compulsion to serve the man's sexual wishes to the point where her own needs are neglected, or … the man's unconscious fear that if he didn't perform, his fiancée wouldn't marry him, may create enough pressure to impair his erectile response.[6]

What is the antidote? Since romance is in the best interest of both (egoism for two) make sure you both experience pleasure. To get pleasure, be conscious at some point of nothing but the pure egoistic pleasure you are getting. To make sure both partners get what they want, take turns if necessary (during sex or even across sexual encounters), so each of you experiences pleasure.[7] Focus on *enjoying* yourself when you are with your partner. That's the selfish path to romance.

Children

We noted in Chapter 16 that partners should not let children undermine their romantic relationship. Michele Weiner Davis writes, "…one of the biggest mistakes I see women make in their marriages is that once the children are born, they forget they have husbands."[8] Tending to your romantic relationship requires that you plan time alone, without the children. There are several options here such as having sex when the kids are asleep, on weekends when the kids are doing things with friends or staying with relatives, and during short romantic getaways. While children require and deserve a great deal of care and attention, so too does your sexual partner. Don't forget that your partner is your top value.

> *Don't sacrifice your own capacity for sexual pleasure by putting it on hold until the kids are out of the nest; instead, cherish your ability to enjoy an ongoing intimacy with your partner.*

Sex is pleasurable, healthy, good, and an essential part of a romantic relationship. Achieving sexual pleasure requires a context; it involves and expresses how you and your partner view yourselves and your entire relationship. It entails the ultimate unity of mind and body—your mutual sexual pleasure reflects everything you feel about yourself and one another. As in the case of love, it requires thought as well as feeling and action, including constant clear communication.

What would an ideal sexual encounter be like? Although there is no one model that fits everyone, we thought the following excerpt from Ayn Rand's epic novel *Atlas Shrugged* illustrates, beautifully

and dramatically, the ecstasy of sexual enjoyment in the context
of a total integration of mind and body. In this scene, the heroine,
Dagny Taggart, makes love to the man who represents everything she
fundamentally values in herself and in life:

> Then she was conscious of nothing but the sensations of her
> body, because her body acquired the sudden power to let
> her know her most complex values by direct perception ...
> her body now had the power to translate the energy that had
> moved all the choices of her life, into immediate sensory
> perception. It was not the pressure of a hand that made
> her tremble, but the instantaneous sum of its meaning, the
> knowledge that it was his hand, that it moved as if her flesh
> were his possession, that its movement was his signature of
> acceptance under the whole of that achievement which was
> herself—it was only a sensation of physical pleasure, but it
> contained her worship of him, of everything that was his
> person and his life. . . . it contained her pride in herself and
> that it should be she whom he had chosen as his mirror, that
> it should be her body which was now giving him the sum of
> his existence, as his body was giving her the sum of hers. . . .
>
> He pulled her head back for a moment, to look straight
> into her eyes, to let her see his, to let her know the full
> meaning of their actions, as if throwing the spotlight of
> consciousness upon them for the meeting of their eyes in a
> moment of intimacy greater than the one to come. . . .
>
> [T]hen she felt, when it hit her throat, that which she
> knew only as an upward streak of motion that released and
> united her body into a single shock of pleasure—then she
> knew nothing but the motion of his body and the driving
> greed that went reaching on and on, as if she were not a
> person any longer, only a sensation of endless reaching for
> the impossible—then she knew that it was possible, and she
> gasped and lay still, knowing that nothing more could be
> desired, ever.[9]

This passion, this unity of body and mind, this ecstasy can be
yours if you make yourself lovable, choose the right partner, treat

your partner as being important, view sex as being both good and important in your lives together, and communicate openly and warmly with your partner.

Exercises

1. What priority does sex have in your relationship with your partner? If it is low, how might you make it higher? List the personal benefits to you of making sex a priority in your relationship:

_____

_____

2. If you find that you are often too tired for sex, ask yourself:
   a. Is my fatigue masking other problems in our relationship? If so, would I be willing to discuss these problems with my partner?
   b. Is my fatigue due to work overload? If so, would I be willing to reduce my work or volunteer commitments to allow for more time alone together?
   c. Can my fatigue be lessened by my partner helping more around the house? Would my partner be willing to help?

_____

_____

3. Do you feel anger at your partner about any issue that detracts from your sexual arousal? Would you be willing to discuss this issue with your partner and try to resolve it?

_____

_____

4. Do you find yourself "spectatoring," judging yourself negatively while making love? For example, do you have anxiety-provoking thoughts, such as: *Does what I'm doing look foolish?* Do you focus not on enjoying the pleasure, but rather solely on pleasing your partner? If so:
   a. Can you gently quiet the anxiety-provoking thoughts by answering them: *I deserve to enjoy the pleasurable feelings*?
   b. Have you thought of experimenting with self-pleasuring to learn more about what you enjoy and then sharing this information with your partner?

    c. Do you allow yourself to receive full, selfish pleasure from your partner?

_____

_____

    5. If you have children, how often do you plan for private time alone? Could you plan for even more?

_____

_____

Notes

1. Kathleen Deveny, "We're NOT in the MOOD," in *Newsweek* cover story: "No Sex, Please, We're Married: Are Stress, Kids and Work Killing Romance?" June 30, 2003, p. 46.

2. Gary Chapman, *The Five Love Languages: How to Express Heartfelt Commitment to Your Mate* (Chicago: Northfield Publishing, 1995).

3. Michelle Weiner Davis, *The Sex-Starved Marriage* (New York: Simon & Schuster, 2003) p. 56.

4. Deveny, *Newsweek,* op. cit., p. 41.

5. Helen Singer Kaplan, *The New Sex Therapy: Active Treatment of Sexual Dysfunctions* (New York: Brunner/Mazel, 1974).

6. Ibid, pp. 130–132, on "Excessive Need to Please Partner."

7. If the male partner suffers from premature ejaculation, so that the woman never gets the full pleasure she wants, there are many ways this can be overcome. We recommend going to a sex therapist or consulting a relevant sex book. Lonnie Barbach has a workbook that is used in therapy: *Ejaculation Control Workbook* (Pennsylvania: Brunner/Mazel, 1997). See also *Sexual Happiness: A Practical Approach* by Maurice Yaffe, Elizabeth Fenwick, and Raymond Rosen (New York: Henry Holt & Co, 1988); and Stephen C. George, et al., *A Lifetime of Sex,* op. cit, pp. 242–245, on premature ejaculation.

8. Davis, op. cit., p. 80.

9. Ayn Rand, *Atlas Shrugged* (New York: Signet, 1992), p. 880.

Part VI: Resolving Conflict

My way of trading is to know that the joy you give me is paid for by the joy you get from me.... A trade by which one gains and the other loses is a fraud.

—Ayn Rand, *Atlas Shrugged*

• CHAPTER 21 •

Causes of Conflict I

*A*ll romantic partners experience conflicts, no matter how strong their love, but there are more and less effective ways to resolve such conflicts.

Above all, partners need good communication skills. If partners can't communicate well when conflicts arise, a gulf will open between them that will widen if not properly addressed. The intimate, loving, soul mate relationship that they started with will likely degenerate into a relationship plagued by feelings of anger, hurt, invisibility, and emotional separation. The end result may well be the destruction of the relationship, followed by bitterness, cynicism, and despair.

Good communication cannot save every troubled relationship. But effective communication is essential to all successful romantic relationships, and it can save many relationships that might otherwise fail. We'll give you some tools needed to make yourself understood, to understand your partner, and to resolve conflicts. Your communication style and skills determine how intense conflicts become; how long they last; how complicated they get (a single issue or a laundry list of complaints); how many people become involved; how many aspects of your life are affected (home, work, sex, family relations); how the conflicts are ultimately resolved; and what emotional scars, if any, such conflicts leave on the partners.

Effective communication requires that you acknowledge areas in which you can improve, have courage to try new ways of approaching conflict, and be determined to avoid becoming defensive. Developing these skills requires practice. You may feel awkward at first, but with time and effort you and your partner can become competent conflict resolvers. In this and the following chapters, we address important issues in conflict management and resolution and answer general questions about the nature of conflict.

In Chapters 21 and 22 we cover:
- Why some conflict is inevitable in all relationships
- How differences between partners may cause
  conflict due to:
     ~ Turning reasonable, optional differences into
        moral issues
     ~ Expectations of mind reading
     ~ Violations of the trader relationship
     ~ Insufficient time together
     ~ Gender differences

In Chapter 23 we look at:
- Communication methods that do not work
- Personality and character attacks
- Global language
- Faking niceness

Chapter 24 surveys rational, practical approaches to conflict resolution:
- Communication methods that do work
- Nipping escalating tensions in the bud
- Healthy assertiveness
- How to actively listen to your partner

Finally, in Chapter 25, we give you some final tips on:
- What and how to compromise
- How to deal with your partner's resistance

Why Some Conflict is Inevitable in All Relationships

Even though you may be similar to your partner in many fundamental respects, inevitably there will be differences in beliefs, values, interests, preferences, tastes, habits, attitudes, and personality traits.

Partners will differ in communication skills and styles and in habitual methods of thinking. In many cases these differences are a source of interest and excitement. For example, an introverted partner may admire how an extroverted mate is so at ease in social situations. Or one partner's interests in dancing or reading history can stimulate the development of similar interests in the other.

Differences that conflict with one's own preferences can be ignored if they are not important enough to make an issue of. Some couples may even agree not to discuss certain issues. For example, a husband loves to golf, but his wife has no interest or desire to participate. However, she recognizes that he gains much pleasure from it. They agree that this is a hobby they will not share, although she, as a loving partner, does ask him if he enjoyed himself when he gets home. Notice that they are not avoiding a significant moral conflict but are avoiding making unnecessary waves about a legitimate personal difference. As the issues become more significant, such as differences in politics or religion, conflicts become more difficult (though not necessarily impossible) to ignore. (Usually such issues will have been considered before a close relationship has developed, but individuals may change over time.)

Differences can cause recurring conflicts. This is obvious in the case of big issues, such as sex, spending money, choosing where to live, philosophy of life, the amount of time spent together, the time spent with relatives, dividing up household chores, whether to have children and if so how many, and how to bring up the children. But there can also be recurring conflicts over small issues, such as how to load the dishwasher, where to leave dirty clothes, when to pay bills, and how and when to interrupt your partner. Seemingly small issues often become larger if they keep recurring and if neither party is willing to change or to simply let it go. Sometimes chronic conflict over small issues (cleaning up the den, spending too much time on the computer with friends) is camouflaging a much deeper conflict that both partners are afraid to address (lack of a satisfying emotional or sexual connection).

Our emotional baggage is a significant factor in our response to conflict as well.

> *Each of us grew up having different life experiences, different ground rules in our families' homes, different ways of managing friendships, different relationship histories, different ways of approaching work and romance.*

We each have an encyclopedic store of experiences, and we have drawn conclusions about the world and ourselves and how we think things ought to be.

Consider Marcie and Doug. When they first met in a sailing class, they were surprised at how similar they were. Both had an adventurous sense of life. Both were soft-spoken. Marcie was pleasantly surprised to discover that Doug shared her love of snorkeling and skiing. Both appeared sincere, with good character, and they were physically attracted to one another. They dated for six months, seeing each other only on weekends. Once, during the holidays, they went on a short Caribbean vacation and had a wonderful time with no major conflicts. Then they decided to live together for the summer in a cottage near the beach, where they could enjoy sailing and snorkeling.

Within two days of moving in together, they were silently at war. Doug's family had been regimented. His dad had treated the family as if they were at boot camp, and there was never any question about keeping a clean home and sticking to the rules. Friends were rarely permitted to visit. On the other hand, Marcie's background was much more relaxed. Her mom gave Marcie an enormous amount of freedom to make her own choices. Her parents never drank alcohol;

it was banned from their lives, due to her grandfather's history as an abusive alcoholic.

As Marcie and Doug were moving their belongings into the cottage, Marcie noticed a few wine bottles among Doug's belongings. Since he had never ordered wine on dates, she assumed he never drank. Now she believed that he, like her grandfather, must have a hidden alcohol problem.

Doug grew very frustrated with Marcie because she dropped her clothes and boxes in a helter-skelter manner as they were moving in. He bit his tongue as he hung up her clothes for her. Why didn't she take responsibility for her own things as he did? Doug was also mortified when Marcie invited her two best friends to visit on their second day there. Marcie had not consulted him and the cottage was in no condition for them to entertain. Both began to harbor doubts about whether they could live together and even whether they liked one another.

Their negative thoughts festered for a week until it finally burst out in an angry exchange. Marcie accused Doug of being a closet alcoholic and a control freak. Doug accused Marcie of being disorganized and lacking in social graces.

Their initial impressions of one another were totally different from what they were seeing in each another now. They were almost ready to split up, but they decided to try counseling.

How Differences Between Partners May Cause Conflict

Two common causes of conflict arise when partners make reasonable *optional* differences into moral issues, and when they have expectations of mind reading. Let's explore both causes of conflict related to partners' differences.

> *Even reasonable, optional differences may cause conflict because one partner feels, on a gut level, that his or her views and habits are morally right and that the partner's are wrong. Accepting such unanalyzed feelings as facts causes many conflicts.*

Making Reasonable Optional Differences into Moral Issues

Sometimes differences do involve moral issues, such as lying, cheating, or stealing. But many differences are morally optional. Doug experienced Marcie's invitation to her friends as being very wrong. His personal rule, ingrained from childhood, had always been that you open your home to guests *only* when it is presentable. (This is a sign of respect for some hosts.) But this was an exception. They were just moving in, the get-together was informal, and Marcie's friends presumably knew her habits well. She was not being rude. But to Doug, it felt like a moral transgression. He needed to understand that the house rules he learned from his father were not the only possible rules—that there were reasonable options.

Marcie, in turn, felt that Doug was morally wrong for having alcohol in the house. She had jumped to the wrong conclusion, automatically assuming that Doug had a drinking problem like her grandfather's. Doug felt hurt that she thought he was an alcoholic. He did have an occasional social drink but never felt or been told that he had a problem. Marcie needed to learn to check her assumptions and the facts before reaching such drastic conclusions.

With better communication, Doug could explain to Marcie that because of his upbringing he felt upset about her asking others over when the house was messy. They might agree that in the future, Marcie would consult with Doug before inviting friends over and she would try to be neater—or he might agree to relax his more stringent standards, which would come in handy if they choose to have children. Marcie could tell Doug that she was very upset at finding the wine bottles because of her traumatic childhood experiences with her alcoholic grandfather. Doug could then describe his actual drinking habits. Thus, by being open and learning more about one another's lives, they would gain a richness of understanding and discover communication skills to distinguish between moral and optional differences.

Since you and your partner—despite differences—have values and ideas in common, there is often a natural assumption that your partner should be able to read your mind and thus always know what you are feeling, thinking, or wanting.

Expectations of "Mind Reading"

Neither Marcie nor Doug spoke up when they first noticed differences that bothered them; they just assumed the other should know better. Marcie should know that Doug likes things orderly and Doug should know that Marcie is highly sensitive to the risks of alcohol abuse. But neither Doug nor Marcie, who had known each other a relatively short time, could possibly "just know" the totality of each other's experiences and values.

Rather than expecting your partner to be a mind reader, communicate what is on your mind directly and assertively while avoiding an attack on your partner's character. Actively seek more information to better understand each other. Had Marcie spoken to Doug immediately upon discovering the wine, and had Doug spoken up immediately about the neatness issue, each would have avoided jumping to wrong conclusions and conflict might have been avoided.

Any time you feel frustration or resentment toward your partner over an issue, don't let the feeling fester. Bring the issue up tactfully and discuss it.

If you have had a lifetime fear of openly expressing your feelings, wants, and desires, consider professional help.

Initially you learn about your partner one detail at a time. After you have gotten to know your partner well—and this may take years—there will be times when you find that you know what your partner is thinking or feeling about many issues, without your partner saying anything, because your acquired knowledge will have become automatic.

Assuming you are an attentive listener and a careful observer of your partner's actions, in time you will know your mate better. But do not assume you will ever know every opinion your partner holds on every issue. Remember, your partner has free will and the power of independent thought. Partners' values, preferences, and viewpoints may change over time. Both partners may encounter totally new ideas and experiences, and their reactions may sometimes be unpredictable. The need to communicate, clearly and with respect, never ends.

Exercises

1. Consider two minor differences you have with your partner that spark chronic nagging of one another, such as leaving the lights on when you walk out of a room. Discuss with your partner whether you can come to an agreement that such minor differences are not important enough to argue over.

2. Think of a recent argument you had with your partner, or a recurring one. Jot down the essence of it:

_____

_____

Ask yourself if this situation involves a truly moral issue, such as lying or cheating, or if you are treating as a moral issue something that is actually an unchallenged personal rule from your childhood—without considering if there are reasonable options. This may open up possibilities of personal growth for you.

3. Do you or your partner typically hold in resentments and let them fester? Name one frustration you are letting build up:

_____

_____

4. Describe some tactful ways you can let your partner know what you're feeling.

_____

_____

5. Think of a time when you felt annoyed because you thought your partner should have known what you were thinking. Was this a valid assumption or an unrealistic expectation that your partner should have been able to read your mind?

_____

——————————— • CHAPTER 22 • ———————————

Causes of Conflict II

*I*n Chapter 21 we covered some ways differences between partners may cause conflict. Now we continue with three more sources of friction: Violations of the Trader Relationship; Insufficient Time Together; and Gender Differences.

Violations of the Trader Relationship

> *The refusal of a partner to trade, even in everyday actions, will be perceived as unfair, a breakdown of the give and take in the relationship.*

We noted in Chapter 3 that love is a trade. This also applies to character and to everyday relations between partners.

Let's say that partners need two incomes to pay the bills. Both have agreed to work, but one partner now refuses to seriously look for a job, preferring to live off the efforts of the other. In addition to being unjust, the partner's refusal to work after promising to do so lacks integrity.

When the trader principle is violated, tensions quickly rise. There is a feeling of betrayal and injustice by the partner who is getting the raw end of the deal.

Sometimes partners feel that one or the other is being unfair, but often neither is intentionally trying to provoke or take advantage of the other. For example, in our last chapter, Doug felt that Marcie was being unfair when she left clothes and boxes scattered all over the house. Doug was neat and organized, and due to his sense of order, he thought she should just know better. He felt put-upon as he picked up after her. Marcie had no idea that such behavior bothered him and resented that he was irritably intruding on her method of unpacking. Such perceived unfairness could have been resolved with better communication. Partners should not keep an accounting ledger to make sure there is fairness; that is far too mechanical. Goodwill and a sense of fairness will often do the job.

Insufficient Time Together

It can be legitimately upsetting if you are not a top priority in your partner's hierarchy of values. Suppose your spouse loves hiking and mountain climbing and spends all his or her spare time in those activities, leaving little time for you. This situation makes a successful romantic relationship unlikely. However, there is no right amount of time that you should spend with your loved one; partners have different preferences and tolerances. Some need time alone and others need a lot of contact.

> *If one or both partners feel neglected or abandoned, this will be a source of conflict.*

Resolving the conflict requires that partners discuss their preferences, communicate frankly and openly, and come to a mutually satisfactory agreement—and then strive to keep it.

Gender Differences

Sometimes gender is a source of conflict. In her book *That's Not What I Meant!*, Dr. Deborah Tannen, international expert on interpersonal communication, explains that in early childhood it is common for girls and boys to play with children of the same gender. Girls often form best-friend relationships with other girls by sharing secrets. This creates a special bond between them. They learn, by sharing intimacies, to express emotions openly. Their priority is establishing close relationships. Often they are brought up to be indiscriminately nice and self-sacrificing.[1] There will always be exceptions, especially with more girls today engaging in rougher, more competitive sports. However, walk into almost any jazz, tap, or ballet class for children and you're far likelier to see more girls than boys and to see the girls focused on establishing close relationships.

Boys tend to play in larger groups, frequently focused around rougher sports. They are more action-focused than verbal and are often encouraged to prove their competence, strength, and toughness rather than to share secrets and more vulnerable feelings. They are frequently taught to go after what they want. Communicating more vulnerable feelings is often seen as a sign of weakness, and they are encouraged to walk it off or are chided if they openly cry.

Women may have trouble understanding why some men seem to be oblivious to emotional issues, and men may be confused when some women get upset instead of just going along or solving problems. In these respects, each feels invisible to the other. When they argue, they are on different wavelengths.

Take the case of Cara and Andres. Cara felt lonely in her marriage to Andres. Although he was a good provider and loved surprising her with special gifts, she felt invisible on the deepest level. He was unaware of her most profound values and feelings. He was of no comfort when she had a fight with her mother or had a bad day with her cranky boss. She wanted Andres to listen to her, to commiserate with her—to understand. She would relate her bad experiences, not with the intent of getting his advice but to feel understood, but Andres would launch into telling her precisely what to say and do. He wanted to fix everything.

Andres, in turn, was frustrated with Cara. Why didn't she take his advice? She was always trying to pry him open, asking him how his day went, what he was thinking, what he felt about this or that— things he never thought much about or even felt compelled to think about. He felt more at home with the guys on the basketball court where there was no pressure to talk or analyze everything. He felt drained by Cara's conversations about their relationship.

Cara and Andres's pattern is common. Both need to learn that such differences in relating often have deep roots in childhood. How would they address those? They would need to understand that such gender differences are common and surmountable. Cara would need to be clear about what she needs. Andres could learn how to be a sympathetic listener and discover ways to open up emotionally. They may do this with some counseling sessions to help them break out of current patterns and to see the value to each of them of learning the missing skills. If they did this, they would feel much more visible to one another.

Emotionally repressed men can learn to read their own emotions and to empathize better with their partners, and self-sacrificing women can learn to be assertive. Both can learn to communicate better.

Exercises

1. What differences emerged as your relationship developed?

_____

_____

2. Do you feel each of you give equally to the relationship? If not, in what way do you feel deprived?

_____

3. Do you spend enough time with your partner? If not, how could this be remedied?

_____

4. Do you notice gender differences in what each of you want? Have you discussed these differences and have they affected your relationship?

_____

_____

Notes

1. Deborah Tannen, *That's Not What I Meant! How Conversational Style Makes or Breaks Relationships* (New York: Ballantine Publishing Group, 1986).

———————— • CHAPTER 23 • ————————
Communication Methods
That Do Not Work

*W*e often communicate in ways that sabotage our
relationships. Most of us have some psychological
baggage that we bring to our relationships and it affects
how we communicate in word and deed. Screaming and swearing,
the silent treatment, interrupting, talking in a cold manner, giving
looks of contempt, smirking—these are a sample of destructive
communication techniques. Here are additional examples of
ineffective communication techniques:

- Sarcasm: "So you think you have all the answers!"
- Name-calling: "You're such a slob!"
- Negative comparisons: "Your brother would never have a
  messy car."
- Giving authoritarian orders: "Clean up this mess right
  now!"
- Threats: "If you don't apologize now, I'm packing my bags
  and leaving!" or "If we don't have sex soon, I'm going to
  find someone else!"
- Global language: "You never listen to me!" or "You always
  manage to be late!"
- Predicting an unhappy future: "You'll never make anything
  of yourself!"

- Lecturing: "You should call your mother more often. I know she wasn't a good mother, but she needs you now and it's wrong to ignore her needs. You should put your own issues aside and be more caring."
- Catastrophizing: "I saw you smile at that salesclerk. You don't love me anymore!"

All of these methods project anger, disrespect, and belittlement. They undermine open communication and a true understanding of one another; they make it difficult to resolve conflicts, and they intensify the problems you may already have.

> *To overcome poor communication patterns: You must first detect any dysfunctional methods that you use and learn to uproot and replace them. Second, you must be able to detect when others use such methods against you and to avoid getting into dysfunctional cycles of attack and counterattack.*

Attacks Using "You" Language

We use the pronoun "you" all the time. For example,

- Thank you.
- You look nice.
- You seem to really love dogs.
- You are so thoughtful.
- You come up with the best ideas.
- You take a right turn at the stop sign.

But when the word "you" is used in a negative way, it is perceived as a personal attack. It is called "you language" or finger-pointing language. Such attacks can involve personality or habits:

- You are so rude.
- You are not very nice.
- You are so messy.
- You are overbearing.
- You are a big know-it-all.

Such attacks are perceived as insults (which they are). But the insults may be even more biting than those above:

- You are an idiot!
- You are useless!
- You are a loser!
- You are a jerk!

When a statement, like one of the above, is thrown at you, your mind automatically signals a warning alarm: *I am under attack!* Responses may vary. The attacked partner may immediately withdraw in hurt, shock, and frustration. Alternatively, they may counter-attack, blaming the attacker for any and all problems. Instead of mutually exploring your differences or working to clarify misunderstandings, your mental energy is consumed battling one another. You may accuse your partner of having bad character or bad motives and the conflict escalates. Real communication ceases; nothing gets resolved. Such battles can also end in withdrawal, emotional distance, and even estrangement.

We've all used or been the target of such digs at some point in our lives. We are familiar with the sinking feelings and hurt that accompanies such moments—not the warm closeness of soul mates, but the emotional turbulence of facing an adversary. We feel anger, hurt, guilt, frustration, helplessness or hopelessness. We feel misunderstood, cast as a villain, accused of things we didn't do and of not doing things that we did do.

This love-destroying cycle, in some relationships, goes on for decades—until death or divorce puts an end to it. When your partner, your best friend, has turned into an enemy, you both lose. The above methods of communication are dysfunctional: they don't work, even when the accusations are true.

"You" attacks can escalate to a more extreme level—that of actual psychological or physical threats.

- You had better do what I say or I'll divorce you!
- If you defy me, I'll wreck the house!
- If you don't go along, I tell a few embarrassing secrets to your parents!
- If you do that again, I'll cut off your money!

- How would you like a fat lip?

The purpose of such threats is to induce fear. They usually succeed in this, along with inducing anger, and may send the relationship into a downward spiral from which there is no recovery. *Motivation by fear* does not accomplish anything; it destroys emotional intimacy or the possibility of it.

Global Language

Once you get into the mind-set that your partner is acting like your enemy, you will selectively focus on negatives in your partner, exaggerating them in your mind and ignoring genuine, positive traits. A tip-off that you are doing this is finding yourself using global words—words that are all-encompassing: "never," "always," "no one," "everyone," "nothing," "everything," "all." Look at the following statements for the global tip-off words:

- "You never do anything right!"
- "You never listen."
- "You're always late!"
- "You always try to hurt me."
- "You find fault with everything I do."
- "Nothing ever pleases you."
- "I'm always left doing all the work."

These statements are usually overgeneralizations. It is rarely true that your partner *never* does anything right and *always* tries to hurt you. If this is really the case, you are clearly with the wrong partner.

When you're on the receiving end, you automatically focus on facts that you feel contradict the global statement. You recall instances when you did things right (arrived early for an appointment, listened, were considerate) and dismiss the entire criticism, which may be partly true. You may feel like throwing a counterpunch even though your accuser made no specific complaint.[1]

The alternative to global criticism is to be *specific and accurate* in your complaint; avoid understating or overstating it. Consider Marcie saying to her husband Doug, "The past three days you told me you'd be home for dinner at six and I planned for dinner to be ready at that time. When you came home at seven-thirty again, I felt angry and abandoned. I wish you had called me. I waited around when I could have gone to the gym."

Doug might then say, "I'm very sorry I didn't call. Thanks for the meals—they were welcome after my hectic days. I'll make sure from now on to notify you as soon as I know my schedule has changed." Had Marcie told Doug that he was *always* late, he would have immediately recalled the times he came home on time or early and would have dismissed her complaint. He then might have mentioned times when she was late (tit for tat). They would have failed to communicate effectively.

To resolve conflict, you must have a mind-set that is respectful of yourself and your partner, not just giving in or being a bully. Your goal is to establish a purposeful line of thinking that works toward a healthy resolution of any conflict. A cooperative, benevolent and solution-focused approach is best. Focus on the area of specific conflict, actively listen to understand each other, clarify misunderstandings and then brainstorm to discover solutions.

Faking "Niceness"

> *If you try to fake a sweet demeanor when you are actually upset, it is only a matter of time before your sweet veneer dissipates. Even if your words come out measured and "sweet," your body language or restrained tone of voice will betray your actual feelings.*

When your tone of voice and body language contradict your words, your partner will react to the non-verbal cues. If your partner says, "But you seem really upset," and you answer, "There you go again—you're always reading into things. I'm just fine!"— communication has been choked. Faking your feelings only masks and compounds the problem, and delays any resolution.

Stifling your legitimate feelings, suspending your thinking, ignoring your own values and nodding "okay" to please or appease your partner is a self-defeating tactic. Stand up for what you want. Then, instead of feeling, "What's the use!" you feel, "We can manage this difference."[2]

We've covered some communication methods that don't work. Personal attacks and threats, global language, and faking "niceness" destroy romance. We will cover some methods that do work in the next chapter.

Exercises

1. Monitor yourself during an argument. Do your arguments involve inappropriate attacks or threats? Global statements? If you do use these methods, how might you re-phrase what you are saying to communicate more effectively?

_____

_____

2. Do you fake "niceness" to avoid conflict? If you find yourself doing this, allow yourself to notice if it resolves the underlying problem or intensifies it.

_____

_____

3. Do you use aggressive "you" language?

_____

_____

Notes

1. We must stress that moral flaws should be treated differently than bad habits. It is true that most liars do not lie all the time. But a lie represents a faking of reality which is much more serious than, say, sometimes not listening. A liar must be told that lying is unacceptable and risks a fundamental breach of trust between partners. Bad habits may become moral issues over time; for example, a person who repeatedly promises to take certain actions and repeatedly fails to do so is showing a lack of integrity, assuming the person is not memory impaired.

2. Douglas Stone, Bruce Patton and Sheila Heen, _Difficult Conversations: How to Discuss What Matters Most_ (New York: Penguin, 1999). This is an outstanding book filled with practical advice which will help you understand the complexity of conversations and give you the skills to effectively manage even your strongest emotions.

• CHAPTER 24 •

Communication Methods
That Work

ow we are prepared to survey rational, practical approaches to conflict resolution. The following methods will help you resolve conflicts with your partner. In contrast to the methods discussed in the previous chapter, these have a proven record of resolving conflict and will help you deal with one another on a rational, respectful, mind-to-mind basis.

Nip Escalating Tensions in the Bud

When people stifle thoughts and feelings, they seethe quietly and anger surfaces indirectly in their body language and tone of voice. People who have stored up a lot of hurt and frustration may suddenly let loose fairly aggressively, using the flawed communication methods we discussed in Chapter 23.

> *Some individuals manage to stifle their feelings for a lifetime and become seriously depressed. They never give themselves a voice, and they betray their deepest desires.*

It is easy for arguments to get out of hand in the heat of emotion. Developing a method that calms things down and restores perspective provides a safe atmosphere in which to deal with conflict. Often this can be done with a touch of humor. Marcie and Doug used a signal system. One time they had gotten into a heated argument about something quite silly: Who would run to the store to get milk? Later they realized how trivial the issue was and had a good laugh about it. From then on, when an argument started to get heated one of them would say "milk run," and they would both smile and calm down.

Another method was to take a brief break from each other. For example, one might go for a walk while the other listened to music. This would give their emotions time to calm down and their minds time to see the argument or conflict from a different angle and to consider alternative solutions.

You should decide in advance how you want to use this last method. Taking a break from the conflict works best if it is a mutually agreed upon method that either of you can initiate, such as: "Let's separate for an hour and come back to this when we're in a better mindset." Continuing to battle it out when you are too upset to think straight or when you are resorting to poor communication methods is counterproductive.

Here are two key skills that you will want to learn or strengthen: active listening and assertively speaking your mind.

Healthy Assertiveness

Assertiveness is very different from aggression. One way to be healthily assertive is to use the pronoun "I." You have every right to say what you observe, think, feel, and expect. Whatever you are trying to express in "you" language can be effectively translated into "I" language. For example:

- You make me angry. → I feel angry.
- You never listen. → I feel ignored.
- You talk to me like I'm stupid. → I feel put down and belittled.
- You drive me crazy! → I am so frustrated.

In each case, the sentences on the left make you and your partner feel attacked. The sentences on the right make you both more likely to listen and talk to one another. When you assertively say, "I feel angry," your partner is much more likely to ask why. You are not battling one another. You are respectfully allowing each other to express yourselves. Now you both have the opportunity to clarify any misunderstandings. Resentments do not have time to fester.

This does not mean that you can never use the pronoun "you." Some "you's" are fine in conversation, for example, when they are used to nonaggressively state facts: "You didn't show up"—as opposed to attacking character with global language: "You are a jerk!" (Of course, your tone of voice and body language should not be hostile, or your partner will experience what you say as an attack.)

There is an exception to the above: if your partner has committed a real moral betrayal, such as adultery, physically hurting you, or stealing money from you, it is fully understandable to show genuine moral outrage and not worry about a constructive discussion initially, assuming you know all the relevant facts. However, it is still more self-respecting and productive to take some time alone to think before engaging in any discussion with your partner. This will give you time to consider if you want this relationship at all.

Here are a few more assertiveness tips that may help you express yourself more effectively.

1. Be as clear as possible when expressing your viewpoint. Giving a specific example helps your partner much more than using global language. Mentally paint a picture of what you experienced: "I was waiting at the restaurant for an hour. When you didn't show up or call, I felt abandoned, angry, and embarrassed." Your partner can easily visualize this, and you are communicating your message more skillfully.

2. Get to the point quickly. Your partner will appreciate your directness, and you will have a better chance of resolving your conflict without further misunderstanding or harm.

3. Limit your complaint to the most pressing issue. Deal with one issue at a time (using examples as needed)—and make it the most important one. Overwhelming your partner with a litany

of complaints will shut down the conversation abruptly. No one can manage even three issues at once.

4. Do not be afraid to express strong emotion—provided this is not done with malice or with "you" language but with frankness. For example: "I'm furious right now. I'll be back in half an hour to talk about what happened." Your partner needs to know the intensity with which some conflict is affecting you.

5. Pause to let your partner digest what you have said. Give your partner time to think, ask questions, and respond. Do not demand that your partner give you an answer or an apology right then and there.

6. Ask your partner to verify that he or she has heard what you said. This will avoid misunderstandings. For example, ask in a genuine tone of caring, "Have I expressed myself clearly?"

7. If you did something wrong, be honest about your mistakes. When you own up to the truth, do not engage in endless battles starting with "I'm sorry, but . . ." The "buts" may put your partner back on the attack again, and they don't work toward resolving the conflict. Furthermore, when you are honest your partner has more respect for you.

Admitting mistakes is not a sign of weakness but of moral integrity. This strengthens your self-esteem.

8. Share the airtime. It is not fair to sit down to dinner and expect your partner to listen to your complaints and concerns non-stop for an hour. Remember that both listening and assertiveness should be used by both partners. Nor is your partner your therapist. If you feel desperately overburdened with problems, seek professional counseling.

Learning why assertiveness skills work so well and how you can become proficient in them is a fascinating endeavor with payoffs in every area of your life, especially for your self-esteem. There are several good resources for more information.[1]

In the following example, Megan shows how she uses assertiveness skills. Megan and Tony went on holiday to a ski resort.

Tony was an expert skier, Megan an anxious beginner. When Tony invited her to join him on the slopes, she hesitated, then asked if he would stay with her on the beginners' trail. He agreed, and they hit the slopes. When they reached the turnoff for the beginners' trail, Tony said, "Hey, let's take Devil's Leap instead—it's fairly easy." Megan saw immediately that it wasn't and refused. Tony lightheartedly said, "Okay, you take the easy trail and I'll take Devil's Leap. We'll meet at the base." As she saw him head down the slope, Megan felt hurt at being abandoned. She took the beginners' slope but was too angry to enjoy it. To make matters worse, she waited at the base but he did not show up.

Megan is at a crucial point. In the past, she would become sullen and quiet, trying to hide her pain, as she often did when in conflict with her parents. When Tony would ask why she was so sullen, she would tell him unconvincingly, "Oh, I'm just tired." She would give him the silent treatment for days. Sex? Forget it—she would have that headache again!

Megan no longer lets resentments build. When she met Tony later, she said, "Hey, I was looking forward to skiing the beginners' trail with you. I felt abandoned. I thought you wanted my company." Tony felt genuinely remorseful and told her that he didn't realize how important skiing the beginners' trail was for her. He apologized and added, "When I got to the bottom of the slope, I was enjoying myself so much that I completely forgot everything else; I took another run. I'm so sorry! Tell me if there is a way I can make it up to you." Tony didn't become defensive and fill the air with phony explanations or "yes, buts." Megan still felt annoyed that he could forget about her so easily, but she realized that this was out of character for him.

Megan felt closer to Tony because he understood why she felt hurt, and she accepted his honest apology. They enjoyed hot cocoa inside the lodge, and she did not have a headache that night.

Had Megan decided to use the silent treatment or go on the attack with "you" language, the whole weekend would have been shot. Speaking up assertively helped her release her strong feelings in a way that Tony was able to acknowledge. She felt better about herself. Tony owned up to having forgotten his promises. Megan again felt at peace with him and was free to enjoy his company. They were happy that they resolved the conflict so smoothly and that it had lasted only a short while.

How to Actively Listen to Your Partner

Most of us believe we are good listeners, but few of us actually listen well. Signs of poor listening include: focusing on irrelevant issues; selectively hearing what you want to hear and avoiding some important point; wishful hearing; jumping to conclusions; tuning out; interrupting your partner; and changing the topic.

In contrast, active listening requires that you:

- *Be courteous.* Do not interrupt or jump in with attacks.
- *Listen with fully focused attention.* Avoid mental drifting. Temporarily set aside your own thoughts and responses to grasp what your partner is saying.
- *Clearly indicate that you are listening.* This requires good eye contact and occasionally letting your partner know you are following by saying, "uh huh" or "I see."

Put yourself in each other's shoes. If you are upset because your partner forgot to pay the electric bill, imagine how you'd feel if the tables were turned. This helps you empathize with his or her feelings.

Help your partner focus on the essential issue. If he or she is meandering, refocus your partner by gently asking, "What is your main concern?" or "How would you sum up the problem?"

Acknowledge strong emotions or non-verbal messages. If your partner is angry, hurt, or sad, you want to acknowledge the strong emotions or non-verbal messages: "You seem to feel strongly about this" or "I noticed that you just winced. What exactly are you feeling?"

Check for misunderstandings. When your partner finishes, briefly summarize what you heard, then add: "Did I hear you correctly that . . . ?" Explore inconsistencies ("You say you're okay, but you seem so disappointed. What's really on your mind?").

Ask for specific examples if your partner uses global language. If your partner says, "You never do anything right!" you can follow up with "Something specific I did must really be bothering you. Tell me what it is."

> *Always apologize if you have hurt or*
> *disappointed your partner.*

If you listen well, you will discover sometimes that you have hurt your partner's feelings. This calls for an apology. Some people find it difficult to apologize because their self-esteem may be based on being perfect. Nothing is more guaranteed to make your partner feel unjustly treated and invisible than your refusal to acknowledge that you have hurt them.

Active listening will go far to put your partner at ease. Your partner no longer has to work to make you understand. You have demonstrated that you have grasped what your partner is saying (without necessarily agreeing with it).

Do not make the mistake of listening intently, agreeing to correct the problem, and then doing nothing about it. This shows a lack of integrity—and you won't get away with it. All your future promises will be viewed as suspect, if not meaningless. You will be seen as someone with poor character. In contrast, if you agree to correct a problem and follow through, you will feel better about yourself and you will have a much better chance of rescuing your relationship.

Exercises

1. Do your arguments tend to escalate? What skills mentioned in this chapter could help stop this pattern and really work to help you understand one another.

---

2. Do you use "you" language or "I" language when asserting how you feel or think? Take something you recently said in "you" language and translate it into "I" language.

---

3. Do you both practice active listening? If not, what goes wrong? Which of the tips we covered would help you remember to actively listen to your partner?

_____

_____

4. Which of the following points do you most need to work on?
- Being as clear as possible when expressing your viewpoint.
- Getting to the point quickly.
- Limiting your complaint to the most pressing issue.
- Not being afraid to express strong emotion—provided it is done in "I" language, and with frankness.
- Pausing to let your partner digest what you have said.
- Asking your partner to verify that he or she has heard what you said.
- Being honest.
- Sharing the airtime.

_____

_____

Notes

1. The following are good resources for books on assertiveness skills:
- Douglas Stone, Bruce Patton, and Sheila Heen, *Difficult Conversations: How to Discuss What Matters Most* (New York: Penguin, 1999).
- Matthew McKay, Martha Davis, and Patrick Fanning, *Messages: The Communication Skills Book*, 2d ed. (California: New Harbinger Publications, Inc., 1995).
- Matthew McKay, Patrick Fanning, and Kim Paleg, *Couple Skills: Making Your Relationship Work* (California: New Harbinger Publications, Inc., 1994).
- Jesse S. Nirenberg, *Getting Through to People* (New Jersey: Prentice-Hall, Inc., 1963).

• CHAPTER 25 •

Compromise and Dealing with Your Partner's Resistance

*F*inally, we give you insights, methods, and the courage to do the difficult: compromise and deal with resistance from your partner.

When Should You Compromise and How Do You Do So Fairly?

It is important that partners resolve conflicts promptly, fairly, and respectfully. Conflicts can often be settled by compromise.[1] We use the word "compromise" here to mean collaborative resolutions in which both parties get at least some part of what they want. Sometimes there can be creative solutions in which both parties get almost everything they want. We are talking about practical compromises, not moral compromises.[1] By talking and brainstorming with your partner, you can make a list of possibilities and then work to find the one that works best for both of you.

Judy and Lance were planning a vacation but disagreed over where to go. Lance wanted to go hiking. Judy wanted to go to a beach resort. Some ways in which they can compromise include:

- Taking separate vacations
- Hiking one year; going to the beach the following year

- Spending half of the vacation hiking, half at a resort
- Doing something else on which they both agree

When you are open to brainstorming, with your goal being a mutually satisfying solution, you have the freedom to be creative.

Tips for compromising successfully:

- Stay solution-focused
- Know what is negotiable and what is not (morally and personally)
- Know basic methods of compromise[2]
- Brainstorm together to find solutions

The ability to compromise is essential when you become parents. The significant responsibility of caring for children throughout their growing years requires that partners have excellent communication skills, including methods of fairly dividing up child rearing responsibilities. Otherwise, misunderstandings grow, small slights ignite large fires, and the soul mate relationship perishes.

Wall Street Journal writer Sue Shellenbarger reported on this phenomenon in a 2004 article titled "And Baby Makes Stress: Why Kids Are a Growing Obstacle to Marital Bliss."[3] Three reasons cited included debt (overspending on the baby); confusion over roles (who should be the stay-at-home parent and who is the breadwinner); and the inability of partners to "talk without fighting."[4]

> *An ongoing process of open communication and compromise can help turn a stressful undertaking like child rearing into a bonding experience.*

A collaborative solution may work at one point but with changing circumstances may fail. A husband may have agreed to stay home with the children weeknights so his wife can work but discovers that he is becoming increasingly frustrated and resentful. He might tell his wife, "Honey, although I originally agreed to stay home, my frustration and resentment are growing. Let's talk about other possible arrangements." Compromise requires a trial period to see if it works, and it is normal to renegotiate if either partner is unhappy. This helps protect a couple from turning one another into an enemy.

Just as healthy negotiation skills are needed in business, they are essential in child rearing to maintain marital happiness.

> *Some things will be non-negotiable because they are relationship breakers.*

If a partner insists you ride behind him on his motorcycle without a helmet and you are terrified of motorcycles, how could you compromise? Drive only half as many miles as he wants? If your partner wants her boorish, alcoholic brother, who is dating a prostitute, to move in for a few months, would you compromise by letting him stay for only a few weeks? What on earth would you gain from such compromises except misery?

Serious moral issues include chronic lying, infidelity, or undependability. Other conflicts might entail deeply held cultural and philosophical views. For example, it may well be a serious problem if you insist that your children go to a religious school and your partner insists they pursue a secular education. You could try persuading one another with principled arguments, but if you cannot find a resolution, you and your partner could be mismatched. This is the type of conflict that should be fully aired before marriage.

Dealing with Your Partner's Resistance

What do you do when your partner resists your efforts to resolve conflicts? And what do you do when your differences can't be resolved?

There are two types of resistance: reasonable and unreasonable. Reasonable resistance involves actively thinking about the issue and openly exploring differences. This includes looking at facts and identifying specific reasons behind your strongly held but differing opinions and feelings. Unreasonable resistance involves manufacturing ploys to avoid thinking or evading the subject: "I'm right, you're wrong! Period!"

Some reasonable resistance is natural. When partners are rational, initial opposition to certain points may indicate they are thinking about the topic and may not yet have processed it from each other's perspective. If you respond with a knee-jerk reaction (becoming angry at your partner's initial resistance), you undercut chances for good conflict resolution and compromise. For example, if Lance responds to Judy's resistance to hiking by telling her, "No way am I going to any stupid beach resort," the possibility of conflict resolution has been sabotaged.

You can reduce reasonable resistance by using methods such as the following:

- Tell your partner that you sense resistance.
- Seek clarity. Understand the details of their viewpoint: "Help me understand you better."
- Inquire into objections or strong emotions—and the reasons for them.
- Avoid saying, "Yes, but," which is often heard as a put-down. Instead try, "I see it differently."
- Handle objections with a solution focus, not a blame focus.
- Do not rush your partner. Give your partner time to digest new ideas or suggestions.[5]

Unreasonable opposition means your partner is not simply misunderstanding you, but also refusing to:

- Understand you
- Grant validity to your carefully reasoned arguments
- Acknowledge relevant facts
- Consider alternatives
- Focus on solving the problem at all

Refusing to use ways to rationally compromise means your partner is beyond reason, is evading the facts, and is acting on the basis of some irrational emotion (such as fear). What can you do when your partner refuses to work with you to resolve conflict?

Sometimes the underlying problem is that partners are not addressing the real issue. The resisting partner may not want to acknowledge or may not explicitly know what the real issue is.

A man may resist planning romantic evenings because he fears the humiliation of impotence. Nurturing, supportive discussion may help him talk about this issue and deal with his fears openly and move toward some solution.

Here are more tips for handling unreasonable resistance: Be persistent. Go into detective mode to identify the real issue. Draw your partner out so that you can both explore his or her reasoning: "Help me better understand why you disagree so strongly." "I'm wondering if something more important is causing your anger." Such comments or gentle questions invite your partner to talk and encourage your partner to be more specific and introspective. If your partner continues to be evasive, persist in addressing the topic and your partner's evasive tactics. You might say, "I noticed that you just changed the subject again—what's really bothering you?" Continue until you conclude that it is truly hopeless. If this happens repeatedly, reconsider the relationship.

Do not get drawn into playing mind games. A reasonable person living with an abusive partner can sometimes be provoked into acting irrationally and out of character (yelling, swearing, throwing the partner's clothes on the lawn). The abusive partner may turn these irrational actions into a false judgment of the rational person's character. It's important to hold context when evaluating yourself in such circumstances.

Get away from partners who try to undermine your self-respect. Use "I" language. If you think your partner is open to listening, try the assertiveness skills discussed earlier.

Break unwritten codes by clearly naming what you see. For example, an irrational spouse might grab your favorite antique and threaten to smash it. He assumes you're too afraid to name what he's doing. In some situations, you may be able to diffuse the anger by openly describing what you observe and your reaction to it: "I see you're grabbing my grandmother's vase. I'm feeling intimidated and afraid. Is that what you're hoping I feel?" It can be disorienting to the irrational person when you name his method of attack. Such a person is counting on your focusing on your own fear and not shifting your focus to his method of intimidation.

Let your partner hear his or her own words. If your irrational partner calls you a coarse name (bitch, pig, ignoramus) or mocks you, you might try repeating their words: "You're calling me a bitch and telling me I'm worthless." Sometimes hearing his or her own words helps the irrational partner to recognize what he or she is doing and to tone it down a bit. If your partner persists in using insulting words, the relationship is likely unfixable.

A word of caution: In situations where your partner may pose a physical danger, you must act to protect your safety first. Take physical threats seriously. If you think your partner might harm you (or already has), get out of the house, move to a secret location and get professional help as soon as possible.[6]

What do you do when differences cannot be resolved? When your partner is consistently irrational (and it is not a momentary anomaly), seriously consider divorce—on moral grounds. You have a moral obligation to yourself (and to your children) to leave. You never have to be stuck with an irrational partner.

Irrationality is one basis for divorce, but often differences are not as serious as just described. Two reasonable people may discover they are seriously mismatched. For example, one may have a career that requires long work hours and the other wants a companion who has more time to spend together. Personalities may conflict—one partner may be formal and quiet and the other extroverted and boisterous. Or they may have just grown in different directions. Not all irreconcilable differences are moral issues. Many are just a matter of decent partners discovering that they are personally incompatible and wanting to find more compatible partners. Both partners have the right to end the relationship with mutual respect.

If you discover irreconcilable differences, read the Appendix. We discuss how to part ways while keeping your self-respect and maintaining—and eventually enhancing—your happiness.

Exercises

1. Have you successfully tried compromise to deal with legitimate differences of opinion (conflicts)? If you were not successful, what went wrong? Can you think of additional methods of achieving agreement?

2. Does appealing to reason, with persistence, work with your partner or is your partner stubbornly irrational? If it is the latter, does your relationship have a future?

3. Have you used any of the following methods to deal with resistance?
- Telling your partner that you sense resistance?
- Seeking clarity?
- Inquiring into objections and strong emotions?
- Avoiding "Yes, buts"?
- Handling objections with a solution focus, not a blame focus?
- Not rushing your partner?

Notes

1. For a detailed discussion of a rational approach to the subject of moral compromise, integrity, and ethics, see Leonard Peikoff, Objectivism: The Philosophy of Ayn Rand (New York: Penguin, 1991). Chapter 8, "Virtue," especially pp. 260–267, presents an expanded discussion on the specific topic of compromise.

2. For an expanded discussion on methods of compromise, see Matthew McKay, Martha Davis, and Patrick Fanning, The Communication Skills Book, 2nd ed. (California: New Harbinger Publications, 1995) pp. 98–101. The authors review examples of "classic methods of compromise," e.g., "I'll cut the pie, and you choose the first piece." "Take turns." "Do both, have it all." "Trial period." "My way when I'm doing it, your way when you're doing it." "Tit for tat." (Tit for tat, in a good sense: "If you walk the dog in the mornings, I'll make you a lunch each day to take to work.") "Part of what I want with part of what you want." "Split the difference."

3. Sue Shellenbarger, "And Baby Makes Stress: Why Kids Are a Growing Obstacle to Marital Bliss," Wall Street Journal, December 14, 2004, p. D1.

4. Ibid.

5. There is an excellent book on this topic: Jesse S. Nirenberg, Getting Through to People (New Jersey: Prentice-Hall, Inc., 1963).

6. If you are in physical danger, we strongly recommend reading Gavin de Becker's The Gift of Fear and Other Survival Signals That Protect Us from Violence (New York: Dell Publishing, 1997).

Epilogue

L ove is too important to give up on unless circumstances simply make it impossible. Even if you've have had struggles in the past, you now have some important new love skills to use. You have the basic concepts that make a healthy romantic relationship possible.

You know that romantic happiness is based not on altruism (self-sacrifice), narcissism, or hedonism, but on valuing yourself and mutually valuing one another. Romantic happiness is based on rational selfishness. You know that:

- It's morally good to seek your own happiness.
- Love is rationally egoistic, not selfless.
- Romantic love is based on the need for visibility.
- Love has causes that can be identified.
- Love requires you to make yourself lovable.
- You need to integrate reason and emotion when choosing a partner.
- Making romantic love thrive requires thought and effort.
- Mutually pleasurable sex is critical to romantic happiness.
- Certain communication techniques work much better than others.
- Many conflicts are rationally resolvable.

Enjoy working to achieve and maintain your own romantic happiness. We did, and for each of us in our own lives we have found a great deal of joy. We wish you the best. We hope you can achieve the romantic joy and intimacy so beautifully expressed in the following poem:

"I Want You"
by Arthur L. Gillom[1]

I want you when the shades of eve are falling
And purpling shadows drift across the land;
When sleepy birds to loving mates are calling—
I want the soothing softness of your hand.

I want you when the stars shine up above me,
And Heaven's flooded with the bright moonlight;
I want you with your arms and lips to love me
Throughout the wonder watches of the night.

I want you when in dreams I still remember
The ling'ring of your kiss—for old times' sake—
With all your gentle ways, so sweetly tender,
I want you in the morning when I wake.

I want you when the day is at its noontime,
Sun-steeped and quiet, or drenched with sheets of rain;
I want you when the roses bloom in June-time;
I want you when the violets come again.

I want you when my soul is thrilled with passion;
I want you when I'm weary and depressed;
I want you when in lazy, slumbrous fashion
My senses need the haven of your breast.

I want you when through field and wood I'm roaming;
I want you when I'm standing on the shore;
I want you when the summer birds are homing—
And when they've flown—I want you more and more.

I want you, dear, through every changing season;
I want you with a tear or with a smile;
I want you [both with feeling and with] reason—
I want you, want you, want you—all the while.

Notes

1. Arthur L. Gillom, "I Want You," is available in *The Best Loved Poems of the American People*, selected by Hazel Felleman (New York: Doubleday & Company, 1936) p. 45. The original line 27 reads "I want you more than any rhyme or reason—". To be more in line with the theme of this book we changed it to read: "I want you [both with feeling and with] reason—."

How to Part Ways and Start Over if You Cease Being Soul Mates

*Y*ou have the right to pursue romantic happiness, and sometimes that means ending a relationship that has failed, despite your best efforts—and starting over.

Whether married or together for thirty months or thirty years, many who contemplate divorce tell themselves, *I just have to make sure I've tried everything.* This is fine as long as "everything" is defined as those things that make sense rationally, and as long as you do not indefinitely keep trying things as a way of escaping a final decision. For example, you try to be more attentive to your partner. If that fails to rekindle romance, you read self-help books on relationships. When that fails, you berate your partner or use guilt. When that backfires, you ask your partner's friends and parents for help to change your partner's mind or actions. When this fails too, you see a counselor. Finally, when nothing works, it is important to gather courage, face reality and make a decision.

Some partners decide to live out their lives together, pretending a soul mate relationship still exists, or they stay together without such pretense—either way remaining in a state of perpetual unhappiness. This is tragic. Why attempt to fake happiness when you have the power to achieve the real thing?

Some partners don't want a divorce, but use the threat of leaving to coerce their partner to do things their way, against their partner's own judgment. This is incompatible with true romance. If you have problems, fix them together or get help, and if that does not work, begin the process of calling it quits.

Calling it quits is not easy. You must be aware of and avoid knee-jerk reactions. You may be tempted to divorce on impulse when feeling intense frustration, anger or loneliness. But with more thought, you may discover that your feelings are a reaction to a temporary situation with an otherwise loving mate. Or you may melt with the affection another person showers on you and long for that person, feeling the temptation to divorce without much thought, and without deep knowledge of the other person. Acting on such impulses is a good way to ruin your chance for longer-range happiness.

Not all divorces require years of thinking, but they should involve a lot more than feeling excited (sexually or otherwise) in another person's presence. Divorce is a major life decision with many consequences and requires careful consideration of key issues. Let's explore some of these issues, which include:

1. Identifying the reasons you're considering a divorce
2. Identifying barriers keeping you in an unhappy relationship
3. Making the final decision: tying all the relevant evidence together
4. Breaking the news to your partner
5. Setting up an atmosphere of respect—even when there are disagreements
6. Helping your children through your divorce
7. Going public with family and friends
8. Making an action plan for your divorce
9. Learning how to live independently and taking new steps toward romantic happiness

1. Identifying the Reasons You're Considering a Divorce

You may poignantly realize you no longer feel special to your partner—you've grown apart with different interests, friends and values. Or you feel you've lost yourself in the relationship—you're living in the shadows of your partner's life. Or you've experienced moral betrayal in some form and can't forgive it. Perhaps you discover your unhappiness by contrast: you meet someone far more attentive and adoring than your partner, and your partner refuses to change.

You might see a contrast between your relationship and that of another couple who seem to be genuine soul mates; you see the tenderness and love missing in your own relationship. Or you realize the battles you've had over the years (regarding finances, kids, sex, the in-laws) left you with painful and unforgettable emotional scars. Maybe there's overt hostility in the relationship and it chronically feels like a war zone. Or maybe a cold indifference has set in; your home is filled with contempt and disdain. Any combination of these situations may prompt you to ask yourself: *Would I be happier without my partner?*

Take that question seriously. Introspect and discover what it is you dislike and you may be able to address the problem and prevent further erosion of your relationship. You may also clearly grasp that you want out. Give serious thought to the reasons you want a divorce. An exercise as simple as writing down the lists of pros and cons of divorcing may help you gain clarity. The time you spend understanding your specific reasons for wanting a divorce will help you feel in command, rather than tortured by self-doubt.

> *Divorce does not have to be tragic or a shameful failure.*
> *When chosen for the proper reasons,*
> *it is self-respecting and liberating.*

Knowing that your marriage has serious problems, including your unhappiness, will bring up another question: *Do I have a moral right to be happy?* Some view divorce as immoral. They view marriage not as a vehicle for mutual happiness, but as a moral duty to be borne at any cost. We strongly disagree. As emphasized throughout this book, the answer to this question is yes—hold the conviction that you have a moral right to seek happiness. (The fact that you have this right does not justify deceit or adultery. As long as you have a committed relationship, trust is an essential element.) When chosen for rational reasons, divorce is, in fact, a moral decision.

2. Identifying Barriers Keeping You in an Unsatisfactory Relationship

The decision to divorce is sometimes relatively easy, as when a partner cheats on you and you choose not to forgive them. The decision may be much harder if your partner has both good and undesirable traits (e.g., has a playful sense of humor but often ignores you). The decision is most difficult when your partner is a good person but just not right for you. Mismatches that were not recognized in the early stages of strong passion come to the fore. Here are some common barriers that keep partners in unhappy relationships:

Guilt at breaking one's vows ("till death do us part"). Marriage oaths are made in the context of what you know about your mate at the time. Partners have free will and can and do change over time. Perhaps they initially misrepresented themselves to you. Or characteristics that were not fully noticed early on come to the fore. There is no way to predict how a relationship will evolve; it may improve or deteriorate. The marriage oath should be taken seriously and you should resist giving up at the first sign of conflict. But there is no moral imperative that requires you to sentence yourself to a life of misery if things cannot be worked out.

Guilt at hurting your partner. No decent person wants to hurt the person they once loved but fear of hurting someone is not the basis for romance. Would you want someone to fake love for you out of pity? The purpose of romantic love is the selfish happiness of both parties, not mutual suffering. To pretend to still love someone when you don't is faking reality.

To stay with your partner out of pity is not a loving gesture. It sentences both of you to mutual, long-term unhappiness. Your partner will feel self-contempt for trapping you. You will feel self-contempt for having abandoned your chances for genuine romance and contempt for your partner who lacks the courage to admit that the romantic relationship is over. No one wants to be a charity case or to give love as alms. If you part ways, the rejected partner is still free to pursue their own happiness with someone else. Reread Chapter 2 and review how staying together out of pity is based on altruism.[1]

Staying together with a genuinely beloved partner who becomes disabled or seriously ill does not necessarily involve pity. If you deeply love your partner, you will not want to desert them. It's important in such cases to give yourself respites from care-taking responsibilities and time to do things for yourself.

Fear of change. Change means dealing with the unknown. This takes courage and the willingness to use your mind to deal with new challenges.

Emotional stress. It's normal to feel a range of upsetting emotions at the prospect of divorce. You may have panic attacks, periods of second-guessing yourself, bouts of debilitating depression, an overwhelming sense of guilt, moments of nostalgia, nightmares, a lack of focus, angry outbursts, headaches, and difficulty sleeping or eating normally. It's no wonder that many retreat back into a bad marriage and grin and bear it. But there may also be moments of joy, optimism, a growing sense of self-confidence, and occasionally an overpowering sense of relief knowing you will soon be out of an unsatisfactory or self-destructive relationship. In fact, one's stress level often goes down when the decision to divorce is made. Professional guidance can help you acquire skills to better manage your stress and deal with the many effects of divorce—earning yourself some peace of mind.[2]

Fear of being alone. Unless you're divorcing after you have found a new partner, the thought of being alone can be terrifying. It's important to keep in mind at such times that everyone is alone within their own soul and every person is separate from every other, whether married or not. You're an individual first and a partner, parent, or friend second.

What you have to fall back on is the same thing you had when you first married: your reasoning mind and your basic values. You may retain some old friends. You may have relatives you like. You may have children. And most important, you have the ability to meet new people, develop new friendships, start new romances, or rekindle old ones. You may be scared, but you can still control your future. Avoid moping and feeling sorry for yourself. Seek professional help if you need it. Get out of the house and pursue your values.

Fear of financial problems. It is often true that a couple is worse off financially living separately than together. It's important to do the math when considering separation. Women who've had a lifetime role as a homemaker face special financial problems and anxieties. They may lack confidence that they can survive independently and may feel that divorce is the end of their happiness. However, divorce can also be framed as an opportunity for personal growth. There's no better or more important gift you can give yourself than to discover that you can survive by the efficacy of your own mind and effort.

Fear of upsetting family or friends. Just remember your life belongs to you (see Chapter 3). One of the great fears partners face when deciding to divorce is worrying that friends and family will feel compelled to choose sides and that they might not choose yours.

> *No one has the right to tell you whom to love or whether you should or should not divorce.*

Your romantic relationship is for your personal happiness; making decisions about marriage and divorce to meet the expectations of others will destroy your chance for happiness. Divorce, like marriage, is your decision. Each family member and friend will judge the breakup according to their own psychology and context of knowledge. Some will judge it accurately, some will impose their personal beliefs on it, some will unfairly cast blame and some will withdraw friendship. Don't take the victim role. Continually judge their responses: Is their response fair? Are these people really your friends? Do they have the necessary information to make a fair judgment about your life? Unless there is a key moral issue at stake (your spouse was abusive or deceitful), it's wrong to ask your friends to take sides. They may continue to be friends with both partners, although social events usually include each partner separately. If it costs you the affection and love of a friend or family member, regard it as a trade-off you must accept. Sometimes divorce helps you discover who your true friends are!

Regrets and nostalgia. The nostalgia factor can be very strong. There was, hopefully, once a time when you deeply loved your partner. You anticipated the best, you shared the excitement of new love, fun times, professional successes, moments of profound sorrow or loss, the birth of your children, the unforgettable vacations, and the inside jokes. When contemplating divorce, there are moments when your mind unrelentingly focuses on better times and causes you to second-guess yourself. You wonder why or how you could ever leave. You feel tortured.

It's normal and healthy to allow yourself to grieve the loss of the good times as long as you keep in mind that this is not the full picture of your relationship—otherwise you would be happily married and not considering divorce. Remind yourself, when tortured by the nostalgia factor, of the full range of facts about your relationship, both good and bad.

Fear of harming your children, if you have children. Many claims have been made about the negative consequences for children when parents divorce. And that tempts unhappy couples to stay in the marriage "for the kids." In a 2000 report known as the Wallerstein study (named for the lead researcher), the authors' argument that divorce is harmful to children included the contradictory finding that half the divorced parents they studied had neurotic difficulties, chronic depression, problems controlling their sexual impulses, or rage.[3] Only a third of the divorced parents in the study were deemed psychologically healthy prior to the divorce. The results imply that a long time before the end of the marriage, a large percentage of children were already in danger. Parents' depression, alcohol problems, erratic angry outbursts or controlling behavior can harm children regardless of whether parents are married or divorced.

A more representative and better-designed study by Professor E. Mavis Hetherington found that 75 to 80 percent of children from divorced families psychologically functioned in the normal range. They adjusted reasonably well and some even became more resilient from learning to cope.[4]

Furthermore, some children who lived in the daily atmosphere of their parents bitter arguments or hostile silent treatment, felt relief at the prospect of their parents getting divorced. A house filled with tension and conflict is not a home. Parents who stay together "for the sake of the children," maintaining the façade of a close relationship until the children are adults, risk causing psychological damage when the truth finally comes out that Mom and Dad stopped loving each other years ago. The children's reactions can include:

- Feeling betrayed, angry, and distrustful because their parents, the most important figures in their lives, have deceived them
- Associating romantic love with self-sacrifice rather than with happiness
- Feeling self-doubt about their ability to judge people: *How could I have been so blind all those years: I thought Mom and Dad were happy. I'll never trust my own mind. People are beyond understanding.*
- Feeling that romantic love is an illusion
- Feeling guilty that they were the cause of their parents staying together and suffering all those years

In homes where conflict is out in the open, the Hetherington study concluded that parents who are "contemptuous of each other, not even with overt conflict but just sneering and subtle putdowns that erode the partner's self-esteem, that is very bad for the kids."[5] Popular and academic literature on divorce "has exaggerated its negative effects and ignored its sometimes considerable positive effects." Hetherington contends that ". . . most [children] do cope and go on to have a reasonably happy or sometimes very happy life."[6]

Divorcing parents can often mitigate the negative effects by the way they handle the situation. Parents can help children comprehend divorce rationally by remaining warm and emotionally supportive, listening to and addressing their children's concerns.[7] Having two loving, supportive parents is best. Even a smooth divorce is not always easy for children; they often go through a transition period that can be very difficult.

Divorcing parents can reduce the risk of psychological trauma and damage by modeling better behavior and explaining that the circumstances are an example of the importance of making self-respecting, rational, long-range decisions. Such parents help their children understand the danger of altruism and self-sacrifice, and the importance of pursuing one's own happiness. In this way, some children will learn from their parents' failed marriage what worked and what led to its downfall, possibly helping them succeed in their own future relationships.

It is crucial to identify the obstacles that keep you trapped in a bad relationship. Identify each barrier individually and give it careful thought. Overcoming those barriers can liberate you from the torture of unanswered questions, moral self-doubt, or selective focus on the good times you used to share. Addressing your personal barriers helps reduce the roller coaster ride of panic attacks, debilitating depression, unearned guilt, second-guessing yourself, angry outbursts, headaches and so on. Challenging such obstacles will increase your confidence and growing optimism that you are able to make the difficult choice to move forward toward your own happiness.

3. Making the Final Decision: Tying All the Relevant Evidence Together

When making a final decision about divorce, ensure that you have all the relevant information and have drawn the proper conclusions from it. This involves integrating all the information you've gained from understanding your reasons for considering divorce (section 1), such as asking yourself: *When did I stop loving or feeling loved by my partner? What changed? Why? Was it due to personality conflicts or major life changes, such as having children or changing careers? Was it due to diverging interests or communication problems? Is there anything we can realistically do to salvage the relationship or is our marriage beyond the point of no return?* Reaching a final decision involves understanding the barriers keeping you in the marriage and addressing each one (section 2).

Clearly identify, in your own words, your fullest grasp of *why* you want a divorce. Self-understanding (processing your thoughts in a journal or with a therapist) will help you avoid needless self-doubt and help build the confidence to proceed. To make a rational decision, ask yourself: *Where are my essential elements of uncertainty?* And then explore the issues in depth until you've gained clarity on each one. Integrating and addressing all your concerns takes time, but it pays off: you will feel in command, rather than tortured by arbitrary, isolated or vague self-doubts.

4. Breaking the News to Your Partner

Even if your partner has some inkling that you're considering divorce, hearing it said aloud for the first time is often a shock to your partner's self-esteem. Your partner is likely to feel deeply wounded and may react with anger, hysteria, threats, withdrawal, and depression. It's important to deliver the news in a respectful manner and at an appropriate time (not in the heat of an argument, in front of the children or during a holiday celebration). Good forethought is the best damage control. The enormity of the values at stake, and the task of making sense of it all, makes divorce one of life's most stressful events.

If your partner has good qualities, make sure to name these up front. "There's so much I admire in you—your honesty, your work ethic and your tenderness toward our kids. I wish I could say we're a perfect match; we're not. Neither of us has been happy for some time and I think at some level we know our relationship is not working." Acknowledging that you've *both* been unhappy (assuming this is accurate) helps put the divorce process on a more equal footing, framing it as a mutual agreement on some of the basic facts. When both partners are basically good people, you can mutually decide to divorce, thus avoiding the dynamics of the "leaver" versus the "left"—avoiding the guilt and hurt that such dynamics add to the painful divorce process.

If your partner has not seriously considered divorce, they may not have been aware of signs along the way. It's respectful to give your partner time to digest this information, without leading your partner on with false hopes. If you are genuinely open to reconciliation, say so. If not, don't mislead or you risk your partner investing energy, time and money in trying to patch things up when you've already decided that reconciliation is no longer an option. Some partners respond to the idea of divorce with fury and may express or harbor revenge fantasies. Threats of violence should always be taken seriously. You may need to move with the children to a secret location and notify the authorities. Even good people can act uncharacteristically when hit with self-esteem-wounding news. Encourage professional help if this happens.

5. Setting up an Atmosphere of Respect— Even When There Are Disagreements

Since you live with the manner in which you divorce for the rest of your life, and the consequences of it, make choices you can be proud of, even if your partner does not always follow suit. Avoid becoming defensive or hostile. Sometimes a more reasonable partner can set a better mood and thus help an otherwise volatile partner act more reasonably.

Acknowledging your partner's concerns ("You seem anxious about the future and your relationship with the kids") may help a partner open up and think more rationally. It can diffuse the "me-versus-you" hostility cycle. When you demonstrate that you understand your partner's feelings and priorities, your partner will be less likely to go to war with you. However, if your partner is abusive or verbally combative, it is important to keep a civil tone at your end and to avoid escalating the anger.

Pick your battles with care. Sometimes you gain more by conceding on a less important issue. You may let go of some possession to which you feel entitled but is causing strife. In return, your partner may soften and be unexpectedly generous in other areas, or you can ask for something even more important to you.

The principle of trade still holds in divorce agreements. Try to be fair. Of course, go to bat for what's most important to you if you have a rational claim to it. If you both want the same thing and have equal claim to it, compromise is needed.

A special warning: Often partners say that they are making a demand "in the best interest of the children," but sometimes this is a rationalization and the real motive may be retaliation or to make their own lives easier. Guard against using this line as a rationalization to hide an ulterior motive. Your kids will be doubly harmed by this since your choices are not truly for their benefit—and they will know it and feel used. You fool no one in the long run, including yourself.

6. Helping Your Children Through the Divorce

Helping your children weather the divorce as unscathed as possible requires careful thought and planning. Be aware that children have often sensed a divorce coming before their parents delivered the upsetting news. Your children may overhear you arguing or discussing divorce, unbeknownst to you; they notice you're no longer hugging or spending time together; they feel powerless when they hear you calling one another names. Such children anticipate divorce and have time to think about it. Unfortunately, some children have no forewarning. This is often more difficult to deal with. Whatever the timing, avoid making the two biggest mistakes: (1) fighting in front of your children and (2) abandoning them physically and/or emotionally. As much as possible, keep arguments private while supporting and comforting your children so that, in spite of their sadness and disappointment, they feel that their world is reasonably safe and understandable.

Parents who genuinely have their children's interests at heart avoid letting marital issues spill over into their children's lives. They remain interested and involved with the day-to-day concerns of their children and sincerely express their love.

The timing of breaking the news to your children is important. It's likely it will always feel like the wrong time to break the news to them but since you have to do it, avoid breaking it on birthdays, special holidays, the night before the prom, exam week and so on. In most cases, it's better if parents cooperate and deliver the new together. They can then invite their children to talk about their fears and concerns. Once the news is broken, be available but don't hover. Children need private time alone to process their feelings and thoughts.

Children worry about all sorts of issues. Commonly they blame themselves for divorce. Sometimes they conjure up reasons such as: *Dad got sick of yelling at me* or *I didn't do my chores and now Mom's moving out.* Kids are quick to douse themselves with unearned guilt. It's essential to address and try to defuse this guilt.[8] There is an excellent illustrated children's book, *Dinosaurs Divorce*, which underscores this point at the outset: "You are not to blame if your parents get divorced."[9] Questions children often ask or privately worry about include:

- Who will I live with, Mom or Dad?
- Will I go to the same school?
- Will we celebrate holidays together?
- Will we take family vacations together?
- What will I tell my friends?
- Will I get to see both of you?
- If Dad or Mom is leaving home, do I have to take over his or her chores (shovel snow, take out the garbage)?
- I don't want a stepmother or stepfather! Will I have to have one?
- Are you going to ship me off to Grandma's?

Children deal with the divorce through how it affects their lives. You may be surprised at the questions they ask. Listen carefully, be prepared to answer honestly and omit details that are inappropriate (information regarding your sex life). Be attuned to your children's lives, rather than involving them in the daily ups and downs of the divorce.

Avoid using your children as surrogate therapists. Children of divorce often report experiences such as: "My mom always tells me her problems with Dad and never listens to my problems with school or my friends. I wish she'd talk with someone else, but I feel so guilty not listening to her when she's crying all the time." Some children resent this. Others feel it gives them a special adult status. But sometimes it causes them to take sides. The child whose shoulder mom is crying on feels compelled to shun dad even though the child loves and misses him. It's important to remain the parent at all times.

Professionals, support groups, friends, family and self-help books are better sources of advice and better "shoulders" to lean on. Your children have their own lives, and their personal feelings about the divorce may not agree with yours. Children who are immersed in a parent's personal struggles are saddled with issues beyond their years when they need to be focusing on their own lives. For more advice, we have listed some books on divorce at the end of the appendix.[10]

One of the sadder side effects results when children interpret divorce as meaning they, too, will fail at romantic love. We often hear of cases like this one, related by a caller to Dr. Kenner's radio program:

> I am divorcing my husband after finding out from my fifteen-year-old daughter that he is cheating on me. Both she and her six-year-old sister heard him talking romantically on the cell phone while in the car. My husband has been physically abusive to me. What do I say to my fifteen-year-old now when she says that somehow she feels it is her fault and that she never wants to get married? Do I have any hope of showing my daughters that all men are not abusive?

Children coming out of such circumstances may always imagine divorce when they think about romantic love. It is particularly important that parents help teenagers put divorce in perspective, since teenagers are at the stage of life when they are exploring what it means to be in a long-term romantic relationship. Conscientious parents and competent therapists can help children by pointing to relationships of people the children know that worked out well— evidence that successful romantic relationships are possible.

Avoid maneuvering the children into unjustly taking sides or belittling the other parent in order to curry favor. Nip in the bud the urge to buy them expensive gifts, or to use the other spouse or grandparents and in-laws as foils, or to interfere with healthy family relationships. Be cautious of what you write in e-mails and text messages. Children are much more sophisticated about computers and technology than most adults are, and many parents have been horrified to find that their children have gotten access to their parents' vitriolic, explicit messages.[11]

Help to frame the divorce and the life to follow in an accurate and positive manner. Don't catastrophize. Some rejected parents falsely portray themselves as martyrs with ruined lives and try to convince their children that they are also victims of the heartless abandonment of the spouse. Although this is a difficult time, don't encourage your children to see life as tragic. There are poignantly sad drawings by children in the book, *Helping Your Child Through Your Divorce*.[12] Children may depict the divorce as a stick figure pulled between mom and dad, or as three lightening bolts striking mom, dad and the child, or a broken globe with the words: "Divorce is what makes the world fall apart." Parents can help their children avoid conclusions such as eleven-year-old Chris did: "I hate life sometimes. Sometimes I'm mad at the whole world."[13]

This book gives specific guidance to help children maintain their optimism and not view divorce as destructive, but as *living differently with two loving parents*. You can help your child frame the process of divorce in a positive manner, while still recognizing their genuine losses. Parents can serve as role models for their children by eventually seeking out a new romantic relationship and modeling the message that rational thinking and behavior is better than wallowing in self-pity.

A word of caution: We advise parents to avoid pretending or glossing over the fact that the other parent may be a thief, an addict, violent, or may indulge in some other dangerous or threatening behavior. Nor is it useful to lie and say that that parent couldn't help stealing, drinking, abusing drugs, hitting, cheating, lying or gambling away the family's finances. Children deserve the truth—in age-appropriate terms. Otherwise, they are left feeling baffled about why you divorced; or when they get wind of the bad parent's character, they will know you lied to them. If they already know about mom or dad's bad character, you are asking them to fake reality. And if you do not tell them about mom or dad's bad character, they may become the victims of this parent in the future.

We recommend, if needed, that children attend family, sibling and/or individual therapy sessions to help them process this major life change, and to process their own thoughts realistically rather than catastrophically. Siblings in therapy have a chance to bond more closely. It helps them to talk through such issues as who mom or dad loves the most, and find ways to remain friends and avoid getting drawn into the tussle between the parents vying for their allegiance. They learn to set the terms of the sibling bond, rather than allow disagreeing parents to split them.

7. Going Public with Family and Friends

Parents should try to collaborate on the best ways to break the news to family and friends. It's a good idea to coordinate getting the message out if you have a reasonably friendly divorce. However, if one partner is an actual victim (of abuse, of deceit, of the other's bad character), then coordination is irrelevant. It's perfectly legitimate in such cases to be honest and receive the sympathy and support from family members. You do not have to act as a united front when there is no basis for unity.

Sometimes one partner lets the cat out of the bag in response to pain, retaliation or trying to garner the upper hand. If that happens, you might be put in the position of having to do damage control. But avoid engaging in retaliatory tactics that can create a cycle of conflict, which can last well beyond the legal divorce.

Relatives, friends or co-workers may ask you, "Isn't divorce the easy way out?" This comment may say more about that person and their own choices than about your choice. They may have settled for less in their own relationship, and resent that you've had the courage to selfishly place a high value on your happiness. People in shaky relationships may feel threatened when divorce crops up in their social circle. People may exhort you to "hang in there" because it's what they've been doing, but outsiders cannot possibly know what goes on inside your marriage on a day-to-day basis. There are family members, friends and associates who do not have the full story, not should they necessarily have it. They may fill in the missing gaps by denouncing you. You can choose to give them the facts or retain your privacy and live with their misunderstanding. Sometimes a simple, "I see that you're thinking I did some pretty awful things. That's not the case, but I value my privacy and prefer not to share the personal details." This allows you to support yourself while not disclosing information for the rumor mill.

With family members, be prepared. If you tell one family member that you are getting a divorce, but add, "Please, keep it secret," it is likely that, with Internet-like speed, the rest of the family will find out. Some family members will be lovingly supportive; some will be condemnatory. Some lead terribly dull lives and your pending divorce adds much needed spice to their days. Remember that it is your decision and that you do not need a cheering or jeering squad. Guard your privacy. The same goes for friends who are married but feel that they have been put in a bind. They sometimes want a reason to take sides, since trying to remain friends with both partners is awkward. They also may simply like one partner more than the other. You and your spouse may lose some friends, and that is another trade-off. You may come to feel like the proverbial "third wheel" when you, as a soon-to-be-ex, go out with a couple. Other friends will be there through thick and thin. Be true to your own rational values. You do not owe your friends a detailed exposé. If they ask, tactfully protect your right to privacy.

8. Making an Action Plan for Your Divorce

One of the strongest emotions one feels at the prospect of divorce is fear of the unknown. Marriage, whether healthy or not, is that old devil you know—the daily routine, home life, steady income, social life, known relationships with extended family and friends, a version of stability. Divorce changes everything and you can't know in advance how it all will turn out. It can feel like being on the edge of a dark, uncharted forest. You have to walk though it, but you do not know what you will find or even if you will emerge on the other side. You can cope with this by using the power of your own mind, your capacity to think.

You'll be flooded with new issues to deal with, including your own strong emotions. To reduce stress, recognize that you cannot deal with all these issues at once. Take your time and be thorough. If your mind is flooded with too many questions, make a list of these issues and note which ones require outside help (legal or financial advice, counseling). Then make an action plan.

An action plan involves ranking issues in terms of importance and then identifying the steps you need to take in each case. Do not rush except with respect to the most urgent issues. You will need time and resolve to process all this information, which may seem overwhelming, and you will have to deal with psychological issues as well. Then there are practical issues: Who is moving out of the home? How much money will I have and who will pay which bills? Who will take the children to school? How and when will I get the shopping done? Will I be able to afford a car? There are social issues: dealing with family, friends and colleagues as a divorced person. There are job and career issues: How will divorce impact my work—will there be disruptions when I have to go to court or pick up the kids? Also, there will be legal issues—how to protect your assets, who gets what, custody issues, the possibility of your divorce case going to trial.

Ask yourself: *What is most important right now?* That issue gets top ranking. It is important to be organized. *The Divorce Decisions Workbook*, by Margorie Engel and Diana D. Gould, gives you a step-by-step guide on how to set up your "divorce business"—a detailed method to organize your divorce and your life, so that you can make educated decisions and be prepared.[14] It is a soup-to-nuts book, which includes different worksheets to help you manage the multiple layers of divorce: visitation schedules, resource and emergency numbers, expenses, personal documents, personal banking accounts, titles and deeds, personal health information, insurance forms (homeowners, automobile), medical forms, division of assets. Being organized, making an action plan for your divorce and for life as a single person, is far better for your mental health (and health in general) than "winging it."

Although it is emotionally upsetting, divorce is still a logical process. You need to educate yourself about the process to make the experience less overwhelming. For many it helps to have a knowledgeable counselor guide them through the many aspects of divorce (emotional, practical, social, legal). Thinking, knowledge, planning and organizing are central to making you feel in control of the process, and as you start making decisions about your future life, you will discover that you feel more and more in control and that this has an emotionally calming effect. Your subconscious, instead of feeding you ideas such as *Oh, my God, this is a disaster, my life is ruined forever; I'm doomed—life is hopeless* will instead start feeding you ideas such as *I can deal with this! I can handle these tasks. I'll survive this. I can control my life—happiness is still possible and the kids will get through this okay.*

9. Learning to Live Independently and Taking New Steps Toward Romantic Happiness

Divorce is an opportunity for personal growth, learning new skills, teaching your children the importance of honesty, and helping them grasp that happiness does not have to be sacrificed by two individuals living together who no longer love one another. When you adopt a self-respecting mindset, reject game playing, take action to cope with loneliness or stress, and refuse to surrender to self-pity—you have taken a potentially damaging situation and emerged psychologically and morally stronger. You have taken steps to bring about your own future happiness.[15] After you have given yourself time to grieve for the losses in your marriage, you can take the first steps toward your future romantic happiness—this time armed with much more knowledge about how to make romance succeed. This is a good time to make a personal assessment. Reread Part II of this book, and ask yourself: *Are there any traits or characteristics that I have that make me less than lovable? If so, what can I do to change them?* Review Part III and ask yourself: *Did I make any errors in picking a soul mate? What have I learned about the right type of person for me—for my needs, wants and desires? What have I learned about judging potential soul mates?* Mutual admiration is a far healthier basis for romance than dependence. Review Part IV and ask yourself: *What did I do or not do to keep the love relationship thriving?*

Having the right mindset, the right philosophy in your life, a self-valuing philosophy, makes all the difference for romance and happiness. Divorce need not be the end of the world. If dealt with rationally, it can be a new beginning—the beginning of a truly happy life with a loving partner. The poet Percy Bysshe Shelley captured the feeling of finding one's soul mate in the following lines:

And we will talk, until thought's melody
Become too sweet for utterance, and it die
In words, to live again in looks, which dart
With thrilling tone into the voiceless heart,
Harmonizing silence without a sound.
Our breath shall intermix, our bosoms bound,
And our veins beat together; and our lips
With other eloquence than words, eclipse
The soul that burns between them, and the wells
Which boil under our being's inmost cells,
The fountains of our deepest life, shall be
Confus'd [Fused] in Passion's golden purity,
As mountain-springs under the morning sun.
We shall become the same, we shall be one
Spirit within two frames, oh! Wherefore two?
One passion in twin-hearts, which grows and grew,
Till like two meteors of expanding flame,
Those spheres instinct [incite] with it becomes the same,
Touch, mingle, are transfigur'd; ever still
Burning, yet ever inconsumable.[16]

Notes

1. Harry Binswanger, ed., *The Ayn Rand Lexicon: Objectivism from A to Z* (New York: NAL Books, 1986; New York: Meridian, 1988). For interesting comments on altruism, egoism, love and more, we highly recommend this resource.

2. Some good books on divorce: Margorie L. Engel and Diana D. Gould, *The Divorce Decisions Workbook: A Planning and Action Guide* (New York: McGraw-Hill, 1992), and Matthew McKay, Peter Rogers, Joan

Blades and Richard Gosse, *The Divorce Book* (California: New Harbinger Publications, 1984).

3. Judith Wallerstein, Julia Lewis and Sandra Blakeslee, *The Unexpected Legacy of Divorce: The 25-Year Landmark Study* (New York: Hyperion, 2000). Also see Stephanie Coontz, "Divorcing Reality," which originally appeared in *The Nation*, November 17, 1997. It is also excerpted in the January–February 1998 *Children's Advocate* newsmagazine, published by Action Alliance for Children and available online: http://www.4children.org/news/198coon.htm

4. Karen S. Peterson, *USA Today* article "Divorce need not end in disaster," January 14, 2002; available online at www.usatoday.com/news/nation/2002/01/14/usatcov-divorce.htm, p. 1 of article.

5. Ibid., p. 5 of website article.

6. Ibid., pp. 2–3 of website article.

7. Website on E. Mavis Hetherington: www.intams.com/review/issues/hetherington82.html, p. 1.

Also see E. Mavis Hetherington and John Kelly, *For Better or For Worse: Divorce Reconsidered* (New York: W. W. Norton & Company, 2002).

8. In extremely rare cases, when a child's bad character is a serious problem that affects the parents' relationship, they should be in therapy as soon as possible. If the child has criminal tendencies, a good book to read is Stanton Samenow's *Before It's Too Late* (New York: Random House, 1989).

9. Laurene Krasny Brown and Marc Brown, *Dinosaurs Divorce* (Boston: Little Brown and Company, 1986).

10. See footnote 2 for some good books on divorce. In addition, we recommend the following books for helping your children: Florence Bienenfeld, *Helping Your Child Through Your Divorce* (California: Hunter House, 1995). M. D. Evans, *This Is Me & My Two Families: An Awareness Scrapbook/Journal for Children Living in Stepfamilies* (New York: Magination Press, Brunner/Mazel, Inc., 1986). We highly recommend the general parenting books by Adele Faber and Elaine Mazlish: *How to Talk So Kids Will Listen and Listen So Kids Will Talk* (New York: Avon Books), and *How to Talk So Teens Will Listen and Listen So Teens Will Talk* (New York: Harper Collins Publishers, 2005), also *Siblings without Rivalry* (New York: W.W. Norton & Company, 1987). Their website is at www.fabermazlish.com.

11. Jeffrey Zaslow, *Wall Street Journal*, "Email Can Make Divorce Worse" December 15, 2005, p. D4.

12. Bienenfeld, op. cit., Chapter 2: "How Children See Divorce."

13. Ibid., p. 36.

14. Engel and Gould, op. cit. (see footnote 2).

15. Edwin A. Locke, "Stress and Coping: An Inductive Approach" (taped course available at http://www.aynrandbookstore.com.

16. Percy Bysshe Shelley, "Epipsychidion," 1821. Some terms had different meanings or nuances in Shelley's time. First, in line 12: "Confus'd in Passion's golden purity" appears closer in meaning to "Fused together in Passion's golden purity." "Fused" seems closest to what the author meant given line 14: "We shall become the same, we shall be one." (This fusing and becoming one, of course, is metaphorical and refers to a state of passionate intimacy.) The closest relevant meaning of "confused" (found on Wordnet) is "blurred" which, although related to "fused," is less fitting in the context of the poem. Second, in line 18 the word "instinct" today is closer in meaning to the word "incite," which is an obsolete meaning of instinct. The poem is available on the University of Toronto website: http//eir.library.utoronto.ca/rpo/display/poem1886.html.

The Selfish Path to Romance
Road Map